Edexcel GCSE
Psychology

Written by Christine Brain,
Julia Russell and Karren Smith

A PEARSON COMPANY

Published by Pearson Education Limited, a company incorporated in England and Wales, having its registered office at Edinburgh Gate, Harlow, Essex, CM20 2JE. Registered company number: 872828

www.heinemann.co.uk

Edexcel is a registered trade mark of Edexcel Limited

Text © Pearson Education Limited 2009

First published 2009

13 12 11
10 9 8 7 6 5

British Library Cataloguing in Publication Data
A catalogue record for this book is available from the British Library

ISBN 978 1 846904 83 7

Edited by Helen Atkinson
Typeset by HL Studios, Long Hanborough, Oxford
Original illustrations © Pearson Education Limited 2009
Illustrated by HL Studios and Julian Mosedale
Cover design by Dickidot Limited
Picture research by Susie Prescott
Cover photo © Gnomus/Alamy
Printed in China (CTPS/05)

Acknowledgements
The author and publisher would like to thank the following individuals and organisations for permission to reproduce photographs:

P 2 Getty/Angelo Cavalli; P 3 Bongarts/Getty Images; P 5 Design Pics/ Imagestate; P 7 Science Photo Library; P 8 L Julia Russell; P 8 M Paul Grover/Rex Features; P 8 R Photographers Choice/Getty; P 10 Creatas; P 10 Ravi Tahilramani/Photodisc/Getty Images; P 12 Kent Knudson/Photolink/ Photodisc; P 13 Mark Newman/Science Faction/Getty Images; P 14 Julia Russell; P 15 T Phovoir/Imagestate; P 15 L Photolink/Photodisc; P 15 R MC Escher company-Holland; P 16 Vintage Image/Alamy; P 17 T Julia Russell; P 17 B Julia Russell; P 18 Julia Russell; P 19 Julia Russell; P 20 Rich Carey/ Shutterstock; P 24 Mary Evans; P 25 L Dan McCoy/Science Faction/ Getty Images; P 25 R Grant Faith/Getty Images; P 27 Julia Russell; P 28 Photolink/Photodisc; P 48 Woodystock/Alamy; P 52 AsiaPix/Getty Images; P 54 Corbis; P 61 Peter Aprahamian/Corbis; P 62 Med.Mic Sciences Cardiff University/Wellcome Trust; P 75 INSADCO Photography/Alamy; P 76 Gareth Boden/Pearson; P 78 Ed Holub/Age Fotostock/Imagestate; P 81 Tom Stewart/Corbis; P 84 Wellcome Images,London; P 85 Bettman/ Corbis; P 86 Solus-Veer/Corbis; P 89 L Hank Morgan/Science Faction/ Getty Images; P 89 R Alessandra Schnellnegger/Zefa/Corbis; P 93 Ingram Publishing/Purestock/Getty Images; P 96 Steve Bloom Images/Alamy; P 97 Michael Brennan/Corbis; P 98 Albert Bandura; P 100 Stock Connection Distribution/Alamy; P 102 Roger Fletcher/Alamy; P 105 Rubberball/Getty Images; P 108 Stewart Cook/Rex Features; P 110

Topham Picturepoint; P 115 AltrendoRR/Getty Images; P 117 Eleanor Bentall/Corbis; P 118 Pearson Education Ltd/Jules Selmes; P 120 Westend61/Getty Images; P 121 Heide Benser/Zefa/Corbis; P 122 BBFC; P 123 BBFC; P 124 Peter Cade/Iconica/Getty Images; P 128 Fiona Hanson/ PA Archive/PA Photos; P 130 Bettman/Corbis; P 134 Serge Krouglikoff/ Stone/Getty Images; P 137 Archives of the History of American Psychology – The University of Akron; P 141 Image Source/Corbis; P 143 TL Eric Isselée/Shutterstock; P 143 BL Les Gibbon/Alamy; P 143 TR John Foxx/Alamy; P 143 BR Blickwinkel/Alamy; P 151 Henrik Sorenson/Getty Images; P 152 Vincent Abbey/Alamy; P 154 Digital Vision/Punchstock; P 156 Uppercut Images/Alamy; P 158 Stockbyte/Getty Images; P 159 Pearson Education Ltd/Lord & Leveritt; P 160 Ami Vitale/Getty Images News; P 164 Andrew Douglas/Masterfile; P 166 Roy McMahon/Corbis; P 168 Richard Bowlby; P 171 Stockbyte/Getty Images; P 172 Age Stock Ltd/ Alamy; P 177 Photos12/Alamy; P 180 John Powell/Rex Features; P 185 AP/ PA Photos; P 186 Dimension Films/Kobal Collection; P 188 Anton Want; P 189 Rex Features; P 191 T Janine Wiedel/Alamy; P 191 B Paul Doyle/ Alamy; P 192 Martin Rickett/PA Archives/PA Photos; P 200 R Rob van Petten; P 200 M Ayzeek/iStockphoto; P 200 B Maryloo/Shutterstock; P 202 Stockphoto4u/iStockphoto; P 202 Masterfile Royalty Free; P 205 Howard Walker/Reuters/Corbis.

The author and publisher would like to thank the following individuals and organisations for permission to reproduce text:

P 26 Current Directions in Psychological Science, 3, 4, 105-111, 1994. Published by Wiley-Blackwell, The Atrium, Southern Gate, Chichester, West Sussex PO19 8SQ; P 30 Memory and Cognition, 3, 519-526, 1975. Published by Psychonomic Society Publications, 1710 Fortview Road, Austin, TX 78704; P 32-33 Bartlett FC (1932) Remembering: A Study in Experimental and Social Psychology, Cambridge University Press: Cambridge; P 34 Journal of Experimental Psychology, 15, 73-86, 1932. Published by the American Psychological Association, 750 First Street, NE, Washington DC, 20002-4242; P 46 Journal of Experimental Psychology, 137, 2, 348-369, 2008. Published by the American Psychological Association, 750 First Street, NE, Washington DC, 20002-4242; P 147 Pedagogical Seminary, 31, 308-15, 1924. Reprinted with permission of the Helen Dwight Reid Educational Foundation. Published by Heldref Publications, 1319 Eighteenth St., NW, Washington, DC 20036-1802. Copyright © 1924.

Every effort has been made to contact copyright holders of material reproduced in this book. Any omissions will be rectified in subsequent printings if notice is given to the publishers.

Websites
There are links to relevant websites in this book. In order to ensure that the links are up to date, that the links work, and that the sites are not inadvertently linked to sites that could be considered offensive, we have made the links available on the Heinemann website at www.heinemann.co.uk/hotlinks. When you access the site, the express code is 4837P.

Disclaimer
This Edexcel publication offers high-quality support for the delivery of Edexcel qualifications. Edexcel endorsement does not mean that this material is essential to achieve any Edexcel qualification, nor does it mean that this is the only suitable material available to support any Edexcel qualification. No endorsed material will be used verbatim in setting any Edexcel examination/assessment and any resource lists produced by Edexcel shall include this and other appropriate texts.

Copies of official specifications for all Edexcel qualifications may be found on the Edexcel website – www.edexcel.com

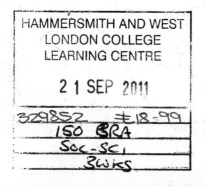

How to use this book

This book has been designed to perfectly match the Edexcel specification, with lots of features to help you understand your course and prepare you for your final exams.

Double page spreads

The book is divided into manageable chunks, set out as a double page spread. The different types of spread each serve a different purpose or relate to a different part of the specification.

Spread numbering

The letter at the front of the spread number matches the **topic** in the specification.

The second letter relates to the **learning point** in the specification.

The first number in the spread number matches a **section** within the specification e.g. 'Explaining the question'.

The last number is given in sequence to spreads covering the same learning point in the specification e.g. A1a has two spreads to cover all the content, A1a1 and A1a2.

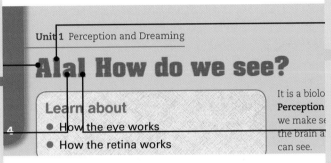

Unit 1 Perception and Dreaming

A1a1 How do we see?

Learn about
- How the eye works
- How the retina works

It is a biolo...
Perception
we make s...
the brain a...
can see.

Topic introduction

The book is divided into 5 topics, each set around a key question. For each topic there is an introduction spread which tells you what is coming up, and what you may already know from your previous studies.

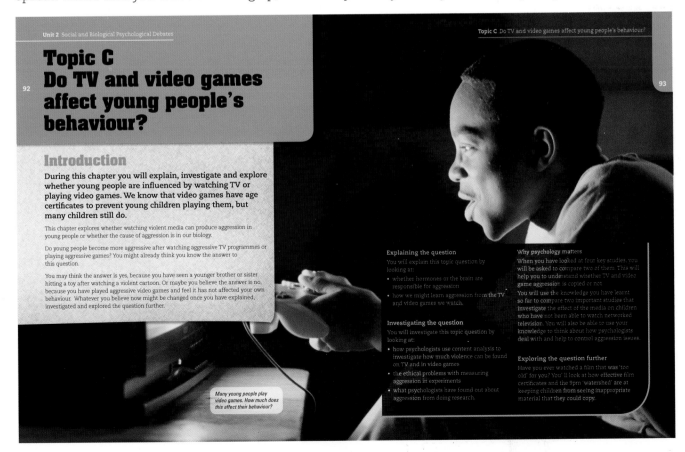

Unit 2 Social and Biological Psychological Debates

Topic C Do TV and video games affect young people's behaviour?

Topic C
Do TV and video games affect young people's behaviour?

Introduction

During this chapter you will explain, investigate and explore whether young people are influenced by watching TV or playing video games. We know that video games have age certificates to prevent young children playing them, but many children still do.

This chapter explores whether watching violent media can produce aggression in young people or whether the cause of aggression is in our biology.

Do young people become more aggressive after watching aggressive TV programmes or playing aggressive games? You might already think you know the answer to this question.

You may think the answer is yes, because you have seen a younger brother or sister hitting a toy after watching a violent cartoon. Or maybe you believe the answer is no, because you have played aggressive video games and feel it has not affected your own behaviour. Whatever you believe now might be changed once you have explained, investigated and explored the question further.

Many young people play video games. How much does this affect their behaviour?

Explaining the question
You will explain this topic question by looking at:
- whether hormones or the brain are responsible for aggression
- how we might learn aggression from the TV and video games we watch.

Investigating the question
You will investigate this topic question by looking at:
- how psychologists use content analysis to investigate how much violence can be found on TV and in video games
- the ethical problems with measuring aggression in experiments
- what psychologists have found out about aggression from doing research.

Why psychology matters
When you have looked at four key studies, you will be asked to compare two of them. This will help you to understand whether TV and video game aggression is copied or not.

You will use the knowledge you have learnt so far to compare two important studies that investigate the effect of the media on children who have not been able to watch networked television. You will also be able to use your knowledge to think about how psychologists deal with and help to control aggression issues.

Exploring the question further
Have you ever watched a film that was 'too old' for you? You'll look at how effective film certificates and the 9pm 'watershed' are at keeping children from seeing inappropriate material that they could copy.

Explaining the question

Each topic in the specification starts by 'Explaining the question'. To match this, each topic in the book starts by doing the same. The 'Explaining the question' pages all have a blue background.

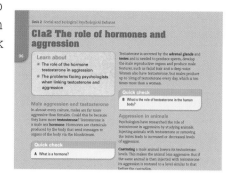

Investigating the question

The next section in each topic aims to 'Investigate the question'. These pages have a yellow background.

Why psychology matters

So that you can understand how the topic you have been studying relates to the real world there is a 'Why psychology matters' section for each topic in the specification. These pages have a green background.

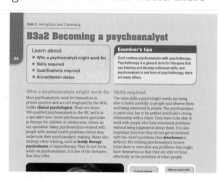

Exploring the question further

In Unit 2 you will look at the topics in more depth, so each of them includes an 'Exploring the question further' section. These pages have a purple background.

Features of the book

Each page of the book is packed with features to help you learn the information in each topic and understand what you need to know for the exams.

Learn about boxes

Each of the main spreads includes a 'Learn about' box that lets you know what you should aim to learn in the next two pages. They can also be used when you revise to help you understand the most important points on the page.

> Learn about

Glossary terms

As you read through the book you will find some words printed in bold. These are words that you may not have come across before, but you will need to understand them to learn the information in each topic.

Key definitions boxes

Some of the new words covered in the glossary are more important than others, and you will need to be sure you understand them properly before taking the exam. These words have been placed in 'Key definitions' boxes on the page where you first meet them.

> Key definitions

Quick check boxes

As you read about the subjects covered in the book you will find Quick Check questions. Try to answer these as you go along to help you understand what you have just read.

> Quick check

Examiner's tips boxes

The examiners who will be setting and marking your exams have also provided tips to help you avoid some common mistakes made by all pupils. These tips have been put throughout the book next to the parts of the specification they relate to.

Examiner's tips

Taking it further boxes

On some spreads you will find ideas for activities you might want to do and websites you might like to visit to help you understand more about psychology.

Taking it further

Some of the boxes will direct you to a website. Links to these websites are provided on a dedicated 'hotlinks' page on the Heinemann website at www.heinemann.co.uk/hotlinks. When you access the site, the express code is 4837P.

Questions boxes

At the end of most spreads in the book you will find some questions about what you have just read. Try answering these as you go along. You can also use them when you are revising for the exams.

Questions

Exam Zone

Exam Zone is designed to help you prepare for your Edexcel exams. You can find information about it on the Exam Zone website at www.examzone. co.uk/home/

This book also includes Exam Zone sections to help you prepare properly for your exams.

Know Zone

At the end of each topic the Know Zone pages will give you a checklist of the main points you need to remember for the exam, as well as providing questions and activities you may want to try as part of your revision.

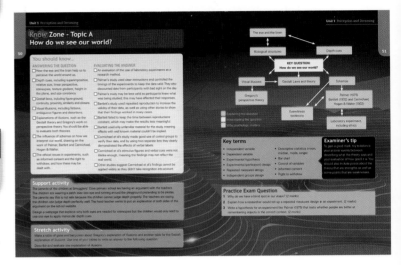

Exam Zone revision pages

At the end of the book the ExamZone pages are packed with tips and hints on how best to prepare for your exams. Taking you from planning your revision timetable all the way to what to do after you have left the exam hall.

Contents

Unit 1: Perception and Dreaming

Unit 2: Social and Biological Psychological Debates

Topic A
How do we see our world?

2

Introduction

Do we see things the way they really are? Or are our eyes (or our brains) sometimes fooled?

You probably already know that you can make mistakes about what you have seen. Perhaps you think this is a 'one off', like thinking you have spotted a friend in a crowd then finding it was a stranger. But you might also be aware that we all see things in the same way, like knowing where a ball is in space. If we couldn't we'd never be able to hit, kick or catch accurately.

You might be surprised to know that we all make similar errors – like thinking the moon looks bigger when it is low in the sky. This chapter will help you to understand how we see things the way we do and why we sometimes get it wrong. You will then be able to *explain*, *investigate* and *explore* how we see our world.

Sometimes perception is wrong: the moon looks bigger when it is close to the horizon.

We can kick a ball because we have a system for judging depth.

Explaining the question

Psychologists call seeing and understanding the world 'perception'. There are two key things about perception to explain:

- how we see distance or 'depth'
- what goes wrong when we are fooled by illusions.

You will learn to explain these problems by studying the eye and the way we interpret visual information. To help you, we will look at how our perception is guided by ideas we already have in our heads and at the way we use rules to guide our perception.

Investigating the question

To find out about how psychologists investigate how we see our world you will look at the way experiments are used. In the laboratory, psychologists can investigate how different things affect the way we see the world. To learn more about how psychologists use experiments you will look at three key studies. These investigate how the way we see and remember pictures and stories can be changed.

Why psychology matters

It is important to know that what we see and remember can change, especially when it comes to criminal trials. It is vital that an eyewitness to a crime sees and remembers the event exactly as it really was. You will use what you have learned about how we see our world to understand some of the problems eyewitnesses have.

A1a1 How do we see?

4

Learn about
- How the eye works
- How the retina works

We use our eyes to see the world. Look around at different objects. Pick something up and close your eyes. It's obvious that you can't see it, but what's missing? You can feel its texture, shape and size, even though you can no longer see those features. You can't see its colour either. Our eyes help us to detect all these things about objects without having to touch them.

When we are not touching an object, we rely on our eyes to give us information about the world. These features include:

- shape
- size
- texture
- colour
- distance from us.

Key definitions

perception: the way the brain makes sense of the visual image detected by the eyes.

retina: the light-sensitive layer at the back of the eye. It is made up of nerve cells called rods and cones.

rods: light-sensitive cells in the retina that respond even in dim light.

cones: light-sensitive cells in the retina that can detect colour.

optic nerve: bundle of nerve cells that leads out from the retina at the back of the eye. It carries information from the rods and cones to the brain.

Perception

Most objects in the world reflect or emit (give out) rays of light that we can detect. Seeing, or vision, is the process of detecting this light from objects.

It is a biological process that happens in our eyes. **Perception** is more than that. Perception is the way we make sense of the visual image. This happens in the brain and allows us to understand what we can see.

Quick check

A Vision and perception are different. Which one is the biological process of seeing and which is the psychological process of making sense of the visual image?

The structure of the eye

The light reflected from an object enters the eye and makes an image on the **retina**, a layer at the back of the eye. The retina is sensitive to light and sends nerve impulses to the brain. This is possible because the retina is covered with thousands of cells which can detect light. There are two types of retina cells:

- **rods**
- **cones**.

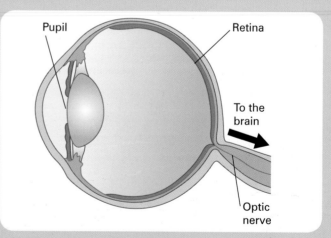

When light reflected from an object enters the eye it is detected by cells on the retina and nerve impulses are sent along the optic nerve.

Examiner's tips

You do not need to learn very much about the structure of the eye for psychology, so don't get bogged down using detail you might have learned in science. All that you will need is on the diagram.

The structure of the retina

Rods are very sensitive to light and they also respond to movement. A rod cell will respond even when only very dim light falls on it. They are found mainly around the edge of the retina. Have you ever noticed something moving 'out of the corner of your eye'? This happens because the light moves across the side of your retina and is detected by rods.

Cones are found mainly in the centre of the retina, in a special area just opposite the 'hole' (the pupil) at the front of each eye. This area helps us to see clearly and in detail as there are lots of cones packed very close together. Cones are less sensitive to light than rods, so they only work in bright light. Unlike rods, cones can detect different colours of light. Our colour vision therefore relies on our cones.

rods	cones
able to work in dim light	only work in bright light
detect light	detect different colours

Have you ever noticed how hard it is to tell what colour something is when the light is dim? Maybe you've tried to find a particular coloured car in a car park at night. It is difficult because there isn't enough light for the cones to work properly.

Nerve impulses from the retina to the brain

Rods and cones are special nerve cells. When enough light falls on a rod or cone, the cell responds by sending a nerve impulse. All the nerve impulses from rods and cones across the whole retina are sent to the brain. The nerve impulses travel along other nerve cells which are bundled together in the **optic nerve**. This looks like a thick stalk at the back of the eye. The nerve impulses in the optic nerve are carried to the brain.

Questions

1 Where are the light-sensitive cells in the eye?
2 What travels along the optic nerve?
3 Which cells would we use to:
   a) detect a bird flying at night?
   b) detect the colour of the bird in bright daylight?

In dim light only our rods work, so we cannot see in colour.

A1a2 The optic nerve and the brain

Learn about
- The blind spot
- Where visual information is used in the brain

We use the words 'blind spot' to mean all sorts of things. Some people say they 'have a blind spot for maths'. That means they can't see how maths works. You might know that when a driver is using their car mirrors to look behind them there is a 'blind spot'. It is an area of road where they cannot see other vehicles. For psychologists, the 'blind spot' means the same thing. It is part of the world we cannot see.

What causes the blind spot?

Page 5 describes how the retina responds when light from an object falls onto the rods or cones and that the optic nerve carries messages to the brain. At the point on the retina where the optic nerve leaves the eye, there is no space for any rods or cones. This little area is therefore 'blind'. If the light from an object falls onto that part of the retina there are no light-sensitive cells to detect it. This area of the retina is called the **blind spot**. There is a blind spot in each eye.

You might be surprised that you don't notice your blind spot. Why isn't part of the world 'missing'? The reason is that the two blind spots don't overlap so even if one eye can't see something, the other one can.

Key definitions

blindspot: the area of the retina where the optic nerve leaves. It has no rods or cones so cannot detect light.

optic chiasma: the cross-shape where some of the information from the left and right eye crosses over to pass into the opposite side of the brain.

visual cortex: the area at the back of the brain that interprets visual information.

You can find the blind spot in one eye by closing the other. Try the demonstration in the picture below.

Quick check

A If you close your right eye and look at the Z in the artwork below, some of the letters in the grid disappear. Why?

Taking it further

Go to www.heinemann.co.uk/hotlinks, enter express code 4837P, and click on the *Metcalfe website*. Watch the video.

Your perceptual system will fill in the gap so you see the whole blue bar when the gap falls on your blind spot.

Examiner's tips

Remember that your blind spots don't overlap. When you have both eyes open you are never aware that part of each visual field is 'missing'.

A	B	C	D	E	F	
G	H	I	J	K	L	
M	N	O	P	Q	R	**Z**
S	T	U	V	W	X	

*Close your left eye. Look at the letter **A**, then read slowly along the rows of letters. On one or more of the letters you should find that you cannot see the big letter **Z**. Keep moving and wait for it to come back. Check again. The **Z** disappears when the image falls on your blind spot.*

The optic chiasma

The information from the retina goes along the optic nerve to the brain. Information from each eye goes to *both* sides of the brain. Some from the left eye goes to the left side of the brain and some to the right. Similarly, some information from the right eye goes to the left side of the brain, some to the right.

Information from the left and right eye crosses over at a point called the **optic chiasma**. It has this name because 'optic' relates to light and the Greek letter 'Chi' is shaped like a big cross χ. This is the shape of the nerves as they cross over on the way to the opposite side of the brain.

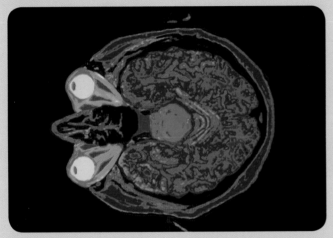

This brain scan shows the cross shape (in green) where some of the information from the right and left eye swaps to the opposite side of the brain.

The brain

From the optic chiasma, visual information is carried to the back of the brain. Many perceptual processes happen in an area called the **visual cortex**. You can see where this is in the artwork below. The job of the visual cortex is to interpret the information from the rods and cones.

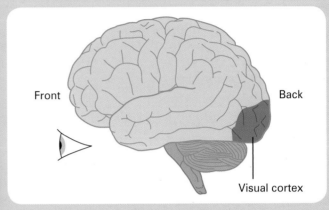

The visual cortex uses this information in perception to understand shapes and distances. It also fills in the gap left by the blind spot in each eye. This is why a pattern seen with one eye looks complete even when part of it falls on the blind spot.

Quick check

B Would a bump on the front or back of the head be more likely to upset your vision?

Questions

1 What is missing from the blind spot to make it 'blind'?

2 Is colour detected at the retina or in the brain?

3 Close your right eye and look at the cross. Move the page towards and away from you and from side to side.

a) What happens to the bird and why?

b) What happens to the bars of the cage?

c) Is this happening in the retina or the brain?

A1b1 Seeing depth

Learn about
- Monocular depth cues
- Binocular depth cues

Look around you. Find three different objects:

- one close to you
- one a long way away
- one somewhere in between.

How did you do that?

This section will help you to understand how people judge distance or 'depth'. By depth we mean how 'deep' into a scene or object a particular point is. In the photo below, the tree looks closer than the wall. It is in the foreground so isn't as 'deep' into the scene. The left wheels of the car seem further away than the right ones because they are 'deeper' into the car.

We can judge distance or depth in a picture.

Depth cues

We can judge depth in the real world, that is, in three dimensions. We can also understand depth in pictures when it is represented in two dimensions. The 'clues' we use to understand depth are called **depth cues**. They are pieces of visual information that trigger or 'cue' our understanding of distance. There are two kinds of depth cues. They are called:

- **monocular depth cues**
- **binocular depth cues.**

We use one eye with a monocle but two eyes with binoculars.

Monocular depth cues

'Mono' means 'one', as in monocle – the old-fashioned single eyeglass. Monocular depth cues are clues to distance that only need one eye. If you close one eye and look around, it is still obvious which things are closer and which are further away. You are using monocular cues to decide.

There are five monocular depth cues you need to understand, which are described in detail on pages 12–17:

- superimposition
- relative size
- texture gradient
- linear perspective
- height in the plane.

Quick check

A Would a person who was blind in one eye rely on monocular or binocular depth cues?

Taking it further

Go to www.heinemann.co.uk/hotlinks and enter express code 4837P. Click on the *Webvision website* which illustrates and defines different monocular depth cues.

Binocular depth cues

The word 'binocular' starts with 'bi'. This means 'two', as in 'binoculars'. Binocular depth cues are clues to distance that need both eyes. Sometimes two eyes are important for seeing depth.

Close one eye and reach both hands out in front of you (as illustrated in the picture below). Waggle them around then try to touch the tips of your index fingers together. This is difficult because you can only use monocular cues. Try again with both eyes open and you should find it easier. This is because you are using binocular cues as well.

Find a partner and ask them to move a finger towards their own nose and watch it. What happens to their eyes? When we are looking at things in the distance our eyes point straight out. As we look at closer objects our eyes point inwards more. This is a binocular cue.

There is another binocular cue to depth called stereopsis. You will learn about this on page 16.

When we only use one eye we are not as good at judging depth as we are when we use both eyes.

Quick check

B When shooting a rifle, you line up the target with one eye. What depth cues could you use?

Key definitions

depth cues: the visual 'clues' that we use to understand depth or distance.

monocular depth cues: information about distance that comes from one eye, such as superimposition, relative size, texture gradient, linear perspective and height in the plane.

binocular depth cues: information about distance that needs two eyes, such as stereopsis.

Taking it further

The cue of stereopsis works because the view from your left and your right eye is different. Go to www.heinemann.co.uk/hotlinks and enter express code 4837P. Have a look at the demonstration on the *Michael Bach website* which shows how seeing the 'tips' of two fingers, one with each eye, can make a sausage appear!

Examiner's tips

To remember which is which with monocular and binocular cues, think of a '*mono*cycle' which has only *one* wheel and a '*bi*cycle' which has *two* wheels.

Questions

1 Which depth cues use two eyes, monocular or binocular ones?

2 Sometimes children play 'pirates' and wear an eye-patch. When they use a toilet roll middle like a telescope, would they be using monocular cues, binocular cues or both?

3 a) Which task relies more on depth cues, hitting a ball with a bat or writing on paper?

   b) In a task that relies heavily on depth cues, would the person be using monocular cues, binocular cues or both?

A1b2 Depth and size

10

Learn about
- Size constancy
- How depth perception helps us to understand the size of objects at different distances

When an object is nearby it makes a bigger image on the retina than when it is far away.

Close one eye and hold your hand in front of your face. You probably can't see much, apart from your hand. The image of your hand completely fills your retina or your 'field of view'. Now stretch your arm out. You can still see your hand, but it fills less of your field of view – it is making a smaller image on your retina.

Size constancy

One advantage of being able to judge depth is that we can tell whether an object is close or far away. This is important as it helps us to judge how big the object is.

Imagine lying on the grass in summer and seeing an ant right beside your face. It would take up lots of space on your retina. Now imagine looking at one when you were standing up. Even though the close-up ant nearly fills your retina, it doesn't look like a 'giant ant' the size of an elephant! This is because we can scale the size of objects up or down. To do this we use information about depth in the scene.

Taking it further

Go to www.heinemann.co.uk/hotlinks and enter express code 4837P. Look at the activity on the *Hanover College website* to help you to understand size constancy.

Our brain is able to scale objects close by or far away.

When an object is close, our brain scales it down in size so that it looks normal rather than enormous. When an object is far away it is scaled up so that it looks its normal size rather than tiny. This is known as **size constancy**. It means that we don't perceive objects as being bigger or smaller just because their distance from us changes.

Key definitions

size constancy: we perceive an object as the same size even when its distance from us changes.

Quick check

A (i) Would a hamster in your hand take up more or less space on your retina than the same hamster the other side of the room?

   (ii) Would the hamster seem to change in size if it ran around the room?

How do surroundings help us to see depth?

We can use information from the whole scene to tell how big an object is in relation to everything else. For example, an ant looks the same size in relation to a blade of grass whether it is nearby or far away. This helps our perceptual system to decide whether to scale the image of the ant up or down. If there was nothing around the image to help judge depth, this scaling would be more difficult. In other words, we need to be able to use depth cues so that we can maintain size constancy.

Size constancy is quite complicated to understand but these two ideas might help you to remember it:

The *size* of an object remains the same, that is, *constant*.

- **d**istant things are scaled **u**p to make them seem **b**igger than the image on the retina (think *d-u-b*)
- **ne**arby things are scaled **d**own to make them seem **s**maller than on the retina (think *ne-d-s*).

Quick check

B If you see a single, little dot of light on a very dark night it is sometimes hard to tell whether it is a big light a long way away or a small one that is closer. Why is this?

The context of the road and hills helps us to understand that the cars are the same size.

Questions

1. Would the image of an aeroplane fill more of your retina if you were beside it looking at it on the runway or if you were on the ground looking at it high up in the sky?

2. a) When does an object make a bigger image on the retina, when it is near or far away?

   b) Imagine you are on a safari and can see a giraffe in the distance. Will the image be scaled up or down? Explain why.

3. A girl is sitting on the beach eating an ice cream with a chocolate flake in it. Far off in the sand, a boy is crying because he has dropped his ice cream and the flake has fallen out. Will the girl's image of each flake be scaled up or down or neither? Explain why.

11

A1b3 Monocular depth cues 1

Learn about

- Relative size
- Texture gradient
- Height in the plane

Key definitions

relative size: smaller objects are perceived as further away than larger ones.

texture gradient: an area with a detailed pattern is perceived to be nearer than one with less detail.

height in the plane: objects closer to the horizon are perceived to be more distant than ones below or above the horizon.

Find two identical objects, e.g. pens or CDs, and put them at different distances from you. Make a circle with your thumb and forefinger and, with one eye, look through the 'hole'. Make the hole bigger or smaller to fit around the nearer object. Now look at the more distant object. It should take up less space in the hole. This difference in size is a cue to depth.

Quick check

A If you were drawing cars on a race track, would you make the cars at the far side of the track bigger or smaller than ones in the foreground?

Relative size

As we saw on page 10, a closer object makes a bigger image on the retina than a distant one. This is used as a cue to depth. It is called **relative size**. Objects making bigger images on the retina are perceived as being closer than ones making smaller images.

Relative size also indicates depth in photographs and drawings. In the photo below of a field of cows, those near to the photographer look bigger than ones in the distance.

Texture gradient

When a scene you are looking at has a surface with texture, such as cobblestones or a sandy beach, this helps you to judge depth. Close up, a textured surface is very detailed. From further away, the texture is less clear.

If you lie down on a carpet you can clearly see the tufts of wool in the area of the carpet very close to you. But if you look across to the other side of the room, you won't be able to see the individual tufts at all. The amount of detail you can see in the carpet would be less and less clear across the room. This is a *gradient*.

If we want to draw a **texture gradient** on paper, we can use patterns such as squares or lines. Where the pattern gets closer and closer together we perceive this to be the background. A clear pattern is perceived to be in the foreground.

We perceive bigger objects as being closer than smaller ones.

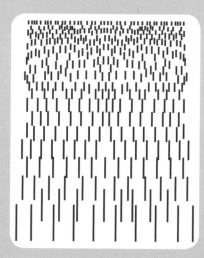

Examiner's tips

Students sometimes muddle up relative size and texture gradient. Remember that a few, separate things that get smaller in the background show relative size. If there is a pattern across all or part of the scene that gets closer together and less clear in the background, it is a texture gradient.

Height in the plane

Sit on the floor in a big room or corridor. Hold your hand flat and about halfway down your nose. Look underneath your hand. You should see the floor. Now look over the top of your hand. You should see a different part of the floor. The area of floor beneath your hand is closer to you than the floor you can see above your hand. This illustrates a cue to depth called **height in the plane**.

The area of floor at the 'bottom' of your field of view is close to you. The area of floor at the 'top' of your field of view is further away. In general, things lower in the scene are closer, those which are higher up are further away.

Quick check

B If there were lots of children in a park, would the children who were closest look higher or lower than those in the distance?

It is interesting that, above the horizon, the order is reversed. If we saw two birds in the sky, the higher one would be closer and the lower one further away. So things nearest to the horizon are furthest away.

Quick check

C Would a helicopter flying in the distance look higher or lower than one flying nearby?

Questions

1 In a drawing of robins, would a nearby robin be bigger or smaller than one further away?

2 The pattern of bricks along a wall is a texture gradient. How would the pattern look different at the near and far end of the wall?

3 a) In a field of rabbits, some make a smaller image on my retina. Why?

   b) In the distance, some of the rabbits make a smaller image than others. Why?

   c) Describe how the grass might look across the field.

   d) Which rabbits would be highest up?

Distant objects are closer to the horizon.

A1b4 Monocular depth cues 2

Learn about
- Superimposition
- Linear perspective

Look around you. Find two objects, where one is in front of the other. Can you tell that part of the object at the back is covered up by the thing in front of it? This helps you to know which one is closer. It is yet another cue to depth.

Superimposition

You might have heard the word 'superficial', which refers to the 'top layer' of something – like skin or someone's personality. 'Super' used in this way means 'on top of' or 'in front of'. The depth cue of **superimposition** is when the *position* of one object puts it *in front of* another. It tells us that the thing you can see must be nearer than the partly hidden object.

Taking it further

Go to www.heinemann.co.uk/hotlinks and enter express code 4837P. Click on the *University of Waterloo website* to see some animations that illustrate monocular depth cues.

We use position to help us to perceive depth. A partly concealed object must be behind the thing that is covering it.

Quick check

A If a dog owner is walking his dog and you can see the whole of the dog but not the lower part of the owner's legs, who is closer to you, the dog or the owner?

Examiner's tips

Although superimposition is sometimes called 'overlap', which is easy to remember, you must learn the proper term too.

Key definitions

superimposition: a partly hidden object must be further away than the object covering it.

linear perspective: parallel lines appear to converge (meet) in the distance.

Linear perspective

Parallel lines are ones that lie side-by-side, like the curb stones on either side of a road. Parallel lines in the real world never meet, they stay the same distance apart.

Imagine that you are looking at a very long, straight road. What seems to happen is that the road appears to get narrower in the distance. The edges seem to get closer and closer together. This is a depth cue called **linear perspective**. Lines which are parallel appear to converge in the distance. The 'lines' themselves do not have to be actual lines. Imagine the tops of a row of trees on either side of a road. They would form 'lines' and provide a linear perspective cue.

Quick check

B A child draws a picture of a house with a garden path. Should the path get narrower or wider towards the house?

14

Due to linear perspective we perceive parallel lines as getting closer together in the distance.

The vanishing point

Artists use linear perspective to help them to give the impression of depth in their work. Lines which represent parallel surfaces, like the buildings on either side of a street, will be drawn closer together in the distance. The parallel lines appear to meet at a point on the horizon called the 'vanishing point'.

Monocular depth cues working together

We don't just use monocular depth cues one at a time. In any scene many or all of the cues may be present. Find some drawings or photographs that have at least two depth cues each. You could use figures in other chapters of this book.

Questions

1 Which depth cue is relevant to the photo below?

2 Put your hand over the left-hand page of this book. Which depth cue tells you that your hand is closer than the page?

3 Draw a picture that contains both the depth cue of superimposition and the depth cue of linear perspective. Label each one.

4 Look at the drawing below by M.C. Escher. Find an example of linear perspective and an example of superimposition in the picture. Explain why the building is 'impossible'.

A1b5 Stereopsis: seeing in stereo

Learn about
- Stereopsis
- The role of the optic chiasma in stereopsis

As we saw on page 9, there are some cues to depth that use both eyes together. These are called binocular depth cues. One important binocular cue is **stereopsis**. This is a cue to depth that the brain works out by comparing the views from the left eye and the right eye. The bigger the difference between them, the closer the object you are looking at.

Pick up something about the size of a mug (an empty one!). Ideally choose something with a picture all over it. Hold it at arms' length. If you close one eye and then the other, it will probably look much the same through your left and your right eye. Now hold it up against your face. Again, close one eye and then the other. Look carefully at what you can see. You should find that the view you have of the object in your right eye is different from the view you have with your left eye.

Key definitions

stereopsis: a binocular cue to depth. The greater the difference between the view seen by the left eye and the right eye, the closer the viewer is looking.

Examiner's tips

Stereopsis seems like a very complex word, but it really just means 'vision using two eyes'. *'Stereo'* means 'two'. Think of stereo music - which comes out of two speakers. The second part of the word, *'opsis'*, means vision. Think about *'**opt**icians'* who help people to see clearly with glasses.

The dominant eye

When we look at an object with both eyes open, our brain forms one perception from the two images. The image on the right retina and the image on the left retina are combined. To do this, your brain has to 'map' one view onto the other. The brain uses one image as 'dominant', and the other image is mapped onto it. For some people the dominant image is the one from the right eye. For other people it is the image from the left eye.

Finding your dominant eye

Make a circle with your thumb and forefinger. Hold your hand out at arms length and look through the circle. Move it around until it fits exactly around an object. Now shut your left eye. If you can still see the object, you are right-eye dominant. If you can't see the object any more, open both eyes and line up the circle and object again. Now shut your right eye. The object should stay within the circle. This means you are left-eye dominant.

Quick check

A If you are right-eye dominant, which eye should you close if you are looking through the lens of a camera?

How stereopsis helps us to see depth

As we saw earlier, some of the information from each eye crosses into the other half of the head at the optic chiasma (see page 7). The brain can then compare the information from the left and right eye. As we have seen, when we are looking at something far away, the two images are very similar. When our eyes are focused nearer to us, the views of the left and right eye are more different. The brain can judge how different the two images are.

This Victorian toy uses stereopsis to produce a three-dimensional view from two photographs.

These photographs are used in a stereoscope. They are made by taking two photographs, moving the camera from the left to the right eye.

Look for differences between the photographs. Which pair were taken of an object close to the camera and which of an object that was further away from the camera?

If there is a lot of overlap between the left and right images, we must be looking at something far away. The greater the difference between the view of the two images, the closer the object we are looking at.

Taking it further

Go to www.heinemann.co.uk/hotlinks, enter express code 4837P and click on the *Optometrists Network website*. This website will tell you more about stereopsis and has some games to test your stereo vision. Around 5% of people in the world cannot fuse the images from both eyes, so have no binocular vision.

Quick check

B A child is looking at some toys in a playroom. With his left eye, the dolls' house looks very different from the way it looks with his right. The train looks very similar with both eyes. Which is closer, the train or the dolls' house?

Questions

1 Can a person who is blind in one eye use stereopsis as a cue to depth?

2 Sam looks out of his window with both eyes open and lines his finger up with a tree trunk. When he closes his left eye nothing happens, but when he closes his right eye his finger seems to jump away from the tree trunk. Is Sam left or right eye dominant?

3 Lucy is looking out of her window. First she looks at the cat just outside on the wall. Then she looks into the distance at a lorry. Will the difference between the left and right eye view be bigger when Lucy is looking at the cat or the lorry?

A1c1 Gestalt laws 1

18

Learn about
- The Gestalt laws
- Figure-ground
- The law of similarity

Seeing patterns

Look around you or out of a window. Can you see anything that stands out against a background? Can you see any groups of things?

When we look at the world around us, we tend to organise what we can see. We separate 'things' and 'not things', 'things that go together' and 'things that don't go together', and edges and solids. This can be explained by a set of perceptual rules called the **Gestalt laws**.

The whole is worth more than the sum of the parts

The Gestalt psychologists tried to explain *whole* situations and experiences. Many of the early Gestalt psychologists were German. Their name comes from the German word 'gestalt', which means 'good form'. They suggested that we build up our perception of the world from the retinal image. We do this by organising the parts of the scene we are looking at. These parts make up what is called the **stimulus**.

Organising these parts of what we can see (the stimulus information) gives us a more complete perception. So the 'whole' that we end up

with is worth more than the total of all the individual 'parts'.

Looking for Gestalt

Take a sheet of paper and cut a hole in it, about 1cm across . Hold the sheet over the picture below. You will only see a few coloured dots. Although you can move your paper all over the figure, at any one time you will only see some meaningless dots. If you take the paper away and look at the whole figure again, it has 'good form'. You can add together all the parts to make a meaningful whole.

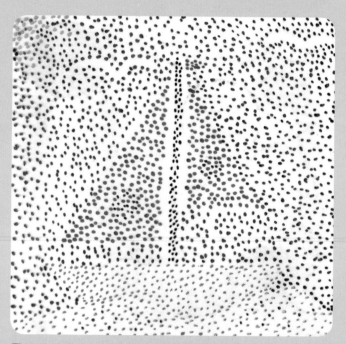

The whole is worth more than the sum of the parts.

Figure and ground

When we look at a scene it is made up of objects against backgrounds. A 'thing' such as a cow is seen as separate from a 'non-thing' like a field. The 'thing' is called the *figure* and the 'non-thing' is called the *ground*. This **figure-ground** relationship helps us to organise the visual scene. Think of the *figure* of a person against a back*ground*.

A figure has several features that make it different from the ground. Compared to the ground, the figure is:

- more complex   • smaller
- more symmetrical.

Key definitions

Gestalt laws: perceptual rules that organise stimuli.

figure-ground: a small, complex, symmetrical object (the figure) is seen as separate from a background (the ground).

similarity: figures sharing size, shape or colour are grouped together with other things that look the same.

The 'ground' is simpler, so it might be plain rather than patterned. It is larger than the figure and tends to fill the whole of the space around the figure. It is also more random or disorganised. The figure is more organised. It may be symmetrical so that one side looks like a mirror image of the other. These differences are illustrated in the table below.

Figure			Ground
Complex		Here the figure is white	Simple
Smaller		Look for a figure of a white cross. It is easier to see on the right	Larger
Symmetrical		The figure on the left is black but on the right is white	Disorganised

Even though the hot air balloon fills more of the scene than the sky, we still perceive it to be the figure as it is more complex. It is made up of lots of different parts, with different shapes and colours.

Taking it further

Go to www.heinemann.co.uk/hotlinks, enter express code 4837P and click on the *Indiana University Southeast website*. Click on each of the links on this page to see a smiley illustrating the Gestalt laws.

Quick check

A Look at this page. Are the letters, or the blue space around them, the figure?

Similarity

If you are in a classroom, look for some books on a shelf. Do they seem to be in sets?

What tells you that the books are grouped? Perhaps they are the same colour or height. We tend to group things that are similar, such as in:

- size
- colour
- shape.

Similarity is what helps us to group together things with the same characteristics and separate them from things which look different. Imagine lots of children visiting the zoo. You would group ones from the same school together because of their uniforms.

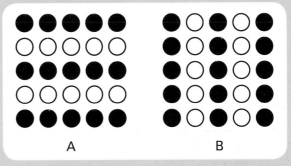

The law of similarity causes us to see rows of dots in (a) but columns of dots in (b).

Quick check

B If you saw lots of trees, would you be more likely to perceive them as a group if they were all the same kind or all different?

Questions

1 Peter watches a dog in a park. Will Peter perceive the dog or the park as the figure?

2 Would a large, simple, disorganised part of a scene be the figure or the ground?

3 Jo looks into her garden and sees different flowers. According to the law of similarity, why might she perceive them as grouped?

A1c2 Gestalt laws 2

Learn about
- The law of proximity
- The law of continuity
- The law of closure

Key definitions

proximity: objects which are close together are perceived to be related.

continuity: straight lines, curves and shapes are perceived to carry on being the same.

closure: lines or shapes are perceived as complete figures even if parts are missing.

Organising the stimulus

Look around and find examples of things that 'belong together'. You might have judged 'togetherness' using figure-ground or similarity, that we looked at on pages 18–19. Alternatively, you might have found things that belong together for other reasons. Here we will be exploring three other reasons why a stimulus can have 'good form'.

Proximity

If you are in a classroom, look at how the desks are arranged. Perhaps they are in rows or blocks, or people might be sitting at desks in pairs. We tend to see some things as grouped because they are close together.

A huddle of students in a corner will look like a group. The same students spread out in the room will not. When objects are near one another or, in other words, in close proximity, we perceive them to be related. This is the law of **proximity**.

The law of proximity makes us see the shoal of fish in the centre as a group because they are close together.

Continuity

Flick through a novel and see if you can find any 'rivers' running through the text. Sometimes the gaps between words on each line almost line up, making it look like there is a diagonal stripe across the page. Even though there is nothing joining the gaps together, we see them as linked. The law of **continuity** says that we will link things that follow a predictable pattern. This makes them look as if they are continuous or joined, even if they are not.

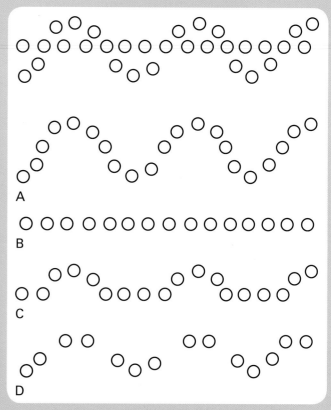

We tend to perceive lines A and B in the top figure rather than lines C and D. This is because lines A and B have good continuity.

We expect straight lines to carry on as straight lines, and curves to continue as smooth curves. This is another example of the Gestalt idea of 'good form'.

The law of continuity also explains why we tend to see regular shapes where we can. The drawing below shows how the same outline can be perceived in different ways if the lines inside are moved around. In each case we perceive the 'best form' using continuity of shapes and lines.

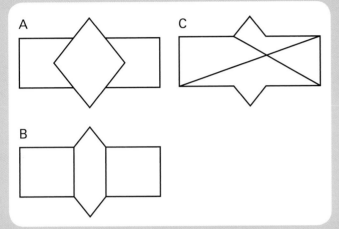

In A we see two overlapping shapes: a diamond and a rectangle. In B we see a long hexagon over a rectangle. Finally, in C we see two straight lines across a big, open shape.

Quick check

A Some primary school children are on a day out. Some are being marched along the pavement two-by-two in a 'crocodile'. Others are standing in little clusters. Which ones would you perceive as grouped because of proximity and which because of continuity?

Closure

We tend to perceive objects as a whole, even if they are not. If you almost draw a triangle but don't join up the last two sides, it still looks like a triangle doesn't it? This is because when we organise perception, we 'fill in the gaps'. This is called the

law of **closure**. Instead of seeing lines, we make the lines into a complete edge and therefore perceive a shape surrounded by the line.

Closure is more likely to happen when the shape produced by joining the lines is a regular one. So we are more likely to perceive a circle or a symmetrical polygon than an irregular shape.

If we see a familiar image, such as an outline of a house or a chair, we don't notice if there are parts missing. Do you notice anything odd about the drawings on the right?

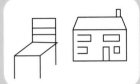

Closure causes us to perceive a hexagon in the figure even though there isn't a whole shape.

Examiner's tips

To help you to learn the difference between closure and continuity, remember that in 'closure' we close a gap to make a whole figure and in continuity we find a flowing 'continuous' pattern to link separate things together.

Taking it further

Go to www.heinemann.co.uk/hotlinks and enter code 4837P. Click on the *Spokane Falls Community College website* which shows you how the Gestalt laws have been used in the design of logos.

Questions

1 If cars in a car park are arranged in rows, which law will cause us to perceive them as related?
2 On a building site, some bricks are scattered on the ground and others are in piles. Which ones will be perceived as grouped and why?
3 Would closure of lines that made us perceive an oval or a random shape be more likely?

A1d1 What are illusions?

Learn about
- Illusions
- Fictions
- After-effects

Have you ever been sitting on a stationary train when the train next to it pulls out of the station? You probably felt as though you were moving in the opposite direction. This is a **visual illusion**.

Confused perceptions

Visual illusions occur when our perception conflicts (disagrees) with reality. We are not seeing the world as it really is. We see an illusion when we misinterpret the stimulus, so the physical reality and our perception disagree.

There are three types of illusion:

- fictions
- ambiguous figures
- distortions.

Key definitions

visual illusion: a conflict between reality and what we perceive.

fiction: an illusion caused when a figure is perceived even though it is not present in the stimulus.

illusory contour: a boundary (edge) that is perceived in a figure but is not present in the stimulus.

motion after-effect: an illusion caused by paying attention to movement in one direction and perceiving movement in the opposite direction immediately afterwards.

colour after-effect: an illusion caused by focusing on a coloured stimulus and perceiving opposite colours immediately afterwards.

Fictions

A **fiction** illusion occurs when you perceive a shape that is not there. Sometimes we perceive edges and believe that a shape exists when there is no actual boundary.

If you look at the illustration below you will see a circle. This is a fiction as there is no physical circle in the stimulus. This is called an **illusory contour**. You perceive a contour or 'edge' that isn't really there in the stimulus, so it is an illusion.

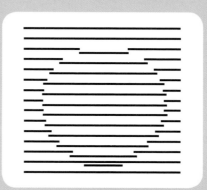

Do you perceive a circle?

Is there actually a circular line in the image?

Quick check

A There is a fiction illusion on page 21. What is the illusion?

After-effects

A special group of illusions are called after-effects. They are like fictions because they involve perceiving something like movement or a shape that is not in the stimulus. This happens when we look at a stimulus for a long time then look away. The after-effect is a perception that is the 'opposite' of the stimulus. Imagine staring at a picture of a black cat on a white background. The 'opposite' would be a white cat on a black background and this is what the after-effect would look like.

You can experience a **motion after-effect** at the end of a film. When the credits roll, watch the words moving upwards. If you look to the side of the screen when they end, the wall or curtains will appear to move downwards! This is an after-effect because you are perceiving movement in the opposite direction from the stimulus.

After-effects also happen with stationary objects. Follow the instructions for the image below. This shows an after-effect with a black-and-white picture. The result is that you perceive a meaningful image that was not present in the original stimulus. The light parts of the stimulus are perceived as dark in the after-effect and the dark areas are perceived as light.

Count to 20 while you concentrate on the white nose in the middle. Then look at an empty space in the margin. What can you see?

Colour after-effects

Just as with motion after-effects, we see **colour after-effects**, when we look at a stimulus, then look away.

This is the Greek letter Psi. It is the symbol that is used to represent psychology. Count slowly to 20 while you concentrate on the dot in the middle of the letter. Then look at an empty space in the margin. What can you see?

You should see a red Psi sign on a green background. This is a colour after-effect. Each colour is replaced with a different one.

Quick check

B In the colour after-effect exercise above, which colour replaces green and which colour replaces red?

Your retina has 'red', 'blue' and 'green' cones. The information from these is used in a special way. Information from the red and green cones is used to tell us about 'yellow'. This gives us perception using four colours: red, green, blue and yellow. The retina has special cells that use these four colours in pairs:

• red and green
• yellow and blue.

The special cells compare the amount of activity in cells for each colour in the pair. So, if you look at something red for a long time, the cells that detect red will get tired. The 'green' cells will be more active. This causes you to perceive a green after-effect. This works in reverse too. So if you stare at a green shape, the green cells get tired and you see a red after-effect. Exactly the same happens with the yellow and blue pair. Looking at a stimulus of one colour causes an after-effect of the other colour.

These effects can happen in different parts of the retina at the same time, causing a mixture of after-effects (see below).

Count to 30 while you concentrate on the black dot. Then look at a white space to the right. What can you see?

Questions

1 Name two types of illusion.

2 What is an illusion?

3 In a colour after-effect, what colour replaces:
   a) red?
   b) yellow?

4 Draw a fiction illusion of your own similar to the one of the hexagon on page 21.

A1d2 More illusions

Learn about
● Ambiguous figures
● Distortions

When someone makes an ambiguous comment, we can't tell what they mean. For example, think of the different ways you could interpret 'They are visiting firemen'.

Ambiguous figures

The same problem applies to some visual stimuli. If you can understand them in two different ways, then they are **ambiguous figures**. When a stimulus is ambiguous, you can only perceive one of the possible interpretations at a time. You can often swap between the two alternatives.

Necker cube

You can see the Necker cube, a two-dimensional picture of a box, as one or other of these:

• a see-through box with a red dot at the back
• a solid box with the red dot on the front.

In the Necker cube illusion, at least one of the possible interpretations is easy to see. For some people it is quite hard to see the alternative, or to flip between them.

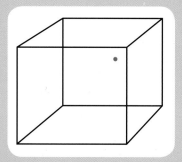

The Necker cube is an ambiguous figure because you can see it in two ways.

Leeper's lady

The picture opposite shows an ambiguous figure called 'Leeper's lady'. In fact, there are two ladies, a young one and an old one. Leeper (1935) showed participants a picture of a young or old face, then the 'Leeper's lady' illusion. The picture they had already seen affected their perception of the

illusion. Participants who had seen an old face identified the old woman first. Those who had seen a young face first interpreted the picture differently, identifying the young woman first.

Swapping between the two different interpretations is often quite difficult. It helps to look at individual features such as the eye, ear, mouth or neck.

Leeper's lady is an ambiguous figure. The two possible interpretations are the faces of a young or an old woman.

Quick check

A Draw a table matching up the facial features of the young woman and the old woman.

Taking it further

Go to www.heinemann.co.uk/hotlinks and enter code 4837P. The *Archimedes' Laboratory website* shows a different ambiguous figure.

Key definitions

ambiguous figure: a stimulus with two possible interpretations, in which it is possible to perceive only one of the alternatives at any time.

distortion illusion: where our perception is deceived by some aspect of the stimulus. This can affect the shape or size of an object.

Distortions

Have you ever known that what you are seeing is wrong? This is a **distortion illusion**. It happens when our perception is deceived by some aspect of the stimulus. A straight line may be perceived as curved or a shape may look bigger or smaller than it really is. If you go swimming, or keep fish, you might be familiar with the distortion when you look at something that is partly under water.

In a distortion illusion we perceive the world incorrectly because we are deceived by the stimulus.

There are some common geometrical distortion illusions. These are ones where shapes are perceived to be different from their actual form. They only work when seen on paper, that is in two

dimensions. If you can see the object in real life and walk around it, the illusion goes away. The images below illustrate several of these illusions. You can use a ruler to check whether you have been deceived.

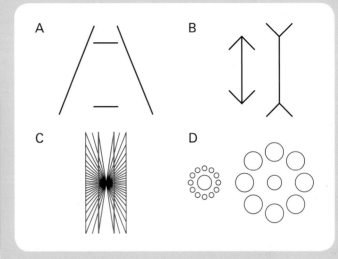

A Ponzo illusion: are the two bars the same length?
B Muller-Lyer illusion: are the two vertical lines the same?
C Hering illusion: are the two blue lines straight?
D Ebbinghaus illusion: are the two central circles the same size?

Taking it further

Go to www.heinemann.co.uk/hotlinks and enter code 4837P. Click on the *Michael Bach website* and the *University of Massachusetts Lowell website* to view more illusions.

Quick check

B Look at this image. Is this an ambiguous figure or a distortion illusion?

Questions

1 Look carefully at this image. You can see either an old man or a rat. What kind of illusion is it?

2 Look at the two lines in this figure. Do they look the same length? Now measure them. What type of illusion is this?

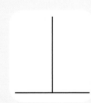

3 What makes an ambiguous figure ambiguous?

4 One group of participants in a study were shown pictures of animals followed by the illusion in question 1. Other participants just saw the illusion. Who do you think saw the rat?

A1e1 The Gestalt theory of illusions

26

> **Learn about**
> - The Gestalt theory of illusions
> - The strengths and weaknesses of the Gestalt theory of illusions

Using Gestalt ideas

The Gestalt laws (see pages 18–21) suggest that our perception organises the parts of a stimulus into a 'whole'. For example, we saw how we perceive groups and continuous lines using the laws of proximity, continuity and similarity. Because of figure-ground we separate 'objects' from 'backgrounds'. Finally, the Gestalt law of closure means that we tend to 'complete' edges and shapes.

We can use these ideas to help us to understand illusions.

Explaining fictions

A well-known illusion is the Kanizsa triangle (see below). A 'brighter than white' triangle is perceived in the middle, even though the edges of the shape are not physically there.

The Kanizsa triangle.

Illusions like the Kanizsa triangle can be explained by Gestalt theory. When we see a figure which is incomplete, our perception makes a 'whole' shape, using closure. We complete the edges to make a regular or familiar shape. This is the 'figure' of the figure-ground relationship. In the case of the

Kanizsa triangle, the arrow heads, 'bitten' circles and the space around them become the ground.

The triangle illusion changes if the circles are replaced with dots.

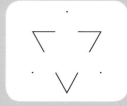

Now we see two interlocking triangles. Similarity organises the dots and lines, and continuity joins the lines to form a triangle.

Which do we recognise first?

Peterson (1994) conducted an experiment to see which we do first, divide the stimulus into figure-ground or recognise the object. She tested participants using stimuli like those shown below.

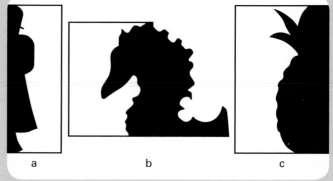

Stimuli from Peterson (1994).

The participants saw the images briefly and judged whether the white or black area was the figure. They generally said it was the black area. She tested them again with the images upside down to make recognising the objects difficult. The participants were slower to judge which area was the figure. This shows that they were recognising the object before they organised their perception into figure and ground.

Explaining distortions

Gestalt theory can explain the Müller-Lyer distortion illusion (see opposite). As you can see, the Müller-Lyer illusion still works when the 'fins' are replaced with circles. This suggests that in perceiving the figure as a whole, we tend to 'add' the fins or circles to the central lines. In Ai and Bi, this pulls the whole together, making it look smaller. In Aii and Bii, the fins and circles extend beyond the central line, stretching the whole figure out, and making the central line look longer.

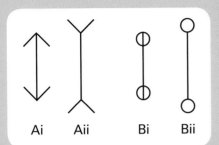

Two versions of the Müller-Lyer illusion.

Explaining ambiguous figures

When we identify an object it is the 'figure' and we separate it from the 'ground'. Normally any part of an image cannot be both. It can only be figure or ground. If we encounter a situation where something could be *either* figure *or* ground it becomes ambiguous, so we see an illusion.

Is the black area of the ambiguous figure shown below the ground? According to the Gestalt explanation, this is an illusion because we cannot tell whether the black or the white area is the figure. Both are meaningful objects. In (b), where the object is more distinct, the illusion is less noticeable. You are likely to see it as a real vase.

Rubin's vase illusion.
(a) Do you see a vase or two faces?
(b) Can you still see the faces?

The Gestalt explanation can account for other ambiguous figures. Look back at Leeper's lady (page 24). The problem is that there are two alternative figures. Because they are made up of the same parts of the stimulus they cannot be seen at the same time. The perception has to be organised differently to see each face.

Evaluating the Gestalt theory of illusions

Gestalt theory provides a good explanation for ambiguous figures. However, it cannot explain any distortions other than the Müller-Lyer illusion. The perspective theory (see page 28) probably explains distortion illusions better because it can explain more of them.

Gestalt theory explains fictions well, although there is a problem. Look back at the Kanisza triangle. The Gestalt explanation suggests that we would use closure to organise this figure. We should make a 'whole' even though there are parts missing. But if we did, we should see a six-pointed star. We don't, we see two triangles. Gestalt theory seems to use different explanations at different times.

A1e2 Gregory's perspective theory of illusions

Learn about
- Gregory's theory of illusions
- How to evaluate Gregory's theory

To understand this theory, you need to remember size constancy (see page 10) and monocular depth cues (pages 12–15). Some important ideas are size constancy and linear perspective.

When we judge an object to be far away, we scale it up because distant objects make small images on the retina. Nearby objects are scaled down because they make a larger image on the retina. This is how we maintain the relative size of objects regardless of their distance from us.

Linear perspective is a depth cue. It is the apparent convergence of parallel lines in the distance.

Distortion illusions often include angled lines, such as the fins of the Müller-Lyer illusion (see page 27) and the radiating lines of the Hering illusion. According to Gregory, we interpret these patterns as if they were depth cues. We then apply constancy scaling and distort our perception.

The Hering illusion
In the Hering illusion, the radiating lines look like a linear perspective cue. The people in the illusion opposite appear bigger towards the back of the scene. Measure them to check that they are all the same height.

The Hering illusion has linear perspective.

If the radiating lines act as linear perspective cues then we would use constancy scaling as if the scene really had depth. The person who appears 'furthest away' would be scaled up so they look bigger. The person who appears closest would be scaled down, and look smaller. This is exactly what we perceive.

The Ponzo illusion
The photograph below is like the Ponzo illusion (see page 25). The top red bar looks bigger than the bottom one. If the railway tracks are used as cues to liner perspective, the top bar would seem further away. As it is perceived to be more distant, it is scaled up so seems bigger than the bottom bar.

The Müller-Lyer illusion
The Müller-Lyer illusion can also be explained using the ideas of linear perspective and constancy scaling. The depth cue of the lines that appear to meet is linear perspective. This gives us an idea of distance. Because we recognise that one line is closer, we scale it down and perceive it as smaller.

Below are two images of a shop window. On the one taken from the outside, point A is closer to you than point B. Remember that we scale down things that are near us. This means that the vertical line on the outside of the building will be scaled down to make it look smaller. This is exactly the same as our perception of the effect of the inward pointing fins in the Müller-Lyer illusion.

On the second image point C is further way from you than point D. Because we scale up things that are further away, the vertical line on the inside of the building will be scaled up to make it look bigger. Again, this is exactly the effect we experience from the outward pointing fins in the Müller-Lyer illusion.

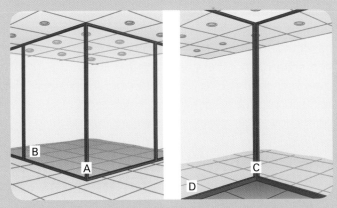

The Müller-Lyer illusion and the perspective theory.

Taking it further

Research the Ames Room on the internet. Look at photographs or drawings of the room and read about how one is built. Explain the illusion using Gregory's theory.

Evaluating Gregory's theory

Gregory's theory is a good explanation for distortions. If angled lines are used as depth cues, this explains many illusions. However, Gregory's theory cannot explain the version of the Müller-Lyer illusion shown on page 25 with circles instead of fins. The circles cannot provide cues to depth so this version of the illusion shouldn't work. But it does.

Cues to depth that form the basis of perspective theory might also help to explain other types of illusions such as ambiguous figures and fictions (pages 22–27).

Gregory's theory can explain some ambiguous figures when the two alternative figures are perceived using depth cues. For example, on Leeper's Lady the nose of the young woman looks further away than the wart on the old women's nose.

The Necker cube (page 24) can be perceived as two different solids. This is an ambiguous figure because the perspective cues can be interpreted in different ways. If this is prevented by adding more information about depth, the illusion goes away.

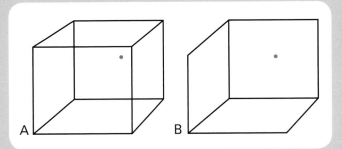

With the additional cue of superimposition, the illusion of the Necker cube disappears.

Depth cues can also explain some fictions. The oval shown below 'stands out'. This impression of depth comes from the position of the lines. The background lines appear closer to the horizon and so further away. By seeming nearer, the lines of the oval are perceived as separate.

A fiction illusion can indicate depth.

However, more of these illusions can be explained by Gestalt theory than by using depth cues.

Questions

1 Is this the inside or outside of a book? Explain how Gregory's theory would account for this distortion illusion.

2 The Zulu people live in circular houses with few straight lines or sharp corners. They tend not to be fooled by distortion illusions. Does this suggest that perception is learned or that we are born knowing about depth?

A1fl Schemas and perception

Learn about
- Schemas
- How schemas affect perception
- How psychologists have investigated schemas

Key definitions

schema (plural **schemas** or **schemata**): a framework of knowledge about an object, event or group of people that can affect our perception and help us to organise information and recall what we have seen.

perceptual set: the tendency to notice some things more than others. This can be caused by experience, context or expectations.

Imagine you are waiting for your friend. She has blond hair. You see a blond head in the crowd and run that way. You were sure you'd recognised her, but it isn't your friend. This shows how expectation can affect our perception.

Visual context and illusions

You have already learned about two explanations of illusions. Neither theory accounts for the Ebbinghaus illusion very well. Measure the central circles in the picture below. You will find they are the same size, even though the left-hand one looks bigger.

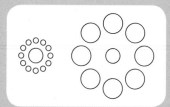

Which central circle is bigger?

This illusion happens because the outer circles provide a context. In contrast to the ring of small circles, the left-hand central one looks large. On the right, the central circle looks small compared to the big circles around it. The rest of the image provides information that causes us to perceive the central circles in different ways.

Visual context in the real world

Visual context is also important in the wider world. Brewer and Treyens (1981) took participants into a room to wait. They were told it was an office. They were then moved to another room and asked what they could remember about the first room. They recalled more objects that fitted with the context of an office, like a desk and chair. They tended not to recall the skull, bottle of wine or picnic hamper. Nine of the 30 participants said they had seen books, even though there weren't any!

Brewer and Treyens' study and the Ebbinghaus illusion suggest that context can produce expectations. One explanation for this is the idea of a **schema**. A schema is a framework we use to make sense of things. It includes our knowledge about something, such as an object or location. This knowledge affects our perception and understanding, helping us to organise information and recall what we have seen. Brewer and Treyens' participants were using an 'office schema' so remembered things that fitted their expectations of offices.

Palmer (1975)
Aim and procedure

Palmer wanted to find out whether context would affect perception.

64 students were tested in a laboratory experiment. They were shown visual scenes like the one of a kitchen, opposite. These scenes were shown for two seconds and provided a context. The participant was then briefly shown an object to identify. The

Key definitions

independent variable: the factor which is changed by the researcher in an experiment to make two or more conditions.

dependent variable: the factor which is measured in an experiment.

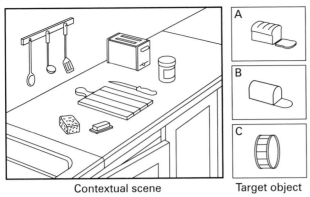

Example of drawings used in the experiment. The presentation of the scene establishes the context for one of the three drawings used as target objects for the scene: a loaf of bread (A), a mailbox (B), or a drum (C).

Examples of drawings used in Palmer's experiments.

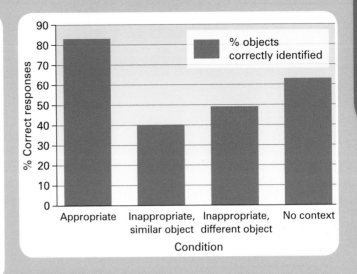

31

objects included a mail box, a loaf and a drum. The participants were given written instructions telling them what to do.

There were four conditions of the context shown to participants. These were the levels of the **independent variable**:

- *appropriate*: e.g. recognising a loaf after seeing a kitchen scene
- *inappropriate, similar object*: e.g. recognising a mailbox which looks like a loaf after seeing a kitchen scene
- *inappropriate, different object*: e.g. recognising a drum after seeing a kitchen scene
- *no context*.

Every participant was tested in each of the four conditions. This is a repeated measures design.

The number of correctly identified objects was counted. This was the **dependent variable**. If the participants gave different names (e.g. 'trash can' or 'garbage can') or named a similar object (e.g. pen/pencil) this was counted as correct.

Results

The participants correctly identified the most objects after seeing an appropriate context and the least after seeing an inappropriate context.

Conclusion

Expectations affect perception. People have a **perceptual set** based on context which affects how accurately they recognise objects.

Evaluation

Strengths:

- Palmer controlled how long participants saw the context and the object for, so the differences in accuracy were not caused by having longer to remember some objects.
- The participants had instructions so they knew exactly what to do.
- Data from two possible participants was not used as they had forgotten their glasses. This is good because poor vision could have affected the results.

Weaknesses:

- Because the participants were told what they would be doing, this might have caused them to try harder in some conditions. Differences between recall in different visual contexts might then have been because the participants were trying to please the experimenter.
- As data from some participants couldn't be used, this means there were fewer results.

Questions

1. What is a schema?
2. How well would one of Brewer and Treyens' participants remember seeing a calculator and an apple?
3. What schema would have helped Palmer's participants to identify a saucepan? Why?
4. Suggest a context that would have helped people to remember the drum in Palmer's study.

A1f2 Bartlett (1932): schemas and remembering stories

Learn about
● What Bartlett did and found
● The strengths and weaknesses of Bartlett's study

Do you remember a children's party game where you whispered a sentence to someone and they whispered it to the next person? This went on all round the group. The final sentence was nothing like the first!

Key definitions

serial reproduction: a task where a piece of information is passed from one participant to the next in a chain or 'series'. Differences between each version are measured.

repeated reproduction: a task where the participant is given a story or picture to remember. They then recall it several times after time delays. Differences between each version are measured.

Ways to study how people remember stories

You have read about research by Palmer on page 30. Like Palmer, Bartlett investigated the effects of schema. He used a technique like the 'Chinese Whispers' game, called **serial reproduction**. A piece of information is passed from one participant to the next in a chain or 'series'.

He also used another, similar, technique called **repeated reproduction**. In a repeated reproduction task, a participant is given some information, such as a story to read or picture to look at. It is taken away and they are asked to reproduce it. After a delay they are asked to reproduce it again.

Quick check

A Suggest one control that should be in place in a repeated reproduction task.

Bartlett (1932)

Aim: to investigate how information changes with each reproduction and to find out why the information changes.

Procedure

All of the tests used a folk tale called 'The War of the Ghosts'. This was a North American Indian folk tale so it came from a different culture from that of the participants. It was deliberately strange, with ideas and names that were unfamiliar to the participants.

One night two young men from Egulac went down the river to hunt seals, and while they were there it became foggy and calm. Then they heard war-cries, and they thought: "Maybe this is a war-party". They escaped to the shore, and hid behind a log. Now canoes came up, and they heard the noise of paddles, and saw one canoe coming up to them. There were five men in the canoe, and they said:

"What do you think? We wish to take you along. We are going up the river to make war on the people."

One of the young men said: "I have no arrows".

"Arrows are in the canoe," they said.

"I will not go along. I might be killed. My relatives do not know where I have gone. But you", he said, turning to the other, "may go with them."

So one of the young men went, but the other returned home.

And the warriors went on up the river to a town on the other side of Kalama. The people came down to the water, and they began to fight, and many were killed. But presently the young man heard one of the warriors say: "Quick, let us go home: that Indian has been hit". Now he thought: "Oh, they are ghosts". He did not feel sick, but they said he had been shot.

So the canoes went back to Egulac, and the young man went ashore to his house, and made a fire. And he told everybody and said: "Behold I accompanied the ghosts, and we went to fight. Many of our fellows were killed, and many of those who attacked us were killed. They said I was hit, and I did not feel sick".

He told it all, and then he became quiet. When the sun rose he fell down. Something black came out of his mouth. His face became contorted. The people jumped up and cried.

He was dead.

Barlett FC (1932) Remembering: A study in Experimental and Social Psychology, Cambridge University Press (original punctuation retained)

● *Serial reproduction task:* The first participant in a series read 'The War of the Ghosts' to themselves twice, at normal reading speed. They then waited 15–30 minutes before telling the story to the second participant. Each participant in a group of 10 repeated their story to the next person. This was done with several chains of participants.

- *Repeated reproduction task:* Each participant was tested separately. They read the story to themselves twice, at their normal reading speed. After 15 minutes, the participant gave their first reproduction. They could not look at the original story. Later reproductions were done at different intervals for different participants (e.g. 20 hours, 8 days, 6 months or 10 years). They could not look at their previous reproductions. Participants did not know the aim of the study. They assumed it was a test of the accuracy of recall. There were 20 participants, 13 men and 7 women.

Findings

Very, very few participants recalled the story accurately. Bartlett analysed the changes in the story and found patterns in the errors.

- *Form:* once a story has a particular outline it sticks, e.g. the order of events.
- *Details:* information such as names and numbers are lost. If remembered, they become stereotyped. Over a very long time they are remembered if they match the participant's interests or expectations.
- *Simplification:* events are made less complex. Details are left out or made more familiar. This can change the meaning of the story, e.g. the idea of 'ghosts' was often lost.
- *Addition:* inaccurate details are put in, e.g. to the building of a fire, one participant added 'probably to cook his breakfast'.

The serial reproductions showed the same changes as the repeated reproductions. They also showed clearly how one individual's interpretation affected all the others in the chain.

Taking it further

Try either repeated reproduction (on yourself) or serial reproduction (with your family or class) using an unfamiliar story. You could find one in a book, make one up or find one on the Internet. Go to www.heinemann.co.uk/hotlinks and enter code 4837P. Click on the *New Zealand Electronic Text Centre website* for some ideas.

Conclusion

Unfamiliar material changes when it is recalled. It becomes shorter, simpler and more stereotyped. This may be due to the effect of schema on memory.

Evaluation

Strengths:

- Both the repeated and serial reproduction tasks were done many times. This helped to show that the changes to the story followed the same patterns.
- Other stories were also used in serial reproductions. This showed that the changes weren't just special to 'The War of the Ghosts'.

Weaknesses:

- By choosing unfamiliar material, Bartlett could not be sure that the changes he found would happen with familiar information.
- Bartlett did not always test the repeated reproduction participants after the same time intervals, so the changes over time cannot be compared fairly.

Questions

1 a) Name two different ways that Bartlett found the story changed.

   b) Describe one of the changes you have named.

2 What is meant by a 'repeated reproduction' task?

3 Bartlett also tested serial reproduction of pictures such as the one below. Suggest one change that might happen to this picture and explain why you think the change would happen.

Original Drawing

A visual serial reproduction figure.

Alf3 Carmichael et al (1932): do words affect recall?

Learn about

● What Carmichael et al did and found

● The strengths and weaknesses of Carmichael et al's study

On page 24 we saw how showing people pictures that related to an ambiguous figure could affect their perception so that they saw one alternative or the other. The pictures set up an expectation or perceptual set. Do you think a perceptual set like this would have a long-term effect? Carmichael, Hogan and Walter (1932) were interested to see if words would remind their participants of a particular schema, and affect their memory.

Carmichael, Hogan & Walter (1932)

Aim to find out whether words shown with pictures would affect the way the pictures were remembered.

Procedure

The research method was a laboratory experiment. Ninety-five participants were split into three groups. They were shown 12 pictures (the stimulus figures below). Between each picture, the experimenter said 'The next figure resembles…' followed by a word from either list 1 or list 2. A control group (of nine participants) heard no verbal labels. These were the three levels of the independent variable. The experimental design was independent groups. The participants were then asked to draw the pictures they had seen. Their drawings were compared to the originals. This was the dependent variable.

Findings

The drawings produced by people who heard list 1 were very different from the drawings by people who heard list 2. In each case the drawings looked like the words the participants had heard.

Carmichael et al looked at how much the reproductions differed from the original figure. There were over 3000 reproductions and 905

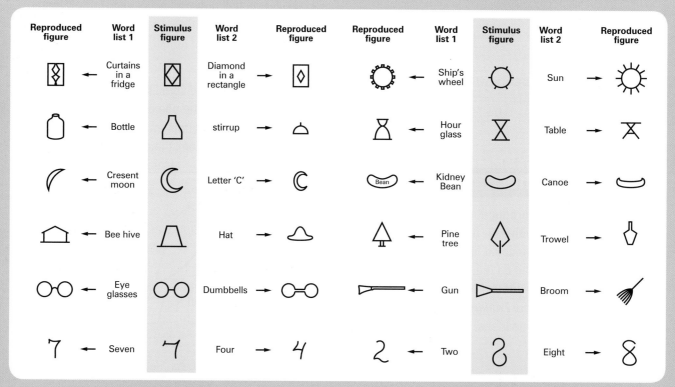

Do verbal labels affect recall of pictures?

reproductions were put in the category of 'almost completely changed'. These were analysed further. In the 'list 1' group, 73 per cent of the drawings resembled the word given. In the 'list 2' group, 74 per cent resembled the word given. In the control group (who had not heard any words) only 45 per cent resembled either one of the words. This shows that the words affected the participants' memory of the drawings.

Conclusion

Memory for pictures is **reconstructed**. The verbal context in which drawings are learned affects recall because the memory of the word alters the way the picture is represented.

Key definitions

reconstructive memory: recalled material is not just a 'copy' of what we see or hear. Information is stored and when it is remembered it is 'rebuilt', so can be affected by extra information and by ideas (like schemas) we might already have.

Quick check

A If the fourth drawing down had been given the verbal label 'mountain', how do you think the participants would have recalled it?

Evaluation

Strengths:

- By using a control group who did not hear any words at all, Carmichael et al could be sure that people's drawings weren't always distorted in the same way.
- By using two different lists they showed clearly that the verbal labels affected people's drawings.
- Having 12 pictures and many participants gave them lots of evidence, so they could be sure that the findings were not just a fluke.
- The findings are supported by recent evidence that verbal labels affect memory (Lupyan 2008 – see page 47).

Weaknesses:

- In real life things are not generally as ambiguous as the stimulus figures were. When we see an object, we can generally tell what it is and any verbal cues tend to match the stimulus, not contradict it. This means that the study wasn't very like real life.
- Prentice (1954) tested the effect of verbal labels on recognition rather than recall. The results showed that verbal labels didn't affect recognition. This would mean that Carmichael et al's findings did not apply very widely.

35

Questions

1 The figure below is similar to the ones in Carmichael et al's study. Explain why the participants produced the two reproductions.

Original figure

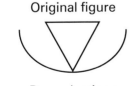

Reproductions

Verbal label 'Flower'

Verbal label 'Cup'

2 a) Draw a simple picture that Carmichael et al could have used in their study.

 b) Write down two words that could have been used to suggest different schemas.

 c) Do two more drawings to show how each of your words could have affected a participant's reproduction of the drawing you suggested in (a).

3 Explain one strength of Carmichael et al's study.

A2al Designing and understanding experiments

36

> ## Learn about
> - What an experiment is
> - What the terms 'dependent variable' and 'independent variable' mean
> - Experimental designs

You will have done experiments in science. Perhaps you've tested plants or chemicals. Psychologists conduct experiments too. They test people (known as *participants*) and animals. Some experiments in psychology are done in laboratories and others use real-world settings.

Psychologists conduct experiments on human participants.

An **experiment** is a way to find out whether one factor affects another. For example, if participants see a picture of an old or young person beforehand, does this affect the way they see the Leeper's Lady illusion (page 24) a few minutes later?

Variables in experiments

Let's suppose we want to find out whether looking at pictures of animals or people would affect the way we see the rat/man illusion.

There are two factors, or variables, involved here:

- which pictures we show first
- what the participants see in the illusion.

The variable we are changing is the kind of picture that is shown first. This is called the independent variable. We expect this to affect our participants. There are always different conditions, or 'levels', of the independent variable. In this case, the different conditions would be whether the participants are shown pictures of:

- animals
- people.

We are expecting these conditions to affect how the participants respond. The experimenter records or measures this change or difference. This is called the dependent variable. In our example, the dependent variable would be whatever the participants see in the illusion. The possible answers are:

- a rat
- a man
- nothing.

Experimental designs

In the rat/man experiment, would you want participants to do both the 'animal pictures' condition *and* the 'people pictures' condition? Probably not. Seeing the pictures and illusion once would affect their reaction in the other condition. It would be better to have two separate groups of participants, one seeing the animal pictures and a different group seeing the people pictures.

Key definitions

experiment: a research method which measures participants' performance in two or more conditions.

experimental (participant) design: the way that participants are used in different conditions in an experiment. They may all do all conditions or different participants may do each condition.

independent groups design: different participants are used in each condition in an experiment.

repeated measures design: the same participants are used in all the conditions in an experiment.

The way an experimenter arranges the participants into conditions is called the **experimental design**. It is sometimes called the **participant design**. When different participants do the different conditions, this is called an **independent groups design**. In the case of the rat/man experiment it would be better to have independent groups of participants seeing *either* the animal *or* the people pictures.

Sometimes it is better to use the same participants in all the conditions. Do you remember Peterson's experiment from page 26? She tested participants on a figure-ground task then tested them again with the same stimuli upside down. When the same participants are used in all the conditions in an experiment, this is called a **repeated measures design**.

Examiner's tips

To learn the names of the experimental designs, remember that in an independent groups design the groups of participants in each condition are *independent* – that is, they don't do the same thing. In a repeated measures design, the participants *repeat* the task because they do two or more conditions.

Taking it further

Go to www.heinemann.co.uk/hotlinks and enter code 4837P. The glossary on the *Gerard Keegan website* might help you with any terms you are finding difficult.

Questions

1 The blind spot illustration (see page 6) can be used to measure the size of a blind spot. The more letters that disappear when you look at the Z, the bigger the blind spot. Peter tests people to see if their blind spot is the same size in the left and right eye.

a) The independent variable is whether Peter is testing the left or right eye. What is the dependent variable?

b) Is Peter's experimental design independent groups or repeated measures?

A2a2 More about experiments

Learn about
- Hypotheses
- How controls are used in experiments

When psychologists do experiments they make predictions. Try drawing you own version of an illusion like the Kanizsa triangle (see page 26). Can you predict what people will see in your new illusion?

What is a hypothesis?

Psychologists use a statement called a **hypothesis** to say what they expect to happen in an experiment. A hypothesis is a statement that can be tested. It describes the difference a researcher expects to find between participants in the different conditions in their experiment. In other words, a hypothesis says how the independent variable will affect the dependent variable.

Key definitions

hypothesis (plural **hypotheses**): a testable statement of the difference between the conditions in an experiment. It describes how the independent variable will affect the dependent variable.

controls: ways to keep variables constant in all conditions of an experiment.

Writing hypotheses

On page 30, we saw how Brewer and Treyens (1981) compared participants' recall of objects in an office. Their independent variable was whether the objects belonged in an office or not. Their dependent variable was the objects that people remembered. The experimental design was repeated measures because each participant saw some objects that belonged in an office and some that didn't.

To write a hypothesis we need to make sure that our statement:

- includes the independent variable
- includes the dependent variable
- says how the independent variable will affect the dependent variable.

For Brewer and Treyens' experiment, the hypothesis would have included:

- the independent variable (whether the objects fitted an office schema or not)
- the dependent variable (which objects were remembered)
- the idea that objects fitting an office schema will be remembered better.

A suitable hypothesis could have said:

Objects seen in an office environment that belong there will be remembered better than objects which don't belong in an office.

In Leeper's experiment (see page 24) he tested the effect of showing participants a 'young woman' picture or an 'old woman' picture. These were the two conditions. He recorded what they saw in the ambiguous figure (either the face of a young or an old woman). He was predicting that the first picture shown, called a priming picture, would affect what the participants saw in the illusion. This can be written as a hypothesis:

The age of the face in the priming picture will affect whether the old or young face is seen in the ambiguous figure.

Quick check

A Using the description of Leeper's experiment and the hypothesis above, identify:

- the independent variable
- the dependent variable.

Which matters most: similarity or continuity?

Quick check

B You might recognise the image above from page 20. This could be used to see which Gestalt law is more important:

• similarity (we should see a line of blue dots and a line of green ones)

• continuity (we should see a straight line of blue and green dots and a wavy line of blue and green dots).

In an experiment to test this, the independent variable would be whether the pattern was coloured in (as here) or not (as on page 20). The dependent variable would be which lines the participants saw. Write a hypothesis for this experiment.

Controls in experiments

To make sure that only the independent variable affects the dependent variable – and nothing else – researchers use **controls**. A control is something that the researcher does to keep variables the same in all conditions.

In Palmer's experiment (page 30) several things were controlled. He made sure that the participants all had the same:

• amount of time to see the context scene
• gap before they saw the object they had to recognise.

These controls were important to make sure that any differences in the participants' ability to identify objects were not due to having seen some of them for more time than others or having longer to forget the context scene.

Quick check

C Suggest a control for Brewer and Treyens' experiment.

Questions

1 Suggest a control for Leeper's experiment.
2 Palmer's experiment (see page 30) investigated the effect of perceptual set. Identify the independent and dependent variables then write a suitable hypothesis for the study.
3 Veronica is doing an experiment testing the number of items of fruit and vegetables people can remember from a scene. She uses two scenes, a supermarket and a classroom. Each participant is tested using only one scene.
   a) Identify Veronica's independent variable.
   b) Identify Veronica's dependent variable.
   c) Write a suitable hypothesis for Veronica's experiment.
   d) Suggest two controls for Veronica's experiment.

A2a3 Dealing with results: descriptive statistics

Learn about
- Averages
- Finding the mode
- Drawing bar charts

When you have done experiments in science, or used data in maths, you might have drawn tables or graphs. The findings of psychology experiments are presented in the same ways.

If you did a science experiment where you tallied numbers, you'd probably put them in a table. What else could you do if you counted the number of people in your class with birthdays in each month of the year? You could find the **mode**.

There are different ways to collect data in psychology experiments. This means we need different ways to describe or summarise the results we find. There are two important ways we might want to describe the data from an experiment. These are called **descriptive statistics** and can tell us:

- a typical or average score
- how spread out the scores are.

Averages

Averages tell us how most people responded. This is useful as it gives us a general picture of the findings. For example, if we do an experiment with two conditions, we usually want to know the average score in each condition. This makes it easy to see if participants have got generally higher scores in one condition than the other. This would help us to decide whether our hypothesis was right or not.

Different kinds of experiments produce different kinds of data. For each kind of data there is a different kind of average.

The three kinds of average are:

- mode
- median
- mean

Our focus here will be on the mode. On pages 42–43 we will look at other descriptive statistics.

Key definitions

mode: an average that is the most common score or response in a set.

descriptive statistics: ways to summarise results from a study. They can show a typical or average score or how spread out the results are.

bar chart: a graph with separate bars. Usually there is one bar for each condition in an experiment.

Using the mode

In an experiment on the Leeper's Lady illusion (see page 24), the dependent variable could be measured using the question 'What do you see?' This would produce data in three categories:

- young woman
- old woman
- something else.

You would use a mode to find the average here because the results are in named categories. Other common named categories are 'yes' and 'no' and answers to questions such as 'Is it red, green or blue?' about an after-effect (see page 23).

Finding the mode

To find the mode, you need to work out the total number of scores in each category. You can do this with a tally chart or table. The category with the highest total is the mode. If there are two (or more) equally high totals, they are all modes.

For example, in an experiment on the duck/rabbit illusion (see page 25), the results were as follows:

Number of people giving each response to the ambiguous figure		
duck	rabbit	nothing
22	21	3

The mode is 'duck', as most people saw the duck in the ambiguous figure.

Quick check

A Zara shows everyone in her class the illusion shown below. She asks them whether A or B is the longer line, or whether they are the same. 19 people say 'A', five people say 'B' and six say they are the same. What is the mode?

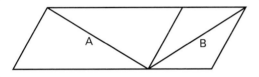

Bar charts

Sometimes we want to show the results of an experiment on a graph. One graph we can use is a **bar chart**. Bar charts can be used for several kinds of data:

- totals of scores from different conditions in an experiment
- the modal score for each condition in an experiment.

They are also used to show medians and means (see pages 42–43).

To draw a bar chart the conditions of the experiment (the independent variable) go along the x-axis (remember x is 'a-cross'). The total or average score goes on the y-axis (up the side).

There would be as many bars on the bar chart as there are conditions in the experiment.

Here is a bar chart for the data in the table on the left, on the duck/rabbit illusion.

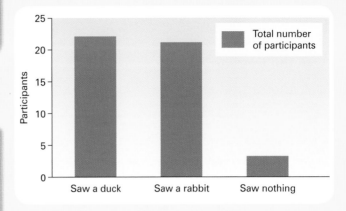

Quick check

B Here is a table of results from a study on the Ebbinghaus illusion (see page 30). Use them to draw a bar chart.

Number of people giving each response		
middle circle on left smaller	middle circle on right smaller	both middle circles are the same
2	18	10

Examiner's tips

Students sometimes draw separate bars for each participant's score. This is wrong! Don't do it.

Questions

1 What are 'descriptive statistics'?
2 What is an average?
3 Here is a set of scores from an experiment. What is the mode in this data set?
6, 4, 7, 3, 6, 2, 8, 6, 3, 2, 1, 8, 9, 5

A2a4 Dealing with results: more descriptive statistics

Learn about
- the mean
- the median
- the range

In science lessons you might have measured people's height. How would you find the typical height of someone in your class? You might also want to know about the tallest and shortest heights. You would need to use descriptive statistics.

More about averages

On pages 40–41 you learned about an average called the mode. There are two other averages: the median and the mean.

Using the median

In an experiment like Bartlett's (pages 32–33), each reproduction of the story could be rated on a scale of 0–10. If it was very like the original it would score 10 and if it was very different it would score 0.

You would use the **median** here because the scores are on a rating scale. Other rating scales include choices like 'very often/sometimes/occasionally/never' because these are in order.

Finding the median

To find the median, you put all the scores in order from smallest to largest. You then find the middle number in the list. You can do this by crossing pairs of numbers off each end of the list. The middle number is the median. If there are two numbers in the middle you add them together and divide by 2. This will also give you the median.

A researcher could test how sure a person was that they could 'see' the Kanizsa triangle.

First we put the scores in order:

1, 2, 4, 4, 4, 6, 7, 8, 9, 9 (you can see the scores at the bottom of the page). Then we find the middle score (or scores). Here there are two middle scores, 4 and 6, so we add them up and divide by 2. 10 divided by 2 equals 5, so the median is 5.

Using the mean

Using a computer, a researcher could show participants scenes and ask them to respond by pressing a key. They press one key if they see an object that fits the scene and another key if the object doesn't fit the scene. The researcher could measure how many seconds they take to press a key.

You would use the **mean** here because the results are measured on a mathematical scale. Measurements like seconds, centimetres and litres are all mathematical scales.

Finding the mean

To calculate the mean all the scores are added together. This total is divided by the number of scores (including any zero scores).

In the Poggendorf illusion below, the diagonal line doesn't look as though it is going directly through the box. This can be used in an experiment where only the black part of the illusion is drawn. The participant has to put in the other half of the line (without drawing across the box). When they have done this, the difference between where their line (the red one) leaves the box and where it should be (the green line) is measured in millimetres.

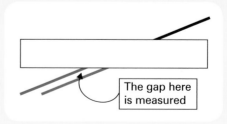

The gap here is measured

The Poggendorf illusion.

Participant number	1	2	3	4	5	6	7	8	9	10
Rating of confidence that they could see a shape	4	9	1	7	9	4	6	4	2	8

Quick check

A Work out the medians from these two tables of data:

Participant number	1	2	3	4	5	6	7	8	9	
Rating of amount of motion in a motion after-effect	6	4	6	2	3	7	1	8	2	

Participant number	1	2	3	4	5	6	7	8	9	10
Rating of brightness of a colour after-effect	7	4	2	3	2	8	7	6	5	1

Participant number	1	2	3	4	5
mm between their line and the correct place	3	2.5	0	1.5	3

The mean is calculated by adding up the scores (3+2.5+0+1.5+3=10) and dividing by the number of participants (5). 10/5=2, so the mean score is 2mm.

Looking at the range

Sometimes a researcher wants to know how spread out the scores are in a group. This is what the **range** shows. The range is worked out by finding the

Key definitions

median: an average that is the middle number in a set of scores when they are put in order from smallest to largest.

mean: an average that is calculated by adding up all the scores in a set and dividing by the number of scores.

range: a way to show how spread out a set of results is by looking at the biggest and smallest scores.

Quick check

B Work out the mean from this table of data:

Participant number	1	2	3	4	5	6	7	8	9	10
Seconds taken to press a key	0.5	1	0.2	0.3	1.5	0.8	0.7	0.6	0.4	1

biggest and smallest scores in the set. Sometimes the range is written as a single number (the biggest score minus the smallest score). If we have two sets of scores we can see which is the more spread out by looking at which has the bigger range.

Look back at the table of results given after the Poggendorf illusion above. The biggest score is 3mm and the smallest score is 0mm. So the range is written as 0–3mm.

We can draw bar charts (see page 41) of medians or means. Draw a bar chart for the medians you found in the tables in question A. The two conditions are 'colour after-effect' and 'motion after-effect'.

Quick check

C Work out the range for the data above.

Questions

1 Name three ways to work out the average.

2 What is the range for?

3 Paul did an experiment to measure the time taken by participants to press a key to say what they saw in the following illusion.

   Should Paul use mode, median or mean on the data?

A2bl Ethics in psychology experiments

Learn about
- Informed consent
- The right to withdraw
- How ethical issues are solved

Think about the psychology experiments you have done. Did you wonder what was going to happen? Maybe you worried about how good your answers were. Everybody feels a bit like this and researchers must make sure their participants are not harmed by what they do. Possible problems like these are called **ethical issues**.

Good ethics | Good controls

One problem for experimenters is that ethics sometimes conflict with the need for controls. Imagine doing an experiment like Carmichael et al's on memory (see page 34). Should we explain to the participants exactly what we expect to happen? No, because this would affect how they behaved and could produce errors in our results. We would need to control the amount they knew. We might even want to hide the real aim of the experiment – and deceive the participants.

Ethical issues

Two ethical issues are:

- **informed consent**
- **right to withdraw**.

If you were a participant in Bartlett's 'War of the Ghosts' study (see page 32) what would you want to know beforehand? Perhaps whether you would be tested alone or in a group. Maybe you'd wonder how many times you had to come to the lab. Or you might not want to come back if you were embarrassed because you didn't remember the story very well. All of these are possible ethical issues.

Informed consent

Participants should know what they will have to do. Imagine volunteering for an experiment on phobias and being shown pictures of spiders if you hated them! Participants might want to know what the task will be, whether they will be in competition with others and what the results will be used for.

Right to withdraw

Participants should not feel they have to carry on with an experiment if they don't want to. If you thought you'd done badly in an experiment, would you do the second condition? Probably not.

Even if the experimenter has paid participants to attend, they should still be able to leave at any time.

Quick check

A Dan is doing a study on memory and gives each participant a card which says 'if you don't want to do the memory test, you can go.' Is this solving the issue of informed consent or right to withdraw?

Quick check

B Neena's experiment is on perception and context. She asks her participants if they are happy to watch a video about gardens and answer some questions. Is this solving the issue of informed consent or right to withdraw?

Ethical guidelines

To help psychologists know how to avoid ethical issues, organisations like the British Psychological Society (BPS) provide ideas to help them. These are not laws but advice, so they are called **ethical guidelines**.

The BPS 'Code of Ethics and Conduct (2006)' gives this guidance:

Informed consent:

- The aims and procedure of the study should be clear to all participants, especially children, vulnerable adults and prisoners.
- If a researcher cannot get informed consent before testing, they should get consent from the ethical committee at their place of work or, if there is not one, then they should ask their peers and colleagues for advice.
- People in public places cannot give informed consent so research should only be done where people would expect to be seen by strangers. Local culture and privacy are important to consider.
- Participants should not be deceived unless:
  - it is essential to the research
  - extra ethical care is taken
  - they are told the truth as soon as possible.

Self-determination:

- Participants should know they can leave at any time.
- Participants can ask for any results that identify them to be removed from the data.

Solving ethical problems

Psychologists often give participants a summary about what will happen in a study. The participant can then choose whether to join in. This is a good way to get informed consent.

For studies done in public places like parks, it is hard to ask everyone if they are happy to participate. Instead, researchers can ask other people, such as colleagues, whether they think people would mind.

Participants might be frightened of coming into a laboratory in case they feel trapped. Researchers can start a study off by saying 'you can leave at any time'. This would help to put participants at ease, knowing they can go if they want to.

Key definitions

ethical issues: potential psychological or physical risks for people in experiments.

informed consent: an individual's right to know what will happen in an experiment, and its aims, before agreeing to participate.

right to withdraw: a participant's right to leave a study at any time and their ability to do so.

ethical guidelines: advice to help psychologists solve ethical issues.

Quick check

C Dheeraj cannot obtain informed consent before testing his participants.
   (i) Who should he ask about this ethical problem?
   (ii) When he tests his participants, why does he have to explain the experiment to them?
   (iii) What else does Dheeraj have to tell the participants before he starts?

Questions

1 a) Name two ethical issues in experiments.
  b) How would you solve these problems?
2 Why might paying participants be a problem and what should a researcher do to make sure they are being ethical if they do?

A2cl Evaluating experiments

Learn about
- The strengths of experiments
- The weaknesses of experiments

In your course you have:

- learned how experiments work
- studied examples of experiments
- done some experiments yourself.

These will all help you to understand how to evaluate experiments.

Strengths of experiments

Informed consent
In a laboratory experiment, you can explain what will happen to the participants. This is ethically good as they can give their consent. If they are told *why* they are doing the experiment this can cause problems. The participants may change how they behave, which would alter the results.

Right to withdraw
When participants come into the laboratory their right to withdraw can be explained. They will then know that they can leave if they want to. This cannot be done if the research is being carried out in a real-life setting and the participants don't know they are in a study.

Only the independent variable (IV) affects the dependent variable (DV)
One of the main strengths of experiments is that the variables can be controlled. The experimenter sets up the different conditions of the IV. This means they can be sure that any changes in the DV have happened because of the changes they have made.

Controls
The experimenter can control other factors that could change the DV. In Palmer's experiment the time that participants saw the stimuli was carefully controlled. This was important as the longer you spend looking at a scene, the more likely you are to remember it. By controlling other variables, the experimenter can be certain that differences in the DV have been caused by the different conditions.

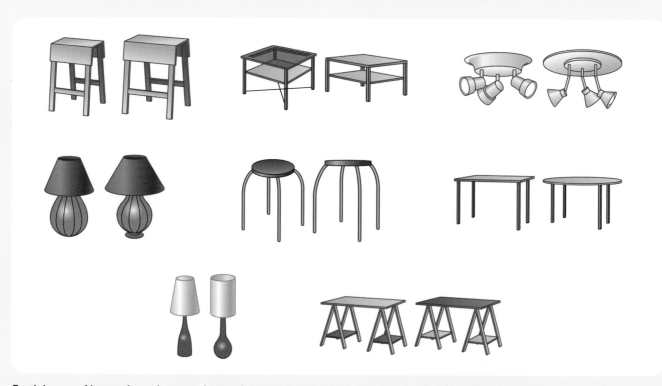

Participants of Lupyan's study were shown pictures of chairs, lamps and tables like the ones shown above.

Measuring the dependent variable
The DV can be measured accurately. This is illustrated in a recent study by Lupyan (2008). In this experiment, participants were asked to look at pictures of chairs, lamps and tables from an IKEA furniture catalogue, like the ones opposite.

Some participants were given a category name for each furniture type. Participants were timed to see how quickly they could recognise the items they had seen in amongst other similar pictures. Lupyan found that people were slower to recognise the pictures if they had been given a category name. Like Carmichael et al (see page 34), he found that labels affected memory.

Lupyan was able to score the DV very accurately. He measured the time taken to recognise the pictures in milliseconds. A millisecond (ms) is one thousandth of a second. Participants took around 300 ms to recognise pieces of furniture.

Weaknesses of experiments

Hiding experimental aims
Sometimes we need to avoid giving participants full information about a study. This is because knowing the aims of the experiment might alter the way that they behave.

Think about how participants might have responded in Palmer's experiment (see page 30) if they had known the aim. They might have deliberately looked for objects that did or didn't match the visual scene and been less affected by context.

Deception
Not knowing the purpose of a study might upset participants. Imagine being in an experiment that you believe is about guilt and innocence. You find the examples of crimes very distressing but do the recall test because you think it's for a worthwhile cause. Later you are told the experiment was really about whether recall is better when you are given key words. You might feel you had been tricked into doing a study on memory which you think is less important than crime and punishment.

Researchers sometimes need to deliberately deceive participants. Even when deception is used, psychologists can minimise harm to participants by:

- avoiding deception unless it is really necessary
- avoiding other ethical problems such as embarrassment
- explaining the real purpose as soon as possible
- allowing them to withdraw their results at the end.

Representing real life
Experiments are often set in laboratories. These are unfamiliar for participants so they might behave oddly compared to normal. The tests that psychologists use can also be unlike real life. We don't often have to identify chairs or find mail boxes in kitchens! This means that the findings from these experiments might not be very like the way people would really perceive or remember in everyday tasks.

Examiner's tips
You can often use the experiments you know to gain extra marks by giving examples to illustrate the point you are making.

Taking it further
Go to www.heinemann.co.uk/hotlinks and enter code 4837P. Click on the *Queen's University Belfast website* to see what to consider when asking for informed consent and a link to a real consent form.

Questions
1 a) Lupyan's participants gave their informed consent. Is this a strength or a weakness?
   b) They also received either $7 or a course credit. Could they still withdraw?
2 Describe one strength of Palmer's experiment.
3 Describe one weakness of Carmichael et al's experiment.

A3al Schemas and eyewitness memory

Learn about

- What an eyewitness is
- Factors that affect eyewitness accuracy
- Why eyewitness accuracy is important to society

Suppose you are coming home from school and notice someone walking ahead of you. They slow down and look through the open window of a car on the roadside. Glancing around, they reach in, pick up something from the seat, walk quickly away and turn down a side street. You could be an **eyewitness**.

Someone who sees a crime being committed is an eyewitness.

Eyewitnesses

An eyewitness is somebody who has seen a crime and can help the police to solve it. What an eyewitness remembers about what they have seen is therefore very important.

The statement the eyewitness gives to the police is called their testimony. Sometimes an eyewitness's testimony is not very accurate. This matters because either an innocent person could be accused of a crime or a criminal could go free. Psychology helps us to understand what can go wrong with an eyewitness's perception and memory of the scene.

Eyewitnesses are often important in crimes such as robberies and fights. They need to be able to accurately report facts such as what individuals looked like, what they were doing and whether they were carrying anything.

Eyewitnesses and schemas

Studies like Bartlett (see page 32), Palmer (page 30) and Carmichael et al (page 34) show that memory is reconstructive. What we see or hear is stored and when it is recalled it is 'rebuilt', so can be affected by expectations, schemas and new information.

Bartlett's participants reconstructed the 'War of the Ghosts' story using their knowledge of fighting, boats and other familiar things. Because the story was unfamiliar, their own ideas made their memory inaccurate. This suggests that things which are unfamiliar to eyewitnesses might be remembered less well.

Key definitions

eyewitness: somebody who sees a crime or aspects of a crime scene and who helps the police to find out what has happened or to catch whoever was responsible.

Palmer found that we recognise items more accurately if they are in the 'right' context. Eyewitnesses might therefore recall events better if they fit in with their expectations.

These ideas are based on experimental situations. However, the ideas do relate to how we perceive people in the real world. For example, you probably have schemas for your teachers. Perhaps one is very strict and she always sets homework. If so, you might also expect her to be cross when you forget your textbook. You might apply this schema to a new teacher who also seems strict, perhaps believing that they will set hard tests.

Schemas are useful because they help us to predict what will happen in the future – we might guess that the new teacher will get angry if we talk in class. As schemas affect the way we interpret new situations, they can affect memory.

Quick check

A If you saw a new teacher telling someone off, you might think they were being harsh because that would fit in with your expectation. Why might you 'remember' the new teacher shouting at the student, even if they didn't?

Taking it further

Use a search engine like Google images to find pictures of teachers at a whiteboard. Ask everyone in your class which teacher they think looks:

- most fun
- strictest.

Does everyone have the same schema for teachers?

If eyewitnesses use schemas to organise information about a crime they have seen, then their recall of events may be affected. Tuckey and Brewer (2003) tested this idea by finding out what people thought was typical of bank robberies. They used this to identify what was in a 'bank robbery schema'. They showed participants a video of a bank robbery that contained three kinds of facts. Ones that:

- fitted the schema – e.g. male robbers, carry bags, escape in a car
- were the opposite of the schema – e.g. the robbers didn't carry guns
- were irrelevant to the schema – e.g. wearing hats, what the getaway car was like.

Participants were asked about what they could recall immediately and then again several times over 12 weeks. Tuckey and Brewer found that they remembered the facts that fitted the schema, or were the opposite, very well. They only forgot things that were irrelevant to the schema. This suggests that eyewitness memory might benefit from schemas.

Allport & Postman (1945) used a picture of two men talking in an underground station in a serial reproduction task (like Bartlett's on page 32). A black man wearing a suit was talking to a white man in overalls, who was holding a razor. In the picture the white man has the razor in one hand and is pointing with the other.

In more than half of the reproductions the black man was falsely recalled with the razor and in some he was reported to be 'threatening' the white man with it. These errors could happen if the participants had a schema that linked black people to crime. If this distortion applied to eyewitnesses, it would make them unreliable.

Boon & Davis (1987) conducted a similar study. They showed participants slides of a violent knife attack by a white man on the London Underground. Some participants then saw two white men fighting, others saw a fight between a black and a white man.

When asked to recognise the scene, many participants wrongly chose the image with the black man holding the knife. But they did not make this mistake when asked to describe the situation instead. This shows that some memory tasks are more likely to be affected by schema. For example, when an eyewitness makes a statement they are recalling information and should be quite accurate. But when asked to identify a person in a line-up (a recognition task) they may be less accurate.

Questions

1 What is an eyewitness?
2 Joe believes old people are crafty. He sees an old lady leaving a shop with a loaf she hasn't paid for. Will Joe think she is forgetful or was stealing?
3 A possible schema might relate bikers to violent crime. Explain how this schema could distort a witness's memory if they see two men fighting and a biker trying to split them up.

Know Zone - Topic A
How do we see our world?

You should know...

ANSWERING THE QUESTION

- [ ] How the eye and the brain help us to perceive the world around us.
- [ ] Depth cues, including superimposition, relative size, linear perspective, stereopsis, texture gradient, height in the plane, and size constancy.
- [ ] Gestalt laws, including figure-ground, continuity, proximity, similarity and closure.
- [ ] Visual illusions, including fictions, ambiguous figures and distortions.
- [ ] Explanations of illusions, such as the Gestalt theory and Gregory's work on perspective theory. You should be able to evaluate both theories.
- [ ] The influence of schemas on how we interpret our world, drawing on the work of Palmer, Bartlett and Carmichael, Hogan & Walter.
- [ ] The ethical issues in experiments, such as informed consent and the right to withdraw, and how these may be dealt with.

EVALUATING THE ANSWER

- [ ] An evaluation of the use of laboratory experiments as a research method.
- [ ] Palmer's study used clear instructions and controlled the timings of the experiments to keep the data valid. They also discounted data from participants with bad sight on the day.
- [ ] Palmer's study may be less valid as participants knew what was being studied; this may have affected their responses.
- [ ] Bartlett's study used repeated reproduction to increase the validity of their data, as well as using other stories to show that their findings worked in many cases.
- [ ] Bartlett failed to keep the time between reproductions constant, which may make the results less meaningful.
- [ ] Bartlett used only unfamiliar material for the study, meaning effects with well known material couldn't be implied.
- [ ] Carmichael et al's study made good use of control groups to verify their data, and by using two separate lists they clearly demonstrated the effects of verbal labels.
- [ ] Carmichael et al's stimulus figures and verbal cues were not lifelike enough, meaning the findings may not reflect the real world.
- [ ] Other studies suggest Carmichael et al's findings cannot be applied widely as they didn't take recognition into account.

Support activity

The parents of the children at Smugglers' Cove primary school are having an argument with the teachers. The children are wearing a patch over one eye and running around the playground pretending to be pirates. The parents say this is not safe because the children cannot judge depth properly. The teachers are saying the children can judge depth perfectly well. The head teacher wants to put an explanation of both sides of the argument on the school website.

Design a webpage that explains why both eyes are needed for stereopsis but the children would only need to use one eye to apply monocular depth cues.

Stretch activity

Make a table of good and bad points about Gregory's explanation of illusions and another table for the Gestalt explanation of illusions. Use one of your tables to write an answer to the following question:

Describe and evaluate one explanation of illusions.

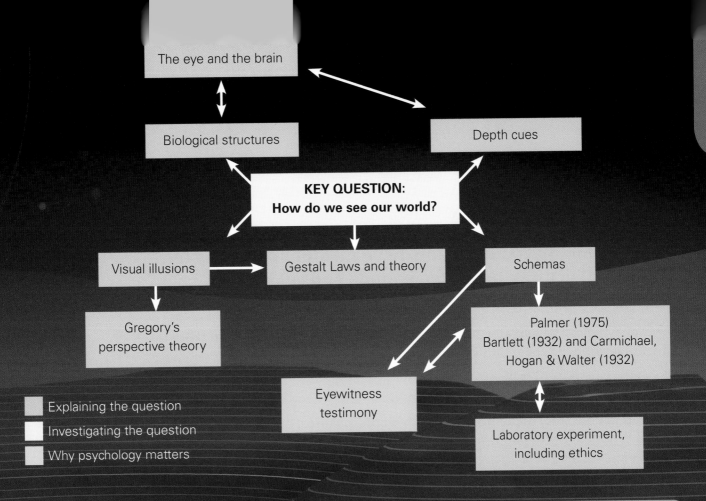

The eye and the brain

Biological structures

Depth cues

KEY QUESTION:
How do we see our world?

Visual illusions

Gestalt Laws and theory

Schemas

Gregory's
perspective theory

Palmer (1975)
Bartlett (1932) and Carmichael,
Hogan & Walter (1932)

Eyewitness
testimony

Laboratory experiment,
including ethics

- Explaining the question
- Investigating the question
- Why psychology matters

Examiner's tip: Stretch activity

To gain a good mark, try to balance your answer evenly between describing what the theory says and your evaluation of how good it is. You should also include points about the theory that are strengths as well as some points that are weaknesses.

Key terms

- Independent variable
- Dependent variable
- Experimental hypothesis
- Experimental (participant) design
- Repeated measures design
- Independent groups design
- Descriptive statistics (mean, median, mode, range)
- Bar chart
- Control of variables
- Informed consent
- Right to withdraw

Practice Exam Questions

1   Why do we have a blind spot in our vision?

2   Explain how a researcher would set up a repeated measures design in an experiment.

3   Write a hypothesis for an experiment like Palmer (1975) that tests whether people are better at remembering objects in the correct context.

Topic B
Is dreaming meaningful?

Introduction

Do you think that your dreams have meaning? Dreams have words and pictures, and often sounds and colours too, so they have meaning for us – they even partly make sense.

However, when we say dreams have 'meaning' we are usually saying that there is something symbolic about our dreams.

What can we say about dreams?

- We can tell the story of our dreams – with words, pictures, colours and sounds.
- But the story of the dream is often not clear at all. We make it make sense.
- A dream may hide deep thoughts, fears and wishes.
- But perhaps a dream is 'just' a biological feature – a random firing of thoughts.

Explaining the question

You will explain the question 'Is dreaming meaningful?' by looking at:

- Freud's work on the meaning behind dreams
- neurons and how messages are sent in the brain
- a theory that says dreams have a biological explanation.

Then you will see how to compare these explanations.

Investigating the question

You will investigate the question by learning how case studies are carried out, and about the terminology researchers use. Case studies are about people – find out how their privacy can be protected.

Is the case study a good research method? What are the good and bad points? See how to evaluate (decide the good and bad points about) a study or theory.

Then you can read about an actual case study that Freud carried out when he analysed the dreams of a young boy.

We cannot know what other people dream, so it is a hard topic to study.

Why psychology matters

Dream analysis is one of the tools psychoanalysts use to help people who are having difficulties. Learn more about what a psychoanalyst does, how they are trained and where they might work.

What happens if we don't get enough good quality sleep? Sleeping and dreaming are crucial to our well-being. Find out about REM sleep and sleep disorders. What can a sleep disorder clinic do to help people who need help with sleeping?

The mind is emotions; dreams are emotions

The brain is biology; dreams are biology

B1a1 Freud's (1900) dream theory

Learn about

● Freud's theory of dreaming
● How dreams reveal powerful unconscious thoughts

Freud thought that dreams have symbolic meaning for the dreamer.

Who was Freud?

Freud is the name you need to remember when talking about dreams having meaning. Over one hundred years ago Freud, who was a doctor living in Vienna in Austria, thought that dreaming was a very important part of a person's life because, through dreams, a person's unconscious wishes and desires could be understood.

What is the unconscious?

Freud thought that a large part of the mind is not accessible and is hidden completely. He called this the unconscious mind. The conscious mind is what we are aware of and what we can remember, discuss and deal with. Some of what is in the unconscious is repressed to help someone to forget or not deal with problems. Repression means something being pushed into the unconscious by the conscious mind, though this is not deliberately done, which means someone would not know what 'dark secrets' they were repressing.

Freud's ideas about the mentally ill

Freud as a young man trained as a doctor and was very distressed at how little was being done for the mentally ill. We would call the 'treatments' at that time cruel, for example shaking patients to shake out demons. Freud wanted to do better and started to wonder about mental health as opposed to physical health. He travelled to France and learned about hypnotism, which he became very interested in. However, he rejected hypnotism because the person could not then remember the sessions, which he thought was important. Nonetheless, he realised that the mind was powerful and could cause mental health problems.

Focus on sexual thoughts

One main reason for Freud being such a well-known figure, even after all this time, is that he focused on how sexual issues were very important for humans. Discussing sexual issues was not socially acceptable in Freud's day. When Freud talked about repressed unconscious thoughts he was often talking about repressed sexual wishes and desires.

Examiner's tips

Freud talked about the unconscious not the subconscious. Don't make the mistake of using the term 'subconscious', because this is not the correct term and had no meaning for Freud.

Taking it further

Go to www.heinemann.co.uk/hotlinks, enter express code 4837P, and click on the *Freud Museum website*.

Quick check

A Why did Freud reject the use of hypnotism?

The power of the unconscious

According to Freud:

- we have conscious thoughts – that we know about and can describe
- we have unconscious thoughts – that we do not know about and cannot describe
- our unconscious thoughts, wishes and desires guide a lot of our behaviour.

Freud said the unconscious is very important and consists of around 90 per cent of our thinking. He thought that through the analysis of our dreams our unconscious thoughts, wishes and desires could be uncovered.

Features of dreams

According to Freud:

- dreams have a **manifest content**, which is the story of the dream that the dreamer tells
- dreams have a **latent content**, which is the underlying meaning of the dream – the hidden content of the dream
- the latent content is what is hiding behind the manifest content.

Quick check

B Omar said he dreamt about falling down the stairs. An analyst said this showed his anxiety about his school work.

(i) Who described the latent content?

(ii) Who described the manifest content?

Dreamwork

Dreamwork is what the mind is doing whilst dreaming – keeping unconscious thoughts hidden and repressed. It is the job of the mind when dreaming to help protect the individual from undesirable thoughts, and dreamwork is the term for this 'job'. Sometimes the term 'dreamwork' is used to describe the analysis of dreams, which is a different meaning from the one used in Freud's theory.

Dreamwork includes condensation, displacement, and secondary elaboration (sometimes called 'secondary revision'). These are Freud's terms that he used to explain the purpose of dreams.

Condensation, displacement and secondary elaboration

- **Condensation:** many ideas appearing as one idea in a dream. These separate elements are important in uncovering repressed material so that one idea needs to be unpicked.
- **Displacement:** something unimportant that seems to be important, in order to shift attention from what is really important
- **Secondary elaboration:** using muddled ideas from dreamwork to build a whole story. The dreamer will add bits to the dream when telling someone what it is about to try to make the dream make sense. This gets in the way of understanding the latent content of the dream.

Key definitions

manifest content: what the dream is said to be about by the dreamer – the story the dreamer tells.

latent content: the meaning underlying the dream. If the symbols from the manifest content are translated by an analyst, they can reveal unconscious thoughts.

condensation: when many thoughts and elements from the unconscious are represented in the dream in one symbol.

displacement: when something that seems to be unimportant in the dream is made central, to shift attention from what is really important.

secondary elaboration: how the dreamer builds a story when telling what the dream is about, adding to and changing things, which makes analysis hard.

Quick check

C What term is used when someone focuses on something in their dream that seems to be unimportant?

Questions

1 What are three features of dreamwork?

2 Explain the terms 'manifest content' and 'latent content'.

3 Explain how some features of dreams according to Freud make it hard for an analyst to uncover the 'true' meaning of a dream.

55

Bla2 Symbols in dreams

Learn about

- Applying condensation, displacement and secondary elaboration to a dream to help uncover themes
- Some ideas (not Freud's) of what symbols in dreams might mean

Dreamwork

As we saw on page 55, an analyst can help to interpret a dream by unpicking themes in the dream and considering how one idea might represent condensation of themes. They might look to see how displacement has changed the focus of the dream on to an unimportant theme, or they might unravel secondary elaboration to get to the original experience of dreaming. As dreams often do not make enough sense to be described exactly to someone, it is hard to see how secondary elaboration can be avoided or how to determine what is secondary elaboration and what is the original dream.

An example of dreamwork

An example can help to show how dreamwork is done, and how analysis can proceed. Beatrice's dream and its analysis is outlined in the table below.

Quick check

A Why is a dreamer likely to use secondary elaboration when describing a dream?

Symbols in dreams

If you dream about falling into a stream with someone you know following you, what does that say about you? Freud did not say that 'falling' or 'someone chasing' always means the same thing. Each individual's dream has to be analysed to find their individual unconscious thoughts and desires.

The meaning of symbols

Freud did not agree with the idea that general symbols can mean the same thing to everyone because, of course, if everyone's unconscious is a personal thing (which it is) then they will have their own underlying meaning of symbols. However, it helps to understand dream analysis if using a general example, so one is given here.

Taking it further

Go to www.heinemann.co.uk/hotlinks, enter express code 4837P, and click on the *Dream Central website* for information on dream analysis. However, remember that Freud did not agree with 'common' interpretations of symbols.

Dreamwork	Possible features
Beatrice sat up suddenly in bed after another strange dream. An eagle swooping to pick up a mouse, just missing it, the mouse running, just reaching shelter, insects buzzing around as if to attack the eagle. A house nearby, a baby crying outside, the eagle refusing to go away. What did it mean?	*Condensation:* Insects 'buzzing around' could be one idea hiding many, such as attacking to protect, feeling reluctant to do so, making a lot of noise, feeling helpless.
	Displacement: The focus is on the eagle, but perhaps it is the running mouse that is the main feature.
	Secondary elaboration: In interpretation the eagle, mouse and insects seem to make a story but the house and baby do not 'fit'. Perhaps the whole dream was told as a story to help it make sense.
	Other ideas: Note Beatrice could be called 'Bee' for short, linking to the theme of insects. You would need to know more about her family, to interpret the importance of the baby perhaps.

Quick check

B Why did Freud think that symbols had individual meaning for each dreamer?

Examiner's tips

Do not confuse 'common' symbols with Freud's theory of dreaming. Just use it to help you understand the idea that dreams have meanings.

Questions

1 Outline how symbols are involved in dream analysis.

2 Explain why Freud would not have agreed with lists of what particular symbols mean.

3 Explain why it is hard for someone else to check symbol analysis to see whether it is reliable. Reliable means that if a study is done again, the same information is found.

'Falling' is often mentioned in the manifest content (the content the dreamer recalls) of a dreamer. Usually the dreamer does not 'land' but is free falling through the air. Usually 'falling' in a dream is interpreted as losing control of life or a situation and there would be a focus on what situation the person is anxious about and what fears they might be repressing. Repression is a way of 'forgetting' by pushing fearful or anxious thoughts into the unconscious, though of course this is done unconsciously.

Dreams should be analysed professionally to reveal an individual's unconscious. However, it is tempting to look at 'common' symbols in dreams. Some examples of what are called 'common' symbols are given in the table below.

'Common' symbols in dreams	Some suggested explanations
Snakes	• Snakes can be a sign of trouble. • Snakes can be a phallic (penis) symbol. • Snakes can symbolise death (afterlife). • Snakes can be about change (being bitten).
Guns	• Guns are linked to males – power, aggression and sexuality. • Being threatened with a gun can mean someone is trying to bully you (the threat is the focus). • If you have the gun this might mean you want power. • If you have a gun (in the dream) and cannot find it, perhaps you are looking to gain power.
Clothes	• Clothes are about how we think others see us. • If you are dressed inappropriately in a dream, perhaps you feel you are not prepared for something. • If you dream of clothing being too tight, perhaps you feel restricted in some way.
Knives	• Knives can be about 'cutting' – perhaps someone has made a cutting remark. • Or perhaps you feel cut off by someone.
Lifts	• Usually if you dream about a lift it is about something going wrong, like pushing the wrong button or the lift going too fast. The lift might symbolise your progress with an aspect of your life and you feel something is going wrong with that progress.

Bla3 Analysing dreams

Learn about
- How Freud analysed dreams
- What is meant by psychoanalysis

Reviewing the process of dream analysis

The analyst starts by listening to a description of the remembered dream (the manifest content). Then analysis takes place.

- The latent content can be uncovered by analysing symbols in the manifest content.
- Unconscious desires 'leak' into the dream via symbols to protect the sleeper.
- Mental health comes from uncovering unconscious desires and dream analysis can be part of the therapy.
- Freud's therapy is called **psychoanalysis**.

Psychoanalysis

Psychoanalysis is a therapy that comes from Freud's idea that mental disorders involve mental processes rather than physical ones. It is a 'talking cure'.

Mental health issues up to the late 1800s, when Freud was working, were mainly treated as physical health issues. Hardly anything was known about the brain and how it worked. People with mental illnesses were put into asylums, mainly because it was not known what could be done for them. People were also thought of as mentally ill if they went against society's rules – for example, young women who became pregnant outside marriage were 'put away' in institutions. It is hard to imagine it now.

Freud treated middle-class patients in the wealthy part of Vienna. His patients told him about their problems, including neurotic symptoms such as inability to move an arm. They talked about disturbing dreams, which led Freud to work on uncovering their meaning. If he could give enough explanation, the patient would consider themselves 'cured'.

Psychoanalysis aims to reveal unconscious wishes, desires and emotions to the patient, who, once knowing about the content of the unconscious, will no longer have psychological problems. As the desires are no longer hidden, they can be dealt with. Psychoanalysis is still carried out today, based on Freud's theory.

Quick check

A Suggest why psychoanalysis is called the talking cure.

Three methods used in psychoanalysis

It is thought that a person uses up energy repressing their wishes and desires – energy that would otherwise be available for moving forward. Psychoanalysis uses unique research methods such as **slips of the tongue**, **free association** and **dream analysis**. By using more than one method, the analyst has more information to work with and to use as evidence for conclusions about unconscious wishes.

Slips of the tongue (also called Freudian slips) describe moments when someone uses one word when meaning another, for example using an ex-boyfriend's name when talking about a current boyfriend. Free association is when someone is asked to say their thoughts out loud, without controlling them, so the analyst can look for associations between thoughts and ideas. Finally, dream analysis can involve the use of free association alongside the usual description of a dream. For example, the patient can be asked to relate dreams to the analyst. Each item in the dream can then be focused on in turn and be used as a starting point for free association. For example, if someone dreams about a boat, they can then be asked to allow a stream of consciousness about 'boat'. The analyst can then look for themes and links that might reveal unconscious emotions or wishes.

Quick check

B What three methods does psychoanalysis include?

An example of a patient undergoing psychoanalysis

Psychoanalysis takes a long time because many dreams have to be related and many sessions undergone before an analyst can start to suggest what the dream might symbolise. The job of a psychoanalyst is discussed in more detail later within this topic (see page 82).

Taking it further

Go to www.heinemann.co.uk/hotlinks, enter express code 4837P, and click on the *Here Be Dreams website* for a brief summary of Freud's ideas of dream analysis.

Questions

1 Outline what is meant by 'psychoanalysis'.
2 Explain why an analyst using psychonanalysis would use more than one method.
3 Explain how free association can be used in dream analysis.

Key definitions

psychoanalysis: Freud's therapy, designed to help release unconscious thoughts.

free association: a method used by Freud in psychoanalysis where the patient is encouraged to express a flow of consciousness. The process helps to uncover links which can then be interpreted.

slip of the tongue: when someone uses the wrong word for something. Freud analysed these slips to help uncover unconscious thoughts.

dream analysis: a method used by Freud to help uncover unconscious thoughts, by analysing dreams and uncovering symbols.

An example of Freudian dream analysis

Ashmur has a dream that could be analysed by a psychoanalyst. To analyse the dream successfully, you would need to spend a lot of time with Ashmur and to know a lot about the background of his case. However, a brief analysis is suggested here.

Ashmur dreamt about being a little boy and being in a large boat about to go under a bridge that was too low. In the dream he was in the boat alone, and there were two people, one on each bank, shouting at him. He was too frightened to get out of the boat and be confronted by those on the banks, and terrified because the bridge was too low.

Analysis of Ashmur's dream

The two people, one on each bank, could be Ashmur's parents. Their shouting could be interpreted as fear that a small boy might have of his parents as they are, to him, in authority. There could have been a past experience of a boat trip that was frightening. Or the boat could represent Ashmur himself, feeling insecure and not on firm ground. The low bridge could represent a block of some sort that in Ashmur's life was holding him back. This could be not being able to be promoted in his job, feeling trapped in his personal life or some other reason for feeling trapped.

B1a4 Evaluating Freud's dream theory

Learn about
- Ways to criticise a theory
- What makes a theory scientific
- What other people make of Freud's theory

When studying psychology you need to be able to **evaluate** the information you learn. This means you need to be able to identify the good and bad points, or strengths and weaknesses, of a theory or point of view.

In psychology it is not always easy to measure the material studied precisely, the way you can in other sciences. For example, people's behaviour and attitudes are not easy to measure. The theories and findings of studies have to be presented and then followed by an analysis of their good and bad points so that a judgement can be made about whether the information is firm enough to call 'true'.

Here, you will look at what others say about the strengths and weaknesses of Freud's dream theory.

Examiner's tips

Although you may have your own ideas about the strengths and weaknesses of Freud's theory, it is important to learn the ones given here. These are the 'common' strengths and weaknesses that examiners will be looking for.

Strengths of Freud's theory

Freud's theory is respected because Freud:

- used unique methods to find data that was difficult to access
- gathered in-depth and detailed information about individuals – **qualitative data** about real life (**valid data**).

Unique methods

Freud used unique methods to uncover unconscious wishes and desires, which, by definition, are not conscious and so are hard to access. He used dream analysis as one of those methods. At that time nobody had considered that problems such as **phobias** could be caused by problems in the mind. Once Freud had realised that there was an unconscious that was strong and guiding much of our thinking, he needed a way to find out what was in that unconscious, which he did creatively. As he instinctively looked for symbols hiding the unconscious, you could say his patients gave him the ideas for his unique methods (e.g. they talked about recurring dreams).

Examiner's tips

Phobias are not only dealt with using psychoanalysis but by other methods, such as classical conditioning (see page 130).

In-depth, real-life data

Freud listened to his patients very carefully over a long period of time. He was only willing to carry out analysis under two conditions. First, he had to know his patients well. Second, they had to co-operate with analysis and contribute by commenting on any analysis. His information, therefore, was about real life and as such was valid. The data were qualitative, containing a lot of detail and depth. Of course the real-life information was often interpreted from the unconscious. However, it was detailed and came directly from the patient, which is a strength.

Quick check

A Outline some strengths of using qualitative data.

Weaknesses of Freud's theory

Freud's ideas are criticised because:

- his sample was biased
- his concepts were unmeasurable
- he interpreted his findings, so they might be biased
- there is an alternative biological theory, activation-synthesis.

This is a photo of the couch Freud used. Freud listened to his patients as they relaxed, and he gathered in-depth detailed information.

Biased sample

Freud was Austrian, working from the late 1800s, and he worked mainly with reasonably well-off Viennese families, so he did not find out about lots of different people in different circumstances Therefore his findings might not be true of everyone in the world. Another way of saying this is to say his results are not **generalisable**.

Hard to measure

The unconscious is not something that exists in the sense that it can be measured, so it is hard to test. Scientific 'truths' have been tested over and over again, for example that water boils at 100 degrees Celsius. Freud's ideas are hard to test in the first place and even harder to test over and over again. So Freud's ideas are 'not science'.

Interpretation

Freud's interpretation of dreams was likely to be **subjective**. This means that another analyst might have a different interpretation. If someone else could come to a different conclusion, it would be hard to call the interpretation 'true'. Science needs data to be **objective** so that the same results are found every time without subjective bias. So, again, Freud's ideas are 'not science'.

Examiner's tips

Be careful not to write 'Vietnamese' instead of 'Viennese'! It's a common mistake.

Quick check

B Define the terms 'subjective' and 'objective'.

Key definitions

qualitative data: data involving stories or attitudes.

valid: refers to findings of studies and means that they are about real-life situations, real-life behaviour or feelings that are real.

generalisable: refers to findings of studies and whether they can be said to be true of people other than those that were studied.

subjective: where the researcher is somehow affecting the information that is gathered, perhaps by their interpretation.

objective: where the researcher's views do not affect the information that is gathered.

Contested by other theories

The other theory you need to learn for your course is the biological explanation for dreaming that is called activation synthesis. You will read more about activation-synthesis theory on page 64.

Taking it further

Go to www.heinemann.co.uk/hotlinks and enter express code 4837P. *The University of Winnipeg website* has a useful evaluation of Freud's theory.

Questions

1 Outline two strengths of Freud's theory about dreams.

2 Outline two weaknesses of Freud's ideas about dreams.

3 Discuss the view that Freud's theory of dreaming is unscientific. (Hint: you could bring in the concepts of objectivity, subjectivity, generalisability and reliability in your answer, though you don't have to use the terms, just the ideas.)

B1b1 How the brain sends signals

Learn about

- What a neuron is and what it is made up of
- How messages are sent around the brain using neurotransmitters

What a neuron is

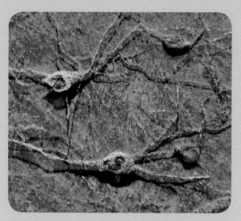

A photo of neurons in the brain.

For your course you need to know the basic structure of a **neuron** and also what it is for. A neuron is a cell in the nervous system that processes and sends information within the body, using chemical and electrical signals. The activity of neurons is central to how the brain and the body works. There are sensory neurons that receive messages from the senses (e.g. touch, light and sound) and motor neurons that are about muscle movement. Neurons respond to stimuli from the environment or inside the body and communicate within the nervous system. The brain and the spinal column make up the **central nervous system (CNS)**, and the CNS processes information from the senses and sends responses for the relevant parts of the body to act upon.

Taking it further

Go to www.heinemann.co.uk/hotlinks and enter express code 4837P. *The Associated Content website* explains how a neuron works.

The different parts of a neuron

A neuron has four important features:

- cell body
- axon
- terminal buttons
- dendrites.

The diagram below shows how these four features link to one another. The cell body has dendrites leading off it and an axon. At the end of the axon are terminal buttons.

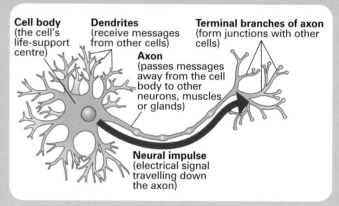

Diagram of a neuron.

Examiner's tips

Study the diagram of a neuron. You will need to know what a neuron is made up of.

How brain messages are sent using neurons

Messages in the brain are sent using electrical **impulses** and chemicals that are called **neurotransmitters**.

Step 1: An electrical impulse is triggered from the cell of one neuron then travels down the axon to the end. The impulse is also called action potential.

Step 2: When the impulse gets to the end of the axon it releases a chemical, called a neurotransmitter, that is found in the terminal buttons at the end of the axon.

Step 3: This neurotransmitter has to cross a gap, called the synapse or **synaptic gap**, to get to the dendrites of the next neuron to continue the message.

Step 4: The neurotransmitter, released by the impulse, goes into the gap – where it could be taken up by the dendrites or could be lost.

Step 5: If the **receptors** at the dendrites of the next neuron are 'suitable' to receive the neurotransmitter that is in the gap, then the chemical gets picked up. This process is explained again later in this section.

Step 6: The neurotransmitter sets off an electrical signal (by changing the chemical balance at the receptor) and then it drops back into the synaptic gap where it can be taken back up to be used again.

Step 7: The change in chemical balance (from the receptors) triggers an electrical impulse from the cell body, which then travels down to the end of the axon... (Return to step 1)

Key definitions

neuron: a cell in the body, including in the brain, that sends information using both electrical and chemical processes.

axon: the 'cable' that leads from a cell body of a neuron down to the terminal buttons that hold the neurotransmitter.

impulse: the electrical signal that travels from the cell body of a neuron to the terminal buttons, where it releases a neurotransmitter.

neurotransmitter: a chemical at the terminal button of a neuron, which is released by the impulse and then goes into the synaptic gap.

synaptic gap: the gap between the dendrites of one neuron and the next.

synaptic transmission: what happens when a neurotransmitter released by an impulse of one neuron goes across the synaptic gap and is taken up at the dendrites of another neuron.

The message continues in this way, as outlined in Steps 1–7. The process of a neurotransmitter passing from one neuron across the gap (synapse) and being picked up by the next neuron is called **synaptic transmission**.

Explaining 'lock' and 'key'

Receptors at a dendrite will be a shape ('lock') to take up only a certain neurotransmitter ('key') and all other neurotransmitters will not be taken up. When someone takes prescribed or recreational drugs, one effect of the drug is to fill the 'lock' of one neuron so that when a neurotransmitter message arrives in the gap, it cannot fit the receptor (which is already full). This means that the message is stopped or 'blocked'. Pain-killers can block messages of pain in this way.

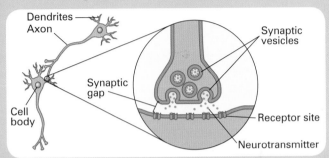

Synaptic transmission – the neurotransmitter passes across the synaptic gap.

Taking it further

Go to www.heinemann.co.uk/hotlinks and enter express code 4837P. Click on the *University of Massachusetts Boston website* to study synaptic transmission.

Quick check

A Imagine that a message is passing from neuron to neuron. Starting from the dendrites, put in order the following terms as the message would 'encounter' them: terminal branches, cell body, dendrites, axon, synaptic gap.

Questions

1 Name two features of a neuron.
2 Put these features of synaptic transmission in order:
   a) Another neuron takes up the message if the neurotransmitter 'fits' the receptors.
   b) The neurotransmitter is released into the gap.
   c) The impulse down the axon triggers the release of the neurotransmitter.

Blcl A biological theory of dreaming

Learn about

- The activation-synthesis theory of dreaming
- What synthesis is
- Terms such as random activation, sensory blockade and movement inhibition

Previous pages in this topic have looked at the meaning of dreams and then at how our brains work biologically. Biologists suggest that dreams are random thoughts which have been put together by the sleeping brain to make some sense of them. You might find this theory less exciting than Freud's because it involves biology rather than the feelings, personality and problems that we all face. However, if you are looking for the truth about dreams, you need to consider that they may 'just' be biological offshoots of sleeping.

The activation-synthesis theory of dreaming

Hobson and McCarley in 1977 came up with a biological theory of dreaming, which is very different from Freud's psychological theory. In fact their theory is known as the activation-synthesis theory of dreaming because it says that dreams are random messages in the brain being interpreted to make a story. Messages are activated randomly, and then synthesised (put together) into a story.

Hobson and McCarley worked at Harvard University in the USA and were biologists not psychologists. Psychologists look at the brain and behaviour, including thoughts, emotions and personality, and biologists look at the physical processes dealing with the brain and behaviour. Biologists are scientists, though psychologists are often thought of as scientists when they use research methods such as experiments and scanning. Hobson and McCarley, from their biological viewpoint, said that there is a dream state generator in the brain and this part of the brain that gives a dream state is switched on during **REM sleep**. REM sleep is explained below.

Quick check

A Explain what is meant by psychological and what is meant by biological.

Stages of sleep

Research has shown that sleep goes through about five cycles of four stages each, and after each cycle of four stages there is REM sleep.

REM sleep is when there is rapid eye movement (when the eyelids can be seen flickering very quickly). This happens around five or more times a night. As dreaming during REM sleep is easily recognisable, scientists can measure electrical brain activity in the brain during REM using an **EEG (electroencephalograph)**.

Examiner's tips

It is not easy to remember names and terms in psychology. Hobson and McCarley could be H&M, which you should be able to remember, and if in the exam you cannot remember their full names, just put H&M to show knowledge.

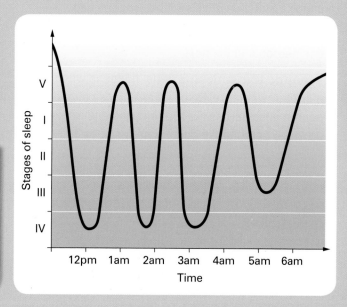

Taking it further

Go to www.heinemann.co.uk/hotlinks, enter express code 4837P, and click on the *Dream Views website* to do further research into the stages of sleep.

Examiner's tips

Terminology is often (though not always) used in psychology exams, so make sure you know what the terms mean. The actual ideas are often not complicated, so it is worth getting used to the terms.

During REM sleep, any incoming information from the senses (sight, sound, touch, taste and smell) is blocked. This is known as **sensory blockade**. Physical movements are also blocked in REM sleep. This is known as **movement inhibition**. So during REM no information is coming into the brain and no outgoing movements are being made by the body.

Key definitions

activation-synthesis model: a model of dreaming proposed by Hobson and McCarley where the brain is active but no sensory information is coming into it. The brain puts the information it has together to make sense of it and this is the dream.

random activation: during REM sleep, when neurons are active randomly not deliberately.

sensory blockade: during REM sleep, when no information enters through the senses.

movement inhibition: the state, during REM sleep, when the body is paralysed and there is no movement.

Quick check

B Explain in your own words what is meant by sensory blockade and movement inhibition.

Concepts in the activation-synthesis theory of dreaming

REM sleep	A stage of sleep that occurs about five times each night, where there is rapid eye movement (REM) which indicates that dreaming is taking place
Sensory blockade	During REM sleep no information is coming in through the senses.
Movement inhibition	During REM sleep the body is paralysed and there is no movement.
Neurons	Neurons in the brain are how messages are passed using electrical (impulses down the axon) and chemical (neurochemicals crossing the synapse) transmission.
Random activation	During REM sleep, neurons are still active – randomly not deliberately.
Synthesis	The brain tries to make sense of the random activation of neurons – and this 'sense' is the dream.

However, during REM sleep the neurons in the brain are activated because there are random impulses that 'give' information as if it were from the senses. This is known as **random activation** and is the 'activation' part of the activation-synthesis theory.

The information that comes from inside the brain itself is known as internally-generated information. The brain then tries to make sense of the 'nonsense' it has generated. It is synthesising the information to make it into a story, and this is the 'synthesis' part of the theory.

Questions

1 Describe what is happening in the brain and body during REM sleep.

2 Explain the activation-synthesis model of dreaming.

3 Explain one difference between the activation-synthesis theory of dreaming and Freud's theory of dreaming.

B1c2 Evaluating activation-synthesis theory

Learn about

Learn about

- Why Hobson and McCarley thought dreaming is to do with the brain's working
- Criticisms of the activation-synthesis theory of dreaming

Evidence for the activation-synthesis model of dreaming

Evidence that Hobson and McCarley gave for their explanation of dreaming is that REM sleep happens regularly throughout a night's sleep, and happens regularly night after night. Sleep labs study sleeping (see page 64) and everyone observed sleeping shows regular patterns of rapid eye movement (REM). As this happens to everyone in a regular pattern, Hobson and McCarley looked for an explanation that would explain this regularity and predictability. Because people have muscular paralysis (movement inhibition – no physical movement) during REM sleep and there is no input from the senses (sensory blockade), Hobson and McCarley felt there must be something happening in the brain itself to produce dreams.

Development of the activation-synthesis model

As with many theories in psychology, Hobson and McCarley's original theory has been developed and added to. For example, Hobson later said (in 1999) that he thought there was 'meaning' in dreams, that some ideas generated by the brain from the random 'firing off' of neurons could be useful and give the individual new ideas. If you wake up and have a good idea, it might have come from your dreams. It is a strength of the theory that it is still being investigated.

Hobson also suggested that this brain activity is likely to be genetic because it is found in everyone. It may be an evolved feature of humans, so there has to be a reason for its survival amongst humans. He thought that it might be there to test brain circuits or that the stimulation of the brain during REM sleep must be important for normal brain functions when awake.

Quick check

A Give one reason for linking the idea of everyone dreaming and experiencing REM sleep with the suggestion that dreaming has a biological explanation.

Examiner's tips

One way of criticising a theory or study about humans is if the study is done on animals. As animals are not exactly like humans, you could say that drawing conclusions about humans from animal studies cannot be accurate.

Taking it further

Go to www.heinemann.co.uk/hotlinks (express code 4837P). The *Here Be Dreams website* gives a simple explanation of activation-synthesis.

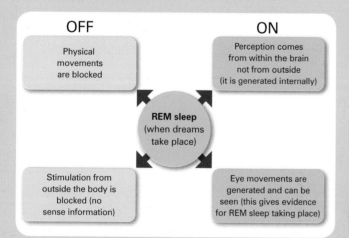

Diagram of the situation during sleep where the brain is a dream generator (according to the activation-synthesis model of dreaming).

Studies giving evidence

To gather evidence for their theory, Hobson and McCarley tested cats to see which areas of the brain were active during REM sleep. They found two active areas – the **pons** and **the reticular activating system (RAS)**. These are the structures that seem to be involved with shutting down physical movement (known as movement inhibition) during REM sleep.

Quick check

B How does evidence that structures generated during sleep are to do with movement inhibition support the activation-synthesis theory?

Other evidence they used was that if the neurons activated during REM sleep are those in the brain that control balance, then the dreamer is likely to dream about falling. This explains why dreams seem to have meaning – they come from neurons that, when activated when the person is awake, have a specific purpose.

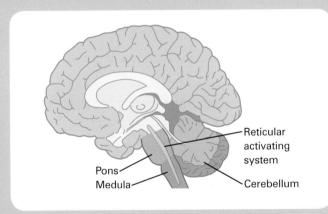

Diagram of the human brain showing the pons. The reticular activating system (RAS) is between the medulla oblongata and the mid-brain, on the spinal cord.

Weaknesses of the activation-synthesis theory

You need to explain criticisms of the activation-synthesis theory, and it is useful to look for problems as this helps you to understand the theory. You will also need to compare the weaknesses of this theory with those of Freud's dream theory (see page 54) for your exam.

Dreams do have more meaning than the activation-synthesis theory suggests. When reporting a dream, many people say they recognise parts of the dream from what has happened the day before or in their lives. This means the thoughts are not really as random as the activation-synthesis theory suggests.

The activation-synthesis theory is based on the idea that dreams often show unusual, bizarre situations and do not make full sense. However, one study that Hobson was involved in suggested that only about 34 per cent of 200 dreams did not make logical sense. Other studies also show that dreams often do make sense. This could be because the dreamer finds sense in the bizarre dream when talking about it. However, if the dream really is strange, this becomes obvious when the person starts to relate the events in their dream.

Lucid dreaming

Another criticism of the theory concerns something called lucid dreaming. This is when people are dreaming but know they are dreaming, and can signal that this is the case when fitted with suitable measuring devices. Lucid dreaming has been tested and found to occur. This idea does not fit with activation-synthesis, as it means dreams are controllable and not random.

Young children

A further criticism is that children under the age of five years seem to have few dreams and their dreams are not very active, yet they have a normal amount of REM sleep. This suggests dreams are not simply linked to REM sleep.

Taking it further

Go to www.heinemann.co.uk/hotlinks (express code 4837P). Research lucid dreaming on the *Dream Views* website.

Questions

1 Give two reasons why Hobson and McCarley thought their theory of dreaming was right.
2 Describe a biological explanation of why people dream.
3 Explain the strengths and weakness of the activation-synthesis theory of dreaming.

B1d1 Comparing dream theories

Learn about

- How to compare two theories
- Making comparison points between Freud's theory and activation-synthesis theory

You almost certainly make comparisons every day, such as deciding which film to watch, which chocolate bar to buy or which CD to listen to. To make the choice you have to list in your mind the various features of whatever you are comparing.

How to compare theories

For your course you are asked to compare Freud's theory about symbols, sexual motivation and the unconscious (see page 78) with Hobson and McCarley's theory that dreaming is a biological feature of sleeping (see page 64). This is similar to making a list of points about the two theories and then comparing them to decide which is 'better' – or which has the most strengths and which has the most weaknesses.

You might not have had to compare theories in psychology up to now. You can use lists of points that you have made yourself, as they will have more meaning for you. Here, though, are some ideas of what can be compared, and how to make a comparison.

Taking it further

Go to www.heinemann.co.uk/hotlinks (express code 4837P). Click on the *Wikipedia website* for a comparison between Freud and Hobson and McCarley's theories.

Comparing using methodology

To compare two theories using **methodology**, list the methodology used in the two theories, as shown in the table below. Then say how it is similar and how it is different, and perhaps what is good and bad about it.

Methodology linked to Freud's theory	Methodology linked to Hobson and McCarley's theory
Case studies Little Hans Dream analysis Free association Slips of the tongue	Neurotransmitter functioning Animal experiments Brain scanning EEG testing (detecting electrical activity in the brain)

Some comparison points

Case studies (Freud's theory) are less scientific than animal experiments and brain scanning (Hobson and McCarley's theory). For example, free association needs interpretation from the researcher, whereas brain scanning, although needing some interpretation, is much more **objective**. So Hobson and McCarley's theory is more objective than Freud's because of the methodology used to find evidence for the theory.

Quick check

A Outline two method differences between Freud's explanation of dreaming and Hobson and McCarley's explanation of dreaming.

Key definitions

methodology: refers to how psychology works, including how data are gathered. It involves considering 'how do we know?'

objective: where the researcher's views do not affect the information that is gathered.

Comparing using the nature-nurture debate

The nature-nurture debate refers to how far a characteristic or feature of humans comes from nature – that is, what they are born with – and how far from nurture – what they learn or experience growing up.

The table below shows what nature and nurture mean, and gives some comparison points between the two dream theories.

Nature	Nurture
• Biology • Genes, hormones, brain structure • Hobson and McCarley's theory is about nature – sleeping and dreaming • Freud's theory has elements of nature as well – the structure of the mind, with the power of the unconscious, for example	• Environment • Upbringing and parents' influences • Freud's theory is about nurture because unconscious desires themselves come from experiences • But it is in our nature to have repressed wishes in our unconscious (it is the wishes themselves that come from nurture)

Quick check

B Explain what is meant by the nature-nurture debate.

Comparing using credibility

A theory is said to be **credible** if it is developed using solid scientific evidence. It is also said to be credible if it agrees with what we usually think. Freud's theory does not use scientific evidence because, for example, the unconscious is not measurable in any scientific way.

On this basis, Freud's theory can be said to lack credibility. It seems a very unlikely theory and many reject it because of that (though that does not make it wrong).

Hobson and McCarley's theory, however, is said to be credible. The evidence comes from scanning and from laboratory studies using animals, so there is credibility in that sense because both are scientific and objective research methods. Also people tend to think of sleeping as a biological feature of humans, so thinking about dreaming in that way too seems logical.

The following table compares the two theories on key issues.

Issue	Freud's theory	Hobson and McCarley's theory
Objectivity	Subjective, as meaning needs interpreting	Objective, as it uses scientific measures such as scanning and experiments
Credibility	Lacks credibility because of lack of scientific methods and unlikely explanation (e.g. sexual interpretations)	Has credibility because of scientific methods and evidence from animal studies
Research methods	Uses case studies and dream analysis	Uses scanning and experiments
Dreams are meaningful	Dreams have meanings with the story giving symbols as clues to unconscious wishes	Dreams have no meaning – they are random and meaningless
Nature-nurture	Both nature and nurture – having a powerful unconscious is nature and its contents are nurture	Nature – dreaming is part of the way the brain and body work

Questions

1 What is the name of Hobson and McCarley's theory of dreaming?

2 Explain the difference between Freud's theory of dreaming and Hobson and McCarley's theory of dreaming in terms of the nature-nurture debate.

3 Compare Freud's and Hobson and McCarley's theories of dreaming in terms of their methodology, including issues of credibility and objectivity.

B2a1 Using case studies

> ## Learn about
> - Features of case studies

If you have already studied some psychology you will know that one of the most important things to think about is how the information is known. For example, how did Freud know that we all have an unconscious and how did Hobson and McCarley know that dreams are about random brain activity? For this topic on dreaming, the 'way psychology works' is investigated through the case study.

What is a case study?

A general definition of a **case study** is an in-depth study that gathers a lot of detail about one person or a small group. Examples of case studies in psychology include studying a person with severe memory loss following brain damage or studying a cult to consider leader/follower relationships.

Examiner's tips

When there are a number of features, such as for a case study, give each feature separately so it is clear that you are giving more than one point. For example: 'A case study is in depth. It is detailed. It is about one person, or it is about a small group.'

A case study rarely involves just one research method. It is a research method itself but involves using many other research methods to gather as much information as possible. The focus is on the individual or small group, so 'case study' is the term that is used to emphasise that focus. However, in order to gather information many different research methods are used, such as questionnaires and observations.

Taking it further

Go to www.heinemann.co.uk/hotlinks and enter express code 4837P. Click on the *Gerard Keegan website* for a description and evaluation of the case study method.

Quick check

A Why would it be useful to use different research methods within a case study?

An aim

A case study has an **aim**, which says what the study is about. The aim is a general idea of why the study is being done and what the researcher wants to find out. Unlike in an experiment, there is no **hypothesis**. A hypothesis is a precise statement of what result is expected in a study (see page 38). A case study looks for detailed information about a person, so a precise statement of what is expected would not be suitable.

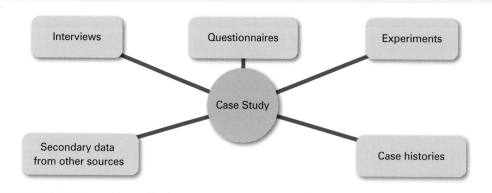

Case studies use many research methods to gather in-depth detailed information about an individual or a small group.

Examiner's tips

When you are talking about qualitative and quantitative data, be sure not to muddle them up. Write the words clearly to make your answer very clear.

Key definitions

aim: a statement of what the study is being carried out to find.

case study: a research method studying an individual or a small group and gathering in-depth and detailed information using different means.

qualitative data: data involving stories or attitudes.

quantitative data: data that involve numbers and statistics, such as percentages.

Qualitative and quantitative data

You need to know the difference between **qualitative data** and **quantitative data**. Qualitative data refers to rich data, which comes from **open questions**, such as asking for someone's opinion. 'Richness' refers to depth, detail, personal information, explanations and examples from the person or small group who are the subject of the study. For example, a case study of someone with brain damage can explore many aspects of what they find difficult and what they find relatively easy, and can be a very personal account. Quantitative data concerns quantity and numbers. It comes from **closed questions** which result in short 'yes' or 'no' answers.

Case studies can gather both qualitative and quantitative data, because different research methods can be used within one case study. For example, an interview could give qualitative data about someone's dreams, explaining the stories. Or a questionnaire can give quantitative data about their dreams, for example if someone rates how frightening their dreams are on a scale of 1 to 5.

Freud's case study of Dora

Freud used case studies to help people overcome unconcious wishes and desires so that they could be freed from such forces holding them back. One such case study was Dora, although she broke off her treatment before a cure was found. Dora was actually called Ida Bauer. A false name was given for confidentiality, but her real name became known. Freud felt that Dora transferred her feelings onto him as the analyst, so he was able to learn a lot about transference from this case study.

Quick check

B What is the difference between qualitative and quantitative data?

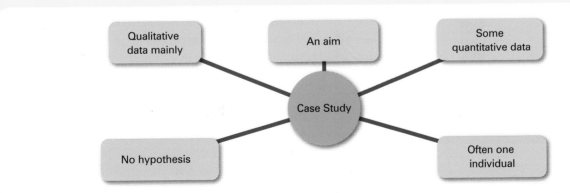

Case studies tend to gather qualitative data (being rich information) but can also gather quantitative data. They involve one person or a small group.

Questions

1 Outline three features of case studies.

2 Explain one difference between qualitative and quantitative data.

3 Explain how an aim differs from a hypothesis.

B2a2 Weaknesses of case studies

Learn about
● Evaluating case studies

Now that you have studied some psychology, you will have noticed that one of the skills you need is to be very picky! You have to read and learn, and at the same time pick holes in everything being claimed! This can be quite fun, but it is also useful to have specific ways of looking for problems with studies and theories, and those ways are suggested here. 'Doing science' involves being picky – it is wise not to accept any evidence without asking 'How do they know that?'

When studying psychology, ask yourself 'How do they know that?'

Quick check

A Outline one reason for criticising research methods.

Weaknesses

There are four major weaknesses in the use of case studies as a research method:

● **generalisability**   ● **subjectivity**
● **reliability**   ● **objectivity**.

You have already come across three of these terms (see page 61) – but we will now look at them in greater depth.

Generalisability

Generalisability means asking whether results can also be said to be true of other situations and other people. For example, a case study of a small boy as he develops is not really generalisable, as it is about one individual, with his unique upbringing and experiences. In contrast a study of 30 people where they are asked to memorise a list of words in certain conditions would, in certain circumstances, be generalisable to the rest of the population. As a rule case studies are said to be not generalisable, because they are not necessarily true of other situations or people. This is a criticism that is sometimes made of them.

Examiner's tips

Imagine you were doing a case study about someone you knew – perhaps focusing on their personality – and you had to make notes about them. Then you were asked to list the factors that would make it hard to say your notes were true of anyone else. What makes them unique? How does this stop you drawing general conclusions about 'everyone'? This should help you to see how important generalisability is.

Reliability

Reliability means that if a study is repeated it gives the same results. Case studies are likely to be difficult to repeat because of the different research methods used and the depth of the data – one person (or small group) at one specific moment in time. If a case study is repeated, the results would be different. As an example, a case study of a small boy's development could not be repeated as he would be older and also possibly affected by the first study. In general, case studies are said to lack reliability.

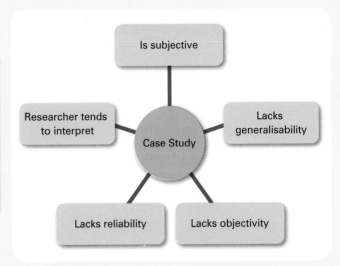

Examiner's tips

Going back to the case study of someone you know, imagine you had to write more notes about the person – perhaps a few months later. Do you think you would be writing the same feelings about them? This might help you to see problems with reliability when it comes to case studies.

Subjectivity and objectivity

Subjectivity in a psychology study means that the researcher has somehow affected the information that was gathered, for example that their own opinions have affected their conclusions.

Objectivity in a psychology study means that there is no **bias** from the researcher and no interpretation involved. The results from an objective study are more scientific because of this lack of bias from the researcher. Objectivity is the opposite of subjectivity. Science requires objectivity.

In general, case studies are said to be subjective because the researcher is deeply involved in the data collection, and the qualitative data gathered (the attitudes, opinions and stories) have to be selected and interpreted by the researcher.

Key definitions

generalisability: refers to findings of studies and how far they can be said to be true of people other than those that were studied. If findings are thought to be true of other people then they are generalisable.

reliability: refers to whether findings from a study would be found again if the study was repeated. A study is reliable if the findings are replicated (found again).

subjectivity: refers to research methods, where the researcher is somehow affecting the results, perhaps by their interpretation.

objectivity: refers to research methods, where there is no bias, for example the researcher's own views have not affected the findings.

Quick check

B Match the definition to the correct term: generalisability, reliability or objectivity.

a) If the study is done again the same information is found.

b) Sampling is done well so that results are said to be true of others, not just those tested.

c) The researcher does not affect the data by the way they look or the way they act.

Taking it further

Go to www.heinemann.co.uk/hotlinks (express code 4837P). Click on the *Gerard Keegan website* to explore the issues raised about case studies.

When making notes about someone you know, how far do you think your own opinions and impressions of them affect your notes? Do you think you are objectively assessing them? This will help you to see the importance of subjectivity and how it can affect the findings of case studies.

Questions

1 Explain what is meant by generalisability, reliability and subjectivity.

2 Evaluate the case study research method including at least two weaknesses.

73

B2a3 Designing case studies

Learn about
- Designing a case study
- Strengths of case studies
- How issues of privacy and confidentiality can be dealt with

Issues to consider

You have had to learn quite a bit about how psychology works for this section. However, this will help if you want to design a case study. Design one in theory now. Here are some issues to consider:

- What would be the aim of your case study?
- Could you make your case study generalisable?
- Could you make your case study reliable?
- What research methods would you want to use in your case study?
- How long would your case study take?
- How would you avoid subjectivity?
- How would you deal with privacy and confidentiality?

A case study on dreaming

Here is an idea for a case study on dreaming. You might have come up with a different idea, in which case explore it further with the list of questions above in mind. That way, you will understood what you need to know when investigating this topic.

- The aim of this case study is to look at one person's dreaming patterns in depth.
- It will cover a period of three months.
- It will use a number of research methods, such as:
  - a dream diary
  - a weekly interview between the person and the researcher
  - a completed form showing time going to bed and time waking up each day
  - a questionnaire for the immediate family of the participant (to find out about the participant's sleeping patterns and to cross-check where possible).

- Conclusions will be checked with the individual to check for validity.
- The case study could be repeated after a few months to test for reliability.
- A few case studies of other people could be carried out after a few months to help to show generalisability.
- When analysing the results the researcher will use only the words of the dreamer to aim for objectivity and avoid subjectivity.

Quick check

A Give one reason why a case study might be useful when studying dreaming.

Taking it further

You could keep a dream diary as if carrying out a case study using yourself. Consider the issues above when analysing your own data. Were your dreams about the events of the day? Did you have dreams that were repeated day after day?

Dealing with privacy and confidentiality

If you carried out the case study on dreaming you would have to keep the participant's name secret to provide confidentiality and privacy. To do this you could use initials or a fake name. If there is information in the study that can identify them, such as the name of the town they live in or the school they attend, then that information must be disguised in a similar way.

Examiner's tips

When discussing ethical issues in research methods, give examples of studies to help your discussion.

For example, an educational psychologist talking about her job and using case studies to illustrate her work might ensure that no cases involving twins or children with certain learning disabilities were referred to if this could lead to individuals being identified.

Taking it further

Go to www.heinemann.co.uk/hotlinks (express code 4837P). Click on the *British Psychological Society website* to look up the issues of privacy and confidentiality.

Strengths of case studies

Case studies have many weaknesses, as we saw on page 72. However, there are also many good reasons for carrying out a case study. Two of the most important of these are that they provide:

- valid (real-life) data
- detail that is hard to find in any other way.

Validity

Case studies are often about one unique person and information comes directly from that person. This means that the data are about real-life situations, which makes them valid. Also, many different research methods can be used to gather other data, again making it likely that the findings are 'real'. Contrast this with experiments where controls mean that data is likely to be from 'unreal' situations.

Detail

Case studies are very detailed and provide information about many aspects of someone's life and what they are like. Not many other research methods achieve this. For example, questionnaires are limited to the questions asked and experiments are limited to the tasks set. Case studies can explore many different angles about someone by asking others for their opinions and asking the person themselves. This detail is rich and in-depth, which is a strength as new theories and ideas can develop from it.

Questions

1 Explain two features, other than ethical issues, to consider when designing a case study.

2 What is meant by 'validity'?

3 Explain two strengths of the case study research method.

People need to be protected so that they do not feel exposed when being studied.

B2b1 Ethics and case studies

Learn about
● Ethical issues relating to case studies

Any study in psychology has to be done ethically. You will hear so much about ethics in your course that you might start to get fed up with the emphasis on ethics. But if you think about what it might be like to be a participant in some of the studies you are learning about, you may realise that it could be quite a stressful experience. Imagine, for example, that you had to tell someone in your class about your dreams, and they had to tell you about theirs. Would it be stressful or make you feel uncomfortable? Perhaps this will help you to see why ethics are important.

Privacy and confidentiality

There are many ethical guidelines that relate to doing psychological studies. In this section you will learn about privacy and confidentiality. You will learn about other ethical guidelines in other parts of your course.

Taking it further

Go to www.heinemann.co.uk/hotlinks (express code 4837P). Click on the *BBC website* and read the case of patient H.M. to find out more about case studies and confidentiality in psychological research.

Privacy is about making sure the identity of the participant is kept secret. The participant has a right to have their results kept private. **Confidentiality** is also about privacy and refers to the participant's name being withheld and their identity being kept secret. For example, if a school and a subject that is taught there could identify a teacher then you would have to withhold the name of the school and/or the subject.

Confidentiality is an important ethical issue.

The case of 'Genie'

One case study often given as an example in psychology is the case of Genie, written up by Curtiss in 1977. 'Genie' was around 13 years old when she was found, locked in a room by her parents. She could hardly walk, could not talk and was frightened of people. She was then cared for by some of the psychologists, who understood her and tried to help her develop social skills and language. However, she did not catch up in her development and ended up in a care home for adults, where she was protected and cared for. Genie was not her real name and until very recently nobody knew where she was. It was reported that she had died.

However, in 2006 she was said to be in the same care home still. Recently there have been rumours that she has been tracked down. It is hard to get accurate information (because of rules of privacy and confidentiality). Usually, in fact, if determined journalists or others want to track someone down they succeed. Initially, however, her privacy was respected and confidentiality was maintained.

Quick check

A Why was Genie given a false name for the purpose of the study?

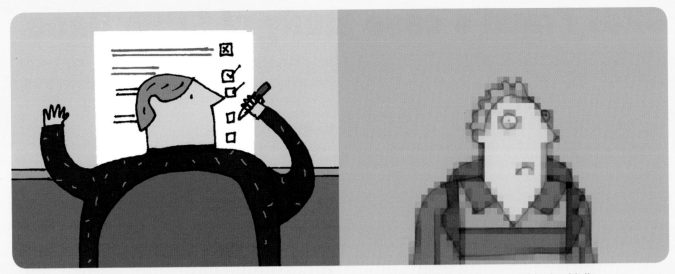

Nobody in a study should be identifiable and their privacy must be protected. Confidentiality is an ethical guideline that must be followed.

Taking it further

Go to www.heinemann.co.uk/hotlinks and enter express code 4837P. Click on the *Feral Children website* to learn more about Genie and other similar case studies.

Competence

Ethical guidelines are given in the UK by the British Psychological Society (BPS) to protect participants taking part in psychological research such as case studies. One important guideline is competence. A researcher must be qualified and capable of carrying out the proposed research. If necessary they must consult colleagues. The BPS also gives guidelines for practitioners, who are practising psychologists, and they must maintain competency, privacy and confidentiality for their clients.

Taking it further

Go to www.heinemann.co.uk/hotlinks and enter express code 4837P. Click on the *British Psychological Society website* which gives a great deal of information about ethical practice.

Key definitions

privacy: an ethical guideline for studies that involve people as participants, which ensures that their names must not be recorded and they must not be identifiable. Privacy is linked to confidentiality.

confidentiality: an ethical guideline for studies that involve people as participants, which ensures that information gained must not be shared with others without permission. There are some occasions when confidentiality must be broken, however, if there are issues of safety for someone else. Confidentiality is linked to privacy.

Questions

1 Outline two ethical guidelines that are important in the study of psychology.

2 Explain, using the issues of confidentiality and privacy, why it is important for studies to be carried out ethically.

3 Explain why it was important that 'Genie's' own name wasn't used.

B2dl Freud's case study of Little Hans

Learn about

- Dream analysis in Freud's case study of Little Hans

Freud carried out a number of case studies, finding out from clients what was causing them problems or holding them back. Often the people he studied had strange symptoms, such as not being able to use their arm, or having bizarre dreams, fears and phobias. Freud tried to help people who had these symptoms by suggesting that they arose from the unconscious.

Taking it further

Go to www.heinemann.co.uk/hotlinks (express code 4837P). Investigate the idea of hysterical symptoms (as they are called), such as not being able to use an arm or becoming blind for no apparent reason, on the *Freud Museum website*.

The Little Hans case study

One of Freud's case studies is the well-known study of a boy Freud called 'Little Hans' (though that was not his real name). The study was done in 1909, so you need to imagine what life was like then, when learning about this study.

Background

Hans' parents were supporters of Freud's ideas. They agreed to log their son's development and send Freud regular letters to keep him informed. Little Hans, although he was only about three years old when the study started, was aware that Freud was studying him. He even sent messages to Freud ('The Doctor') through his parents' letters. However, Freud only met Little Hans once or twice.

Horse phobia

Little Hans' main problem was his phobia of horses. He was afraid to go out of the house, and was particularly frightened of horses. Freud analysed what Little Hans said, including his dreams, to find out what it was in Hans' unconscious that was causing the phobia. This was so that these wishes and desires could be revealed to Little Hans and so cure the phobia.

This is traditional psychoanalysis – listening to what is being said and dreamt, considering how these issues are symbols of hidden unconscious desires, and then interpreting the symbols to uncover the desires. (See page 82 for more about psychoanalysis.)

Little Hans saw an accident in the street involving a horse, so his phobia could have come from that.

78

Quick check

A Explain what is meant by the conscious and the unconscious.

An early dream

Little Hans' father reported that one day, just before Little Hans was five years old, he woke up in tears and when he was asked why he was crying he said to his mother that he thought that she was gone and he had no mummy.

Freud said this was an anxiety dream, and showed he was anxious that his mother would leave him. This links to Freud's theory of the **Oedipus complex**. According to Freud, a boy of about five years old will have feelings for his mother and be jealous of his father as well as feeling guilty for wanting to take his father's place with his mother. These conflicting emotions cause the boy fear and anxiety. Unconscious wishes (wishing to possess his mother, in this case) are repressed and will 'leak' out in dreams. When Little Hans dreamt that his mother would not be there, this was showing his desires for his mother.

Freud thought that Hans, like other children of his age, was in the **phallic** stage. The phallic stage, according to Freud, is the third stage of development, happening from about the age of three or four years old until about five years old. In the phallic stage, sexual interest is focused on the genital area both for boys and girls. For boys at this stage, sexual interest is transferred onto their mother. Freud thought that a boy wanted to take his mother away from his father, but feared his father's anger and also felt guilty about these desires. Note that all of these emotions are unconscious – the person is not aware of them.

Quick check

B Explain the Oedipus complex according to Freud.

To resolve his feelings, of guilt for wanting to take his mother away and of fear of his father, a boy would identify with his father and 'become' his father. There is a similar idea that girls have feelings for their father and identify with their mothers to overcome fear and guilt in a similar way. Freud interpreted the phobia of horses as being symbolic of Little Hans' fear of his father.

The 'giraffe' dream

Little Hans also had a dream about giraffes. In the dream there was a big giraffe in the room and a crumpled one. The big giraffe shouted out because Little Hans (in his dream) took the crumpled one away from it. The big giraffe stopped calling out and Little Hans says that in the dream he sat down on the crumpled giraffe.

Freud and Little Hans' father both thought that the big giraffe was a symbol for a penis, but Hans himself denied this. Freud discussed the dream with Hans' father and they linked in the fact that Little Hans liked to get into bed with his parents in the mornings – something Hans' father did not like. It was thought that the big giraffe who was shouting out was Little Hans' father and the crumpled giraffe was his mother. When the big giraffe shouted at Little Hans for taking the crumpled giraffe away, this was interpreted as showing that Little Hans wanted to take his mother away from his father. This again was taken as evidence for the claim that a young boy has sexual feelings for his mother and also fears his father and feels guilt.

Key definitions

phallic: term used to refer to anything that is related to or said to represent the male penis, or the term can refer to the penis.

Oedipus complex: the idea that a boy from about the age of four years old will have unconscious feelings for his mother and want his father out of the way, though then fears his father and feels guilty too.

Questions

1 Explain why 'Little Hans' was given a false name.
2 Explain how Freud gathered the data in the Little Hans case study.
3 Describe Little Hans' giraffe dream.
4 Outline Freud's explanation of the giraffe dream.

B2d2 Evaluating dream analysis

Learn about
● Evaluation of dream analysis as a research method

Evaluation of dream analysis as a research method

Dream analysis is one of the methods used by Freud in his case studies. It is mainly done by those following Freud's theoretical approach and is unlikely to be used on its own as a research method. From what you have learned, especially when considering the Little Hans case study, you might conclude that dreams are always analysed for strange sexual content so you might dismiss them. However, in some modern counselling situations dreams are considered to be relevant areas for discussion. They are used to reveal interesting emotions and thoughts – and not always sexual ones.

Strengths of dream analysis

Dream analysis has many strengths. Its main strengths are that:

● it can access hard-to-reach information
● it is usually accepted by the client
● it uses information from the client directly.

Accessing hard-to-reach information
Dream analysis is useful in uncovering hard-to-reach information buried in the unconscious. The unconcious is not known to the individual so they cannot access or deal with any information there. Dream analysis is a way of tricking the brain to reveal some of its unconscious wishes and desires.

Quick check
A Why is the information to be accessed by dream analysis called 'hard to reach'?

Accepted by the client
Dream analysis is also seen as a good research method because people usually accept the analysis. Because they often agree with it, this helps them to be 'cured' of whatever they went to analysis for. For example, a study (Hall, 1947) reported the dream of a 20-year-old female college student. She dreamt she volunteered to go overseas as a teacher and went to Italy to teach children. Her dream was about leaving her family and getting married soon after arriving in Italy. The conflict is clear, as much of the dream is about leaving home. She said herself that she thought the dream was about her fear of leaving home and accepted the analysis.

The dreams are offered by the client
Dream analysis comes from the clients themselves, who offer their dreams as part of what is troubling them or as a way towards a solution of their

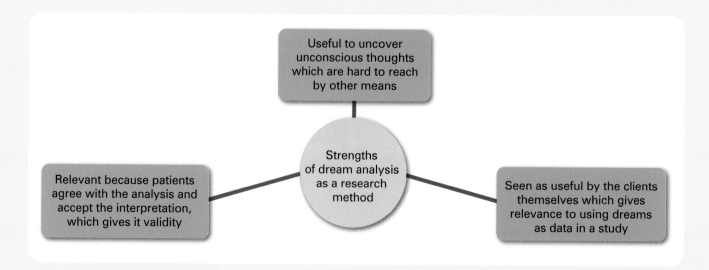

problems. If dreams are *thought* to be useful, relevant and meaningful to a person undergoing counselling or analysis, then to that extent dreams are relevant and dream analysis is a legitimate method to use as part of a case study or therapy.

Weaknesses of dream analysis

Dream anaylsis also has weaknesses. The main ones are:

- there may be ethical problems
- it involves interpretation that is subjective.

Ethical problems

There can be ethical problems with dream analysis, as the interpretation can be wrong and yet accepted, which can lead to **false memories**. A false memory is when, in analysis, it is 'revealed' that something is being repressed and that 'memory' is brought to light – but it is not a real memory, it is a false one. An example is when a client 'remembers' childhood incest, although it didn't actually occur. If a false memory is accepted as 'true' and involves perhaps another member of the family, then that person can be accused of something they didn't do and family splits or worse can occur. There is evidence that this has happened.

Dream analysis can also be distressing for the client, as they are taken back to possibly stressful situations from their childhood. However, a therapy that is distressing is not necessarily unethical if guidelines are followed; it depends how the situation is handled.

Taking it further

Go to www.heinemann.co.uk/hotlinks (express code 4837P). Look up false memory syndrome on the *Skeptic's Dictionary* website.

Interpretation

Dreams have to be interpreted by the analyst, which means information might be affected by subjectivity. The same dreams could be interpreted differently by another researcher. If data can be subject to someone's ideas, it suggests they might not be 'true' and are not reliable (remember that reliability is when a study is done again and the same results are found). And if someone interprets data then they are perhaps not valid either, because they represent that person's interpretation rather than real life.

Quick check

B Is 'science' more likely to look for objectivity or subjectivity?

Key definitions

false memory: any memory that is not true and can be given by someone else 'remembering' an event and telling another person who then 'remembers' it as true. Freud's definition refers more to false recovered memory, where a childhood memory (e.g. of abuse) is suggested by the analyst and accepted, then later found not to be true.

Quick check

C What is meant by 'false memory'?

Questions

1 Outline two evaluation points about dream analysis as a research method. (Evaluation points can be strengths or weaknesses.)

B3al The job of a psychoanalyst

Learn about
- What a psychoanalyst might do
- How a psychoanalyst might use dream analysis

Most psychoanalysts work with people with mental health issues, such as **obsessive compulsive disorder (OCD)**, phobias or anxiety. Sometimes they work with someone who is having problems with relationships or managing their life, rather than someone with a diagnosed mental illness. There are different types of psychotherapy, including **cognitive behavioural therapy (CBT)**, humanistic therapy, general **counselling**, and **hypnotherapy**, but psychoanalysis is specific to Freud's ideas. The aim of psychoanalysis is to uncover unconscious wishes and desires to find the reasons for the patient's problems, which will help to solve them. Some psychoanalysts train other psychoanalysts, and don't work with patients.

What a psychoanalyst does

The psychoanalyst listens and observes, focusing on emotions that the patient shows. They work with clients individually and gather both verbal and **non-verbal information**. Having carefully gathered information in this way, the psychoanalyst then helps the person to understand their emotions. The idea is that this understanding – making the unconscious conscious – will release underlying issues, freeing the person from the behaviour that is causing the problem. The analyst records the information from each session carefully. Psychoanalysts tend to work part-time, rather than full-time, and don't usually work weekends and evenings, but can do so.

Quick check

A Explain two features of what a psychoanalyst does in their job.

The experience of psychoanalysis for the client

The client usually undergoes analysis about four times a week, which is clearly a huge commitment. Each session lasts just under an hour. The analysis can go on for a very long time, because there is a lot of listening and observing to do before enough information is available. The analysis takes place in a quiet and comfortable room, so that the client can relax and feel able to talk freely. The client is often settled comfortably on a couch, with the analyst just behind them and out of sight, so as not to affect the client's flow of information. Each session costs about £50, so the treatment is quite expensive. It is unlikely that psychoanalysis would be available through the NHS or that funding would be available, so a client would have to pay for the treatment themselves. However, some psychoanalysts work on a 'sliding-scale' basis, which takes the client's ability to pay into account.

Quick check

B Describe the experience of the client when undergoing psychoanalysis.

The use of dream analysis

During dream analysis the client describes and talks about their dream (as well as showing emotions, which are also noted). The psychoanalyst uses this information, as they use other information such as data from free association when a client gives a stream of consciousness, or information from the client about their background and current situation. They listen, observe and record. Then they analyse and present ideas to the client for their acceptance. With regard to dream analysis the analyst considers the manifest content and then draws out symbols to uncover the latent content (see page 55). The analyst does this using all the other information they have gathered about the client, and will not just analyse the dream on its own.

How often dream analysis is used

A psychoanalyst may use dream analysis but will not always do so. Dream analysis is not the main focus of psychoanalysis now. **Transference** and **countertransference** have more focus, revealing things about the client just as other methods do. Transference describes the way a client will transfer their emotions – love, hate or anger – on to the analyst, who must be prepared for this. Countertransference is the word used for the way an analyst is likely, in turn, to transfer their own feelings back onto the client. Again, very importantly, they must be trained to deal with this. By recognising which emotions are being transferred onto them, the analyst can find out what emotions are involved in any possible problems that the client has.

A survey in 1995 of the use of dream analysis within the private practices of 228 analysts found that 17 per cent never use dream analysis, 57 per cent use it sometimes, 17 per cent moderately often, and only 9 per cent use dream analysis frequently. Of those who do use dream analysis frequently, only 4 per cent said they used it almost always. However, this survey covered different types of psychotherapist, not just those focusing on Freud and psychoanalysis.

Another study, carried out by Schredl et al in 2000, was carried out in Germany, using 79 psychoanalyst participants. They found that dream analysis was used in about 28 per cent of the therapies carried out by psychoanalysts.

It was also found that very often (64 per cent of the time) it was the client who introduced the idea of analysing a dream rather than the therapist. So in only about one third of the cases was the idea of dream analysis introduced by the analyst.

The Schredl et al survey in 2000 showed that about 70 per cent of clients had benefited from the dream analysis. In general it was thought by psychoanalysts to be successful to a large extent. Clients rarely rejected the analysis of their dreams.

Psychoanalysts who were working using dream analysis were those who worked within the guidelines of Freud (and another psychoanalyst, Jung). Psychoanalysts worked with dreams two or three times a month with clients.

Quick check

C How often is dream analysis used in psychotherapy in general?

Bar chart showing results of a survey asking about psychotherapists' use of dream analysis.

Questions

1 How is dream analysis used in psychoanalysis?
2 Discuss whether dream analysis is used often in psychoanalysis.
3 Explain why it is relevant that clients accept the analysis that a psychoanalyst may suggest.

B3a2 Becoming a psychoanalyst

Learn about

- Who a psychoanalyst might work for
- Skills required
- Qualifications required
- Accreditation status

Examiner's tips

Don't confuse psychoanalysis with psychotherapy. Psychotherapy is a general term for therapies that use listening and develop individual skills, and psychoanalysis is one form of psychotherapy; there are many others.

Who a psychoanalyst might work for

Most psychoanalysts work for themselves in private practice and are not employed by the NHS, unlike **clinical psychologists**. There are about 300 qualified psychoanalysts in the UK, and it is a specialist area. Some psychoanalysts specialise in therapy for children or adolescents, others do not specialise. Many psychoanalysts worked with people with mental health problems before they undertook their psychoanalytic training. Many also undergo other training, such as **family therapy**, **psychodrama** or hypnotherapy. They do not focus solely on psychoanalysis; it is one of the therapies that they offer.

Skills required

The main skills a psychologist needs are being able to listen carefully to people and observe them and being interested in people. The psychoanalyst, in particular, has to be patient and build a strong relationship with a client. They have to be able to work with people who have emotional problems without being judgmental about them. It is also important they that they do not get so involved with the client's problems that **detachment** is difficult. The training psychoanalysts receive helps them to overcome any problems they might have themselves so that they are able to focus effectively on the problems of other people.

Melanie Klein, who died in 1960, was a well-known psychoanalyst who worked with children. She built on Freud's work and developed the object relations school.

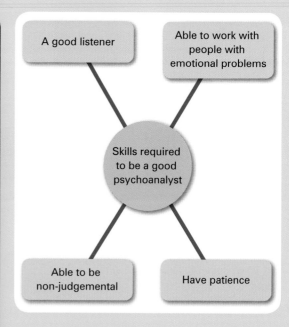

A good listener

Able to work with people with emotional problems

Skills required to be a good psychoanalyst

Able to be non-judgemental

Have patience

Quick check

A Explain three skills that a psychoanalyst would need.

Qualifications required and accreditation status

To become a psychoanalyst you have to undertake training that is approved by the International Psychoanalytic Association. There are only two providers of training in the UK: the Institute of Psychoanalysis and the British Psychoanalytical Association. Before this training you would need a degree or the equivalent of a degree.

To be accepted on a training course you would have to go through more than one interview. Very often those who apply for training are **psychiatrists** or other professionals who already work in the NHS or in the field of mental health in some way. In fact, because 'psychoanalyst' is not a protected term, anyone can claim to be a psychoanalyst.

Taking it further

Go to www.heinemann.co.uk/hotlinks (express code 4837P). Click on the *Institute of Psychoanalysis website* to find out more about the work of a psychoanalyst.

Quick check

B What does it mean to say that anyone can call themselves a psychoanalyst?

Training to be a psychoanalyst

- The training lasts four years and is part-time.
- The person being trained must undergo psychoanalysis themselves for four or five 50-minute sessions a week.
- There are also seminars and theory sessions. For the first year the training focuses on general theory and Freud's views, for example. Then more theories are explored.
- The final part of the training is the psychoanalysis of two patients whilst being supervised by a qualified psychoanalyst. These sessions start in the second year and the trainee sees a client for 50 minutes each day four or five days a week. This lasts for two years. A second client is seen in the third year of training and the analysis of this second client lasts for one year.

Like Freud, Carl Gustav Jung focused on the power of the unconscious and on dreams. However, his ideas on the subject were quite different.

Continuing Professional Development

Like other professional people, psychoanalysts must provide evidence of **Continuing Professional Development (CPD)** to show that they are keeping up with new issues and practising professionally.

Questions

1   Why would a psychoanalyst have to provide evidence of Continuing Professional Development? (You might want to refer to information on other psychologists to add detail to your answer – see pages 116, 154, 190)

2   Outline the qualifications required to be a psychoanalyst.

3   Explain what would make someone a good psychoanalyst.

B3b1 Psychological sleep disorders

Learn about
- The importance of REM sleep
- What psychological sleep disorder is

Taking it further
Do you have trouble sleeping? If you have a bad night for some reason, how does this affect you the next day? Does it affect your friends the same way?

The importance of REM sleep

You have already learned about REM sleep, which is the period of rapid eye movement and dreaming (see page 64). Research has shown that without REM sleep for a prolonged period – about two weeks – we experience disorientation and worse (for example memory difficulties, illusions and **paranoia**). Rats that have been kept awake have died! It is REM sleep that is important – but that means sleep too, of course. So, difficulties with sleeping are taken seriously and various hospitals have sleep labs and sleep departments to study sleep disorders and help people.

Snoring is one issue that a sleep disorder clinic will investigate, as well as problems with breathing that affect sleep. However, in your course you will be looking at psychological sleep disorders, rather than physiological ones. Psychological issues are to do with the brain and mind, and are about mental health. Physiological issues are about physical health.

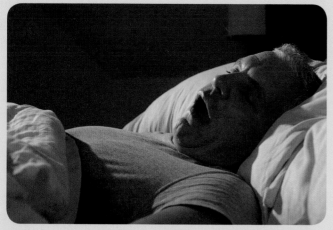

Many sleep disorders, such as snoring, have a physiological cause. However, there are also psychological sleep disorders.

Types of sleep disorders

The symptoms of psychological sleep disorders are listed in what is called the Diagnostic Manual, which doctors use to diagnose mental illnesses. There are two types of sleep disorders: primary and secondary. **Primary sleep disorders** are not related to any other problem, but are problems in themselves. Examples are problems going to sleep, problems staying asleep or problems with waking up. **Secondary sleep disorders** stem from another problem, such as pain (keeping someone awake), jet lag or stress (affecting the person's sleeping patterns).

Quick check
A What is the difference between primary and secondary sleep disorders?

One way of dividing up sleep disorders is to put them into four categories:

- insomnia
- hypersomnia
- circadian rhythm disorders
- parasomnias.

Insomnia

The most common sleep disorder is insomnia, which means someone cannot go to sleep or cannot stay asleep. Insomnia is diagnosed if the lack of sleep is affecting someone's activities in the day. Insomnia is more common as people get older. Some prescribed drugs can cause insomnia, as can other mental illnesses, or stressful life events. Often insomnia is treated using prescribed drugs, rather than a sleep disorder clinic. Other treatments available include teaching the sufferer to relax or teaching them to focus on positive thoughts when they go to bed. These treatments can be carried out in a sleep lab but don't have to be.

Hypersomnia

The second category is hypersomnia. This means people feel very sleepy at all times of the day. There are conditions that can cause hypersomnia, such as narcolepsy, which is a brain disorder where people have sudden attacks of sleep in the day. Hypersomnia can also be caused by not sleeping properly through the night, perhaps because of breathing difficulties rather than from any psychological problems.

Taking it further

Go to www.heinemann.co.uk/hotlinks (express code 4837P). Click on the *BBC website* to investigate narcolepsy.

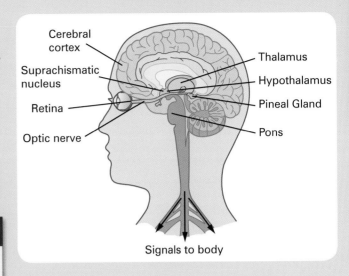

Signals to body

Circadian rhythm disorders

The third category involves disorders of the sleep-wake cycle and these are called circadian rhythm disorders because they cause problems with the body's circadian (24-hour) rhythm, or 'body clock'. The sleep-wake cycle is the pattern of sleeping at night and being awake in the day over a regular 24-hour (more or less) period. The sleep cycle refers to the nightly pattern of about five waves of the different sleep stages (see page 64). If there are problems with the sleep-wake cycle then the body clock can be badly affected. Problems can occur when people have different shifts at work that require them to go to bed at different times, so their body clock cannot settle to one pattern. However, in other cases of circadian rhythm disorder there are no obvious explanations. Using bright lights at certain times can reset the body clock.

Parasomnias

The fourth category includes parasomnias. These are disorders that occur when someone is asleep, such as nightmares, sleep-walking and sleep terrors. Sleepwalking happens during non-REM sleep and is more common in children than adults – as well as being more common in males. Sleep terrors are when someone wakes up in non-REM sleep because they feel very agitated. Again, this is more common in children than in adults. Teeth grinding and bedwetting are also problems that are featured in parasomnias.

Narcolepsy tends to activate the muscle paralysis associated with REM sleep. REM sleep behaviour disorder does not activate the muscle paralysis, resulting in violent movement.

There are REM sleep behaviour disorders (RBD), which involve violent movements and violent language, in contrast to the usual paralysis (see page 65) in REM sleep. Drugs such as benzodiazepines are used to treat RBD.

Psychotherapy (see page 84) can be used to help parasomnias, as can medication. Relaxation therapy is also used.

Quick check

B What is the difference between the sleep cycle and the sleep-wake cycle?

Examiner's tips

Be careful not to confuse the sleep-wake cycle of 24 hours, with the sleep cycle, which refers to patterns of sleep over the night.

Questions

1 Name two types of psychological sleep disorder.
2 Explain the difference between parasomnia and insomnia.
3 Using examples, explain what a psychological sleep disorder is.

B3b2 Sleep disorder clinics

Learn about

- What a sleep disorder clinic is
- How psychological sleep disorder is treated at a sleep disorder clinic

Do you have trouble sleeping? If you have a bad night for some reason, how does this affect you the next day? It is common to have problems sleeping sometimes, but there has to be more to it for a sleep disorder to be diagnosed.

Many sleep problems are dealt with by the sufferer, taking advice and helping themselves. They may, for example, avoid drinking coffee after a certain time of day, try to get more exercise during the day, and establish a regular pattern of going to bed. Sleep problems may be dealt with by a doctor, who can prescribe medication such as sleeping tablets or anti-depressants. However, medication is only a short-term solution as it can be detrimental to a person's health in the long term.

Treatments at a sleep disorder clinic

Physical problems such as snoring are probably the most common type of disorder dealt with by sleep disorder clinics, and treatment may involve lasers and surgery. However, psychological sleep disorders, including insomnia, parasomnias and narcolepsy, can also be dealt with at a sleep disorder clinic.

A sleep disorder clinic is also involved in the assessment and diagnosis of the problem. Blood testing can help with diagnosis – for example, it can be used to see if there is a genetic link for someone who has narcolepsy. (Narcolepsy itself is not diagnosed using blood testing.)

Observation and other measures can also help with diagnosis. Someone suffering from a sleep disorder is likely to spend a night in a clinic for observation and monitoring while they are asleep. An EEG (electroencephalograph) can be used to study a person's sleep cycles. The researchers may simply watch the individual sleeping, recording any rapid eye movement shown, or watch for the amount of restlessness the individual exhibits. They may look for patterns of when or how often the person wakes. They may also monitor the sleeper's temperature.

Taking it further

Go to www.heinemann.co.uk/hotlinks (express code 4837P). Click on the *Private Healthcare UK website* to investigate sleep clinics.

Many sleep clinics are privately run and offer a variety of services. Often they explain that they use a **holistic** approach, which means they deal with people of all ages and take the person's lifestyle into account, treating them as an individual. Holistic means whole – looking at the person as a whole rather than just as someone who snores, for example. To assess a sleep disorder, the clinic will monitor someone's mood, temperature, activity levels and environment, as well as other aspects of their life, to gain an overall picture.

Quick check

A What are two functions of a sleep disorder clinic (what are two things they do)?

How psychological sleep disorders are treated in a sleep disorder clinic

Treatments of psychological sleep disorders include:

- medication
- cognitive behavioural therapy (CBT)
- **acupuncture**
- hypnotherapy.

Medication

Prescribed drugs are often used to help with sleeping disorders. For example, some drugs help to regulate sleeping and waking patterns and are prescribed for narcolepsy and other disorders. The use of benzodiazepines for sleeping behaviour disorders has already been mentioned (see page 87).

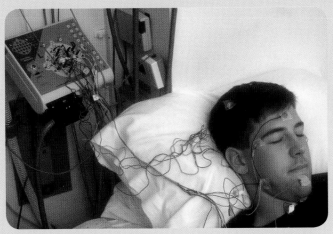
Sleep disorder clinics monitor sleeping and waking patterns to try to identify causes of sleep problems.

Acupuncture can be used for psychological sleep disorders.

Cognitive behavioural therapy (CBT)

Cognitive behavioural therapy can also help. Sleep problems are often related to anxiety, and cognitive behavioural therapy addresses unhelpful thinking. For example, the way a person sees sleep might not be appropriate. They might be very distressed by waking up every night and, as a result, view sleep negatively. By changing their negative thoughts about waking up in the night to more practical, positive thoughts about how to manage that time, it may reduce their anxiety, and actually help them sleep better. In fact the individual may not need as much sleep as they think, and CBT can help them recognise this. CBT finds a way of replacing automatic negative thoughts with more positive ones.

Acupuncture

Acupuncture is a form of Chinese medicine. The treatment involves inserting needles at certain related points on the body. This 'map' of connected points along pathways (called meridians) was identified by Chinese therapists in ancient times. There is some scientific evidence that this treatment works and it is now fairly widely used. Acupuncture can be used to help the body clock to readjust when the sleep-wake cycle is out of step.

Hypnotherapy

Hypnotherapy involves the client relaxing thoroughly with a therapist so that the therapist can help uncover any problems the client has and can make suggestions about overcoming their sleep disorder. This therapy is used with insomnia and parasomnias, such as night terrors.

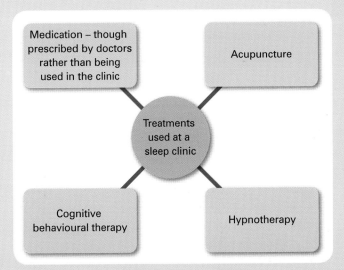

- Medication – though prescribed by doctors rather than being used in the clinic
- Acupuncture
- Treatments used at a sleep clinic
- Cognitive behavioural therapy
- Hypnotherapy

Quick check

B Name four treatments offered for psychological sleep disorders at a sleep disorder clinic

Questions

1 Give an example of an automatic negative thought.
2 Explain how CBT is used to treat psychological sleep disorders.
3 Explain, using examples, the work of a sleep disorder clinic.
4 Explain how hypnotherapy is used to treat psychological sleep disorders.

KnowZone - Topic B
Is dreaming meaningful?

You should know...

ANSWERING THE QUESTION

☐ Freud's theory of dreaming (1900) – dreaming is meaningful and that dreams reveal our emotions, uncovering our unconscious thoughts and desires.

☐ Hobson and McCarley's theory of dreaming (1977) – dreaming is not meaningful because it is a biological activity. They also agree that dreams are about how we think, so they are meaningful to an extent.

☐ The basic structure and function of a neuron – helps to understand Hobson and McCarley's theory.

☐ The case study as a research method and related terms – evaluate the use of the case study as a method of research.

☐ Ethical issues in case studies – privacy and confidentiality and how they can be dealt with.

☐ The dream analysis involved in Freud's 'Little Hans' case study – evaluation of dream analysis.

☐ The role of the psychoanalyst – what they do, qualifications and skills, how they might use dream analysis to help a patient.

☐ The work of a sleep disorder clinic.

EVALUATING THE ANSWER

☐ Freud's theory developed in Viennese high society in the 1900s and arose from repressed desires – his theory might only be relevant to that time.

☐ Hobson and McCarley worked in the 1970s in a much more scientific society – treated dreams as being a scientific part of our makeup.

☐ Freud used case studies and qualitative data as his method of research – findings are hard to repeat in order to test (they are not reliable).

☐ Using qualitative data and in-depth methods, Freud's findings are about real people and issues (they have validity).

☐ Hobson and McCarley used scientific methods, such as experiments with animals, which can be repeated (they are reliable).

☐ Using animals and experiments are both artificial procedures for finding out about humans – Hobson and McCarley's findings might not be relevant for people (they might not be valid).

Support activity

Summarise the work of a psychoanalyst (pages 82–85) as either a poster that would be suitable for a careers day, or as a leaflet aimed at someone interested in having psychoanalysis.

Stretch activity

Use what you have learned about experiments as a research method (pages 36–39) and what you have learned about the case study research method (pages 70–77) to answer the following question:

Describe how experiments and case studies could be used to study why people dream and compare the two research methods.

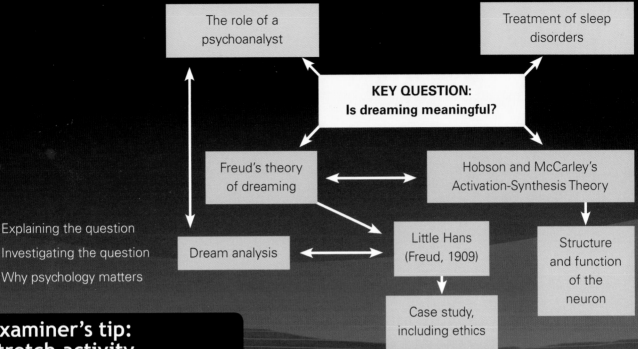

The role of a psychoanalyst

Treatment of sleep disorders

KEY QUESTION:
Is dreaming meaningful?

Freud's theory of dreaming

Hobson and McCarley's Activation-Synthesis Theory

- Explaining the question
- Investigating the question
- Why psychology matters

Dream analysis

Little Hans (Freud, 1909)

Structure and function of the neuron

Case study, including ethics

Examiner's tip: Stretch activity

Briefly describe what is meant by an experiment and what is meant by a case study using terms from Topics A and B. Then give one suggestion of how an experiment could be used to study dreaming and one suggestion of how a case study could be used to study dreaming. Hobson and McCarley drew on experiments whilst Freud drew on case study material so you could base your suggestions on their work.

The final part of the question asks you to compare the two methods. You could consider whether they are different in terms of reliability, validity and subjectivity/objectivity. End by considering which research method enables more knowledge to be uncovered about dreaming, or which is more scientific.

Key terms

Freud
- Manifest content
- Displacement
- Latent content
- Condensation
- Dreamwork
- Secondary elaboration

Hobson and McCarley
- Random activation
- Movement inhibition
- Sensory blockade

Basic structure and function of a neuron:
- Neuron
- Neurotransmitter

- Axon
- Synaptic transmission
- Impulse

Methodology:
- Aim
- Confidentiality
- Case study
- Generalisability
- Qualitative data
- Reliability
- Quantitative data
- Subjectivity
- Privacy
- Objectivity

Practice Exam Questions

1   Outline the activation-synthesis theory of dreaming.

2   Describe one case study where Freud used dream analysis.

3   Outline what is meant by dreamwork in relation to Freud's theory of dreaming.

4   Explain one similarity and one difference between Freud's theory of dreaming and Hobson and McCarley's theory of dreaming.

5   Explain one treatment offered in a sleep disorder clinic.

Topic C
Do TV and video games affect young people's behaviour?

Introduction

During this chapter you will explain, investigate and explore whether young people are influenced by watching TV or playing video games. We know that video games have age certificates to prevent young children playing them, but many children still do.

This chapter explores whether watching violent media can produce aggression in young people or whether the cause of aggression is in our biology.

Do young people become more aggressive after watching aggressive TV programmes or playing aggressive games? You might already think you know the answer to this question.

You may think the answer is yes, because you have seen a younger brother or sister hitting a toy after watching a violent cartoon. Or maybe you believe the answer is no, because you have played aggressive video games and feel it has not affected your own behaviour. Whatever you believe now might be changed once you have explained, investigated and explored the question further.

Many young people play video games. How much does this affect their behaviour?

Topic C Do TV and video games affect young people's behaviour?

93

Explaining the question

You will explain this topic question by looking at:

- whether hormones or the brain are responsible for aggression
- how we might learn aggression from the TV and video games we watch.

Investigating the question

You will investigate this topic question by looking at:

- how psychologists use content analysis to investigate how much violence can be found on TV and in video games
- the ethical problems with measuring aggression in experiments
- what psychologists have found out about aggression from doing research.

Why psychology matters

When you have looked at four key studies, you will be asked to compare two of them. This will help you to understand whether TV and video game aggression is copied or not.

You will use the knowledge you have learnt so far to compare two important studies that investigate the effect of the media on children who have not been able to watch networked television. You will also be able to use your knowledge to think about how psychologists deal with and help to control aggression issues.

Exploring the question further

Have you ever watched a film that was 'too old' for you? You' ll look at how effective film certificates and the 9pm 'watershed' are at keeping children from seeing inappropriate material that they could copy.

C1a1 The role of the brain and aggression

Learn about
- How the brain might control aggression
- Which parts of the brain might affect aggression levels

What do you think when you see someone being aggressive? Do you think it's because of the way they were brought up? Some psychologists believe that some people are aggressive because they were born that way or that parts of the brain are linked to **aggression**.

The biological reasons for aggression

A person can be aggressive because of their biological make-up; they are aggressive people naturally. Some psychologists have conducted research into whether aggression has a genetic basis, but scientists have not found a gene responsible for aggression. Research has focused more on how the brain functions and how areas of the brain are involved in aggression.

Looking at the brain

There are two areas of the brain that we need to look at more closely, because they are involved in aggression:

- the **limbic system**
- the **amygdala**.

Examiner's tips

There are some difficult words to learn in this chapter. It would be useful to start your own glossary of new terms that you come across. This will help you remember them and make it easier to revise.

The limbic system

The limbic system is a set of brain structures that lies in the middle of the brain. It looks a bit like a wishbone (see the picture below). The limbic system is called the 'emotional area' of the brain because it is responsible for emotions needed for survival, like fear and aggression.

Quick check

A What is the role of the limbic system?

People with emotional disorders have been shown to have had damage to the limbic system. The limbic system is made up of many structures that are jointly responsible for recognising, controlling and producing aggression, but some research has focused on the amygdala.

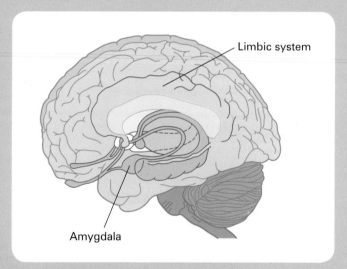

The limbic system and amygdala are known for their influence on aggression.

The amygdala

The amygdala is a structure in the brain that recognises emotion. If someone smiles we know they are happy, and if they frown we know they are sad. The amygdala also creates emotional responses. You have probably seen a frightened cat; it bares its teeth and hunches its back. This is the amygdala producing a fear response.

The amygdala is also responsible for producing aggression. In animal studies, if the amygdala is removed the animal becomes very calm and does not respond to threatening situations with aggression. Damage to this area of the brain may cause increased levels of aggression.

Quick check

B What is the role of the amygdala?

Some human **case studies** do offer some evidence that the amygdala might cause aggression. King (1961) described a case of a woman whose amygdala was electrically stimulated during an operation. She became threatening and verbally aggressive until the electrical current was turned off.

In 1966 Charles Whitman killed 13 people from an observation tower at Texas University, after killing his wife and mother. He left behind a note asking doctors to examine his brain as he was convinced that something was making him aggressive. He was found to have a brain tumour pressing against his amygdala.

Quick check

C Name one case study that links aggression and the amygdala.

Difficulties researching human brain biology

Humans and animal brains are similar, but not similar enough for us to make a direct comparison. The problem with using animal studies as evidence is that they are very different from humans. However, we cannot of course purposefully damage an area of the human brain to see if it results in aggression, and stimulation of the brain is very risky. So, it is difficult to tell whether the limbic system and amygdala are involved in aggressive behaviour or not, as there is limited direct proof.

Quick check

D Outline one problem with animal studies.

Taking it further

Go to www.heinemann.co.uk/hotlinks (express code 4837P). Click on the *Wikipedia website* to read more about Charles Whitman.

Evaluating the link between biology and aggression

Strengths:

- Animal studies that have involved damage to or removal of the amygdala offer evidence for its link with aggression.
- The case study of Charles Whitman and the case described by King (1961) are evidence for its link with aggression in humans.

Weaknesses:

- Studying the human brain is difficult and can be very risky, so there is no way of making sure areas of the brain are linked to aggression.
- Animals and humans are different in many ways, so animal research suggesting a link between the brain and aggression may not be applicable to humans.
- Case studies are **unreliable**, as the reason for an individual's aggression may be unique to that individual.
- Aggression could equally be explained by the way children copy the media. (This issue will be covered in more detail on page 98.)

Key definitions

amygdala: a brain structure thought to be involved in aggression.

limbic system: an area of the brain involved in emotion.

Questions

1 Describe a biological cause for aggression.
2 Describe one source of evidence that supports the idea that aggression has a biological cause.
3 Explain one problem with the source of evidence you have described.

C1a2 The role of hormones and aggression

96

Male aggression and testosterone

In almost every culture, males are far more aggressive than females. Could this be because they have more **testosterone**? Testosterone is a male sex **hormone**. Hormones are chemicals produced by the body that send messages to organs of the body via the bloodstream.

Quick check

A What is a hormone?

Testosterone is secreted by the **adrenal glands** and **testes** and is needed to produce sperm, develop the male reproductive organs and produce male features, such as facial hair and a deep voice. Women also have testosterone, but males produce up to 10mg of testosterone every day, which is ten times more than a woman.

Quick check

B What is the role of testosterone in the human body?

Aggression in animals

Psychologists have researched the role of testosterone in aggression by studying animals. Injecting animals with testosterone or removing the testes leads to increased or decreased levels of aggression.

Castrating a male animal lowers its testosterone levels. This makes the animal less aggressive. But if the same animal is then injected with testosterone its aggression is restored to a level similar to that before the castration.

Male tigers display aggression because of high levels of testosterone.

This is strong evidence that testosterone is responsible for aggression. But would we be able to say the same about humans? We would not be able to test this in a psychological study, as it is not **ethical** to deliberately increase testosterone in men to study aggression levels.

Instead, psychologists use animals, although they are naturally different from humans in many ways, both physically and behaviourally. Aggression in humans is less instinctive than in animals; humans consider the consequences of their actions and are more reasoned in their actions than animals.

Aggression in humans

Psychologists can take blood from humans to see what level of testosterone they have and compare this to how aggressive they feel or act. Some **correlation studies** (studies that see if there is a link between two variables) have found a relationship between high testosterone levels and questionnaire results showing greater reported aggression. However, it is not certain whether testosterone causes increased aggression or aggression causes increased testosterone.

Quick check

C Outline one way that psychologists have researched testosterone and aggression in humans and one way in animals.

Evaluating the role of testosterone on aggression

Strengths:
- In animals, there is a clear cause and effect relationship between testosterone and aggression.
- Human studies show a relationship between aggression and testosterone in correlation studies.

Weaknesses:
- Not all humans with high testosterone levels are aggressive. Some have greater sporting ability or are driven in their careers. Testosterone creates a drive, but this need not be a violent one.
- Correlation and animals studies have weaknesses. Animal studies may not apply to humans, and correlation studies just look for relationships and are not direct evidence.
- If testosterone is the cause of aggressive behaviour, why are some women more violent than some men, and why aren't all men violent?
- This explanation of aggression completely ignores the huge impact of upbringing and social circumstances on our behaviour.

97

Women can be as violent and aggressive as men.

Key definitions

hormones: chemicals produced by the human body that send signals to organs around the body via the bloodstream.

Questions

1 Outline the evidence that suggests testosterone produces aggression.

2 Explain two problems facing psychologists who want to study the link between aggression and testosterone.

C1a3 Social learning theory

Learn about

- Using the social learning theory to explain aggression
- The link between watching TV and playing video games and aggression.

The media always talk about the films we watch, music we listen to or video games we play. Unfortunately there have been several recent murders involving children shooting schoolmates in the USA and Finland. Each time, the media focus on the influence of violent TV or video games to provide an answer for their behaviour.

Do you think that violent TV and video games alone could cause these tragedies?

Social learning theory as an explanation of aggression

Observational learning

Children learn through watching other people. When we try to teach a child to eat with a spoon, complete a jigsaw or use a pen, we often demonstrate the skill first. The child remembers and copies this action and performs it itself. This is called **observational learning**.

Modelling is the act of copying an observed behaviour. If a parent frequently reads books, the child may model this behaviour by picking up books, opening them and turning pages.

Bandura's study (1961) showed how children imitate adults.

Observational learning can take place without modelling; we don't copy everything we see, but we still learn it. It involves four steps:

- Attention: paying attention to the person being observed.
- Memory: being able to remember what we have seen until it is needed.
- Reproduction: being able to act out what we see – this is modelling.
- Motivation: the incentive to copy what has been seen.

Role models

The person we observe and learn from is called a **role model**. This can be anyone we watch, such as a sporting hero, celebrity, teacher or parent. David Beckham is a role model for most children who like football. They model him by wearing 'his' football shirt and copying his football tricks.

Identification

We are more likely to model a person who is popular, attractive, a similar age, or the same gender as us. We identify with role models who are like us or that we look up to. **Identification** is when we adopt the behaviours, attitudes and beliefs of a role model. We become like them and believe that we can do what they do.

Quick check

A What is meant by the term 'identification'?

Vicarious learning

We are more likely to imitate someone if we think that there will be a reward in it for us. Vicarious learning is when we learn from the fortunes or misfortunes of others. If we see a friend being praised for helping tidy away after a class, we are more likely to model this behaviour. This is known as **vicarious reinforcement**, because the reward we see others receive will motivate us to copy them and get a reward too. However, if we see a friend receiving a detention for being noisy in class we are less likely to model this behaviour. This is known as

98

vicarious punishment, because if we copy we might get a detention too.

Essentially, we are learning through the consequences of other people's actions. We do not have to receive reward or punishment ourselves.

In the 1960s the psychologist Albert Bandura found that children were more likely to copy an adult attacking a large inflatable doll (known as a bobo doll) if the adult was rewarded for it. If the adult was punished the child would be less likely to copy. Bandura's study seems to support the idea that children can learn aggression. He also found that boys were more likely to copy physical aggression than females.

Do children copy TV and video games?

If we use social learning theory to understand how TV and video games change the behaviour of young children, then we should believe that watching violence could make children aggressive. Young people do watch programmes and play games that are not suitable for their age group, and observational learning of aggression or violent behaviour can occur.

Key definitions

observational learning: the process of learning from watching others.

modelling: observing, identifying with and copying the behaviour of a role model.

role model: a person who is looked up to and copied.

identification: a feeling of similarity with a role model that leads to the imitation of their behaviour – we believe we can be like them.

vicarious reinforcement: learning through the positive consequences of other people's actions rather than firsthand – we are more likely to copy if they are rewarded.

Many children act out the behaviour of their favourite television or video game characters. You only need to watch small children for a little while to be able to pick out the fighting moves of their favourite superheroes or the dance steps of their pop idols.

Children identify with characters on TV and in video games and believe they can be like them. Many of these characters are rewarded for their behaviour, even if it is aggressive, motivating children to copy them because they feel they will receive a similar reward.

Evaluating social learning theory as an explanation of aggression

Strengths:

- Bandura's (1961) study supports social learning theory because he found that children do copy aggression.
- Many tragedies, such as school shootings, have been linked to TV and video game violence.

Weaknesses:

- It could be that aggressive children watch aggression on TV and play violent video games rather than being affected by them. They could be naturally aggressive.
- Many children watch violence but not all children copy it.
- Watching violent TV and video games can actually lower aggression. This is because it acts as a release for natural aggression.
- It is difficult to study observational learning because modelling may take place a long time after it has been observed or may never have taken place at all.

Questions

1 Alex likes to dress up as his favourite cartoon characters and act out their superhero moves. Using social learning theory, explain Alex's behaviour.
2 Outline one strength of social learning theory.
3 Outline one weakness of social learning theory.

C1b1 Comparing theories of aggression

Learn about

- How the biological and social learning theories of aggression compare
- How these theories relate to the nature-nurture debate

The biological and social learning theories clearly disagree on the cause of aggression. So, how do they compare with one another? Comparing two things means that we need to weigh one up against the other to see what their views, strengths and weaknesses are. This puts us in a better position to judge them.

Comparing the biological and social learning theories of aggression

The biological approach sees aggression as something that comes from within us, whereas the social learning theory believes that aggression is copied from others external to ourselves.

The focus of the social learning theory is on how we 'learn' aggression rather than whether we have the tendency to be aggressive because of the way our brain functions. Social learning theory argues that we are likely to be motivated to copy aggression through vicarious reinforcement (see page 99), whereas the biological approach emphasises amygdala damage or testosterone imbalance (see pages 94–97).

Examiner's tips

It is not unusual in psychology to have theories that do not agree with one another. Sometimes it is not as simple as right or wrong. Both theories can offer good reasons for aggression. Try to remember that there are many sides to a story. It is better to be aware of them than try to dismiss all but one in search of the truth.

Difficulties with each theory

It is difficult to decide which theory to side with, because both are difficult to study. Observational learning may not lead to modelling or it might be modelled at a later date, so we cannot be certain that the observed behaviour has been learnt. Similarly, studies of the brain and hormones are difficult or unethical, and we have no direct evidence that testosterone or the amygdala cause aggression.

Another similar problem with both theories is that not all individuals with high levels of testosterone or who watch violent TV and video games are actually aggressive. Neither theory takes account of differences between individuals.

Both have been criticised because the reverse of each theory might be true. Aggressive children might seek out aggressive media rather than the media affecting their behaviour. Similarly, aggression might cause high testosterone levels rather than testosterone causing aggression.

Is aggression caused by biology or learning?

The nature-nurture debate

The **nature-nurture** debate is an ongoing discussion about whether our behaviour is caused by our biology (nature) or the environment we have been brought up in (nurture).

Nature

As we have seen, the biological side of the discussion says that the way we behave is determined by how our brain and hormones function. The brain controls our behaviour, and if it is damaged in some way it can affect how we behave. If we have a hormone imbalance, this can affect our behaviour too. High levels of testosterone can increase aggression according to this theory. This is the nature side of the debate because the cause of aggression comes from within us.

Quick check

A What is meant by nature?

A conclusion

Whether children are naturally aggressive or learn aggression from TV and video games is not yet understood. It does seem sensible to explain aggression in terms of a combination of both factors. Maybe biologically aggressive children seek out violent TV and video games, and then copy what they see. This means that both theories are correct, as both contribute to aggression in children. Nowadays most people believe that it is a combination of nature and nurture that makes us who we are and influences how we act.

Taking it further

Draw a line with nature at one end and nurture at the other. Now think of a skill or talent you have and decide where on that line you would put it. Maybe you are a skilled musician. Did your parents push you to get your musical grades or do your parents also possess the same musical skill?

NATURE ← ——————————————→ **NURTURE**

The biological explanation of aggression:
- limbic system
- amygdala
- testosterone

The social learning explanation of aggression:
- observational learning
- modelling
- identification
- vicarious reinforcement

Summary of the biological and social learning explanation of aggression

Nurture

The nurture side of the debate says that our environment causes our behaviour. This includes the way we are brought up, the people we learn from and the experiences we have. All of these guide us to behave in a certain way. Social learning explains how we identify with others and model their behaviour. It argues that aggression is caused by the environment in which we live – whether we are exposed to aggressive media or not.

Quick check

B What is meant by nurture?

Key definitions

nature: what we are born with.

nurture: what we learn from the way we are raised.

Questions

1 Outline both theories in relation to the nature-nurture debate.

2 Describe a difference between the two theories in explaining aggression.

3 Describe a similarity between the two theories in explaining aggression.

C1b2 Ramirez et al (2001): culture and aggression

Learn about

- What Ramirez did to find out if aggression differs between cultures
- Whether Japanese and Spanish people show different levels of aggression
- The strengths and weaknesses of this study

Culture and aggression

Try to picture in your mind a Japanese person and a Spaniard. Your images will probably be **stereotypical**. A person from Spain may have tanned skin and dark eyes, probably a man waving a red coat at a bull! Someone from Japan, however, will be quiet, hardworking – perhaps a Japanese woman, wearing a kimono? Now try to imagine how each would respond to a threatening situation. It is easy to imagine the temperamental Spaniard throwing his hands in the air and shouting, but it is more difficult to imagine a Japanese person even making eye contact with an aggressor, let alone displaying any aggression.

The study by Ramirez et al (2001)

Martin Ramirez and his colleagues wanted to investigate whether aggression varied between cultures. They were also interested in the different levels of aggression between males and females.

Procedure

The study involved 400 psychology students, who volunteered to take part. Half of the students were at university in Japan and the other half in Spain. All students were asked to complete a questionnaire that measured different types of aggression, including:

- verbal aggression
- physical aggression
- anger
- hostility.

Questionnaires

The questionnaires included Likert-style questions, where the participants respond by saying to what extent they agree with each statement. You will learn more about this on page 138.

The questions covered different areas, for example:

Verbal aggression:

- I tell my friends openly when I disagree with them.

Physical aggression:

- Once in a while, I can't control the urge to strike another person.

Anger:

- Some of my friends think I am a hothead.

Hostility:

- I sometimes feel that people are laughing at me behind my back.

Some cultures are more aggressive than others.

The participants had to answer each question using a 5-point scale:

1 = extremely uncharacteristic of me
2 = somewhat uncharacteristic of me
3 = neither uncharacteristic nor characteristic of me
4 = somewhat characteristic of me
5 = extremely characteristic of me.

Taking it further

Go to www.heinemann.co.uk/hotlinks (express code 4837P) and access the questionnaire on the *York University website*.

Quick check

A What type of question did the questionnaire contain?

Findings/results

Ramirez uncovered some key findings:

- Japanese students showed more physical aggression than Spanish students.
- Spanish students showed more verbal aggression and anger than Japanese students.
- Males showed more physical and verbal aggression and hostility than females in both cultures.
- Males and females in both cultures showed the same level of anger.

Examiner's tips

Many of the issues dealt with in Unit 2 require you to recall information from Unit 1. Make sure you revise the methods from both Units 1 and 2 to prepare for your exam.

Conclusion

Despite the cultural stereotypes of the Japanese culture being shy and not showing emotion, this study found that Japanese males and females were more physically aggressive than Spanish students. The finding that Spanish students are more verbally

aggressive is consistent with the stereotype of Spaniards being expressive of their emotions. The study supports previous theories that males are more aggressive than females. This may be because of the way men are raised, as masculine, or because of hormonal differences between the sexes.

Strengths and weaknesses of the study

Strengths:

- The questions produce **quantitative data** (see page 71) so cannot be interpreted differently by researchers.
- All the students were volunteers and fully aware that the results would be published. This means that it is an ethical study.

Weaknesses:

- Some questionnaires are criticised because the answers can be interpreted in such a way that they meet the expectations of the researcher (although this is not the case with the Ramirez study). Open-ended questions would be an example of these (see pages 138–9).
- All the participants were psychology students and may have tried to guess the aim of the study (response bias) or answer questions in a socially desirable way. (You will study these problems with questionnaires on page 138.)
- Students may have answered the questions according to how they think they would act, but in a real-life situation they may be unlikely to behave that way.

These are the problems with self reports/ questionnaires compared to experiments or observations.

Questions

1. What did Ramirez want to find out by conducting this study?
2. What do the findings of this study tell us about gender differences and aggression?
3. What do the results of this study tell us about cultural differences and aggression?

C2al Content analysis as a research method

Learn about

- What content analysis means and why it is used
- How to carry out a content analysis
- The issues with doing a content analysis

Content analysis is a research method used to measure the number of times a behaviour or event occurs within one or several forms of media.

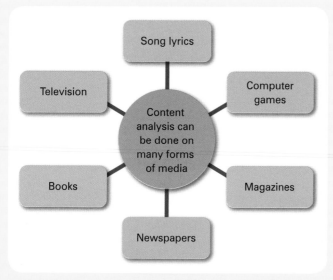

Many forms of media can be used for a content analysis.

Conducting content analysis

Researchers who wanted to see how much aggression occurred on television would use content analysis as a research method. They would have to take a number of steps to do this:

1 Decide what aggressive behaviour is.
2 Develop a list of behaviours or categories that could be measured as aggressive.
3 Decide on the sample they need to study (e.g. which television programmes or adverts, what times of day).
4 **Tally** (count) the times aggression occurred.
5 Assess the reliability of their results.

Quick check

A What is meant by the term content analysis?

Tallying

The table below is an example of a tally chart.

Categories	Tallies
Kicking	⫲⫲⫲ = 5
Punching	⫲⫲⫲ ⫲⫲⫲ ‖ = 12
TOTAL number of aggressive acts	17

Once they have selected a sample of programmes to watch, the researcher uses a tally to record how many times they witnessed the aggressive acts on their list. A tally is a mark that shows a behaviour occurring once. These are added up to give the total number of aggressive acts so that they can decide how much aggression is on television.

Examiner's tips

You may be asked to plan or discuss a content analysis in the exam, so why not have a go and bring this research method to life. Practise using a tally chart to measure the aggressive acts in one of your favourite cartoons or TV programmes. Conclude your findings and see if your analysis uses appropriate categories and is reliable.

This process is quite straightforward, but there are a few things you need to be aware of. You are asked to consider a content analysis again when looking at censorship and the watershed on pages 122–125.

Quick check

B (i) Make a list of aggressive acts that might be found in
  a) a children's cartoon
  b) a children's drama.
 (ii) Construct a tally chart to record the aggressive acts you have listed.

The choice of categories

The list of behaviours needs to be a good example of what is being measured. So, putting a category such as kissing as a measure of aggression would clearly not be appropriate. It could even be more subtle than this. For example, if a category of pushing was on the list, it might not be a good measure of aggression if you are watching a game of tag in a playground as it would appear as if children were more aggressive than they actually were.

Sometimes it is difficult to interpret behaviour. This game of tag might be seen as either aggressive or playful.

Sampling

Good content analysis depends on looking at a good sample of programmes, books or other forms of media to study. Even the time of day or type of programme can lead to a **biased** sample. For example, if you only look at television programmes after the watershed (9 p.m.) they are more likely to include violence than before the watershed. This may lead you to conclude that more television is violent than is the case. A good sample of television programmes should be at different times of the day, on different channels and different days of the week.

A poor sample means that the study findings will be **unrepresentative**. This means that the programmes in the sample cannot be said to be similar to all television programming or media forms being analysed.

Reliability of content analysis

When a researcher does a content analysis they might record tallies that other researchers would not, like the example of pushing in a playground. Another researcher might see this as playful and not give it a tally.

Each researcher has their own views, and this means that the results of a study might not be **reliable**. This could lead to researchers coming to different conclusions.

Quick check

C What is meant by the term 'reliability'?

One way of overcoming this is by getting two or more researchers to do the same study. Everyone's results can be compared and only those that are agreed upon are used as a result. If more then two people agree on them then we can assume that most people will too.

Key definitions

content analysis: a research method used to measure the number of times something comes up in a book, newspaper article, television programme, etc.

tally: a single mark on a chart to show that a behaviour/category has been found during a content analysis.

unrepresentative: limited so that it might not apply to everyone.

reliability: refers to whether findings from a study would be found again if the study was repeated.

Questions

1 How would you conduct a content analysis to investigate how teenagers are portrayed in newspapers?
2 Kylie wanted to study the type of toys children played with in books. Make a list of girls' and boys' toys that she might investigate.
3 Kylie's friend did the same study but found something different. Explain why Kylie and her friend came to have different findings.

C2bl The ethics of psychological research

Psychologists are bound by a strict set of ethical guidelines that are regulated by the British Psychological Society (BPS). These guidelines help protect participants of psychological research and make sure that the research conducted is carefully considered. Ethical guidelines are moral rules that prevent us from doing harm.

Ethical guidelines

There are six main ethical guidelines, of which one directly relates to the **protection of participants**. The others are:

• **Consent**
• **Right to withdraw**
• **Deception**
• **Debrief**
• **Competence**.

Protection of participants

Participants of psychological research should not experience physical or psychological harm. Psychologists have to consider the rights and welfare of participants and weigh this up against the benefit or gains of the research. Clearly participants cannot be physically harmed by a study, as this is unjustifiable. Psychologists also have to consider whether the study might cause psychological harm, such as embarrassment, distress, anxiety or concern.

Quick check

A Why might psychologists feel it is necessary to not inform participants?

However, it is worth considering the rest of the guidelines, because all are there to safeguard the physical and psychological wellbeing of participants.

Consent

Participants should give consent to taking part in psychological research and, if possible, psychologists should try to fully inform participants about the nature and aim of the study. The purpose of this guideline is to allow participants to refuse permission if they don't want to be part of a study. Without information, participants do not have the knowledge to be able to say no. This can cause distress or embarrassment when they find out later, so consent should be informed consent.

Right to withdraw

Participants should be able to withdraw their consent to take part at any point in a study. If they feel stressed, distressed or embarrassed they should be able to leave the study so they are not harmed.

Deception

Participants should not be lied to unless absolutely necessary, because it can make them feel humiliated when they eventually find out. Finding out you have been lied to is not a nice feeling, particularly if the research pressurises you into doing something you would not normally do. Anderson and Dill (page 108–109) lied to their participants so that they could test aggression. If the participants had known the truth about the study they might not have been aggressive. Although the deception in this study meant that the researchers could measure natural behaviour, the participants would have probably been annoyed, and also felt guilty about harming someone else.

Quick check

B Describe the ethical guidelines of consent and deception.

Debrief

Participants should be told the real aim of the study when it is over. This is to ensure that they are left in the same state as when they started the study. However, a debrief is not an excuse for deception. That would be like saying sorry to someone after kicking them in the shin.

Competence

A researcher must be qualified to conduct the study. Also, if they are chartered psychologists, they might need approval from the British Psychological Society. See what it means to be 'chartered' on page 119. As well as needing to be qualified, researchers might also seek advice from colleagues if they are not sure how the study will affect participants.

How ethical?

A study by Anderson and Dill (2000) (see page 108) could be said to be unethical because they did not protect their participants physically or psychologically. The participants of the study received loud blasts of noise up to 100 decibels through headphones. This would be similar to standing near a rail track as a high-speed train went past, or putting your iPod on the loudest setting.

Medical research suggests that more than 15 minutes exposure to such noise can result in permanent tissue damage to the ear, and even hearing loss. Did the study cause physical harm? Well, the researchers did not expose participants to the loud noise for very long (0.5–1.75 seconds) and it was not always set at the highest level of 100 decibels. Most blasts of noise were 55 decibels, about the same level as a normal conversation.

Key definitions

consent: permission to take part in a study.

right to withdraw: a participant's right to leave a study at any time and their ability to do so.

deception: being lied to.

debrief: being told the truth about a study when it is over.

competence: a psychologist's ability to conduct a study.

protection of participants: looking after the rights and welfare of participants to ensure no physical or psychological damage.

Participants also had to administer blasts of noise to someone they believed was an opponent. Although the opponent did not actually exist, participants may have felt distress because they thought they were harming someone else. Participants may have been embarrassed and felt guilty about their aggressive behaviour when debriefed, because they were deceived and not fully informed. However, the researchers tried to make sure they felt valued.

Quick check

C Name two ethical guidelines that Anderson and Dill did not implement in their experiment.

How can we protect participants?
- Before research is carried out, we should make sure that all risk of harm is identified, and minimised where possible.
- Psychologists should seek professional help from colleagues or advisors about the risks identified.
- Researchers should inform participants where possible about any risks involved.
- Participants should always be given the right to withdraw at any point in the study. Even if they are not fully informed about the study aim, at least they can choose to leave the study if they begin to feel distressed or embarrassed, etc.
- Counselling or other professional services should be provided if the participants have been affected by the study. There should be a follow-up of all participants to ensure that they have not suffered any long-term damage.
- When debriefing participants, they should be reassured that their participation will be confidential and that their participation in the study has been of great value.

Questions

1 Outline why it is important to have ethical guidelines for psychological research.
2 Describe the ethical guideline 'protection of participants'.
3 Describe one way that could be used to make sure participants are better protected.

C2c1 Anderson and Dill (2000): video games and aggression

Learn about

- A study that looked at how video games can affect aggression
- What Anderson and Dill did and what they found
- The strengths and weaknesses of this study

Eric Harris and Dylan Klebold (in the back row) as students at Columbine High School.

In March 1999 Eric Harris and Dylan Klebold went to school, Columbine High in Colorado. They gunned down 13 fellow students, then committed suicide. The Columbine High massacre was linked to *Doom*, a violent video game that both boys enjoyed playing. On that day the boys seemed to re-enact the game to murderous result. Could this tragedy have really happened because of a video game?

The study by Anderson and Dill (2000)

Aim

Craig Anderson and Karen Dill wanted to see whether people who played violent video games became aggressive.

Procedure

They conducted a laboratory experiment in which 210 psychology students were split into two groups and asked to play either a violent or a non-violent video game for 30 minutes. The **independent variable** was the type of video game participants played. The **dependent variable** was the level of aggression shown after playing the game. The video games were:

- *Myst*, a non-violent fantasy adventure game
- *Wolfenstein 3D*, a violent and graphic 'shoot-em-up' game.

The participants were told that the study was about the development of motor skills, not that it was a study of aggression, so they would not guess the aim of the study.

Each participant was placed in a cubicle and told to play a video game against an opponent who was in another cubicle. In fact there was no opponent – the cubicle was empty.

After 15 minutes playing time, they were asked to begin a competitive game with the opponent, involving a reaction test. The person who pressed the button fastest would be able to give the opponent the punishment of a blast of loud noise. The winner would be able to set the volume and duration (length of time) of the noise inflicted on their opponent.

Once the study was over, an experimenter entered the cubicle and fully debriefed participants and answered any questions they might have.

Quick check

A What was the independent variable? How did the researchers manipulate this variable?

B What was the dependent variable? How did the researchers measure this variable?

Results
Anderson and Dill found that the loudest and longest blasts of noise were given from participants who played *Wolfenstein 3D* – the violent game. Interestingly, women gave greater punishment to their opponents than men.

Conclusion
Playing violent video games such as *Wolfenstein* increased the level of aggression in participants, particularly women. The researchers believed it made them think in an aggressive way and that long-term use could result in permanent aggressive thought patterns.

Quick check
C The video games used in this study were from 1997. How might video games have changed in the last decade and what might the effect of this be today?

Evaluation
Strengths:

- It was a laboratory experiment so researchers had a lot of control over the participant and their experiences. They made sure all participants received the same instructions and procedure; the only difference was the game they played. This makes sure the results are reliable because the study can be repeated exactly and the same results are likely to be found again.
- The findings of this study have useful applications in the real world. It tells us that we are right to have age restrictions for video games because they might adversely affect the behaviour of young people.

Key definitions
independent variable: the factor which is changed by the researcher in an experiment to make two or more conditions.

dependent variable: the factor which is measured in an experiment.

Weaknesses:

- Even though participants were told this was a study about motor skills, they may have guessed the aim of the study anyway. After all, participants knew it was a psychology experiment.
- We normally play video games at home or in arcades, where behaviour is not monitored or recorded. These participants had to play the games in a cubicle and knew they were being watched. This is not a realistic study and participants may not have acted naturally.
- The study violated some of the ethical guidelines that psychologists should stick to when conducting research. First, they did not fully inform participants about the true aim of the study; they deceived the participants and did not tell them the whole truth. However, the participants may have changed their behaviour if they were informed of the real study aim. Second, the participants may have been stressed by receiving loud blasts of noise or believing that they were harming someone else with loud blasts of noise. This goes against the ethical guideline to protect participants. However, the noise did not last long, so was unlikely to result in long-term damage. (Full coverage of ethics can be found on pages 106–107.)

Taking it further
Investigate the latest video game releases and make a list of ones that are violent and ones that are non-violent. Which list is longer?

Questions
1 How were the participants of this study deceived?
2 What might have happened if the participants had been told the truth about the study aim?
3 Outline one weakness of this study other than an ethical consideration.

C2c2 Charlton et al (2000): St Helena study

Learn about

- The island of St Helena, and Charlton's famous study
- Whether researchers found introducing TV increased aggression or not
- Some of the strengths and weaknesses of the study

Houses on the remote island of St Helena.

St Helena is one of the most isolated islands in the South Atlantic Ocean. Around 2000 kilometres from mainland Africa, it is only accessible by boat. The community on St Helena is small, with a population of around 5000 inhabitants, including just over 1000 children of school age. Imagine living in a small close-knit community where everyone knows each other.

Charlton's (2000) study

Tony Charlton and his colleagues from the University of Gloucestershire have spent many years studying the island of St Helena because it did not have any access to television before March 1995. They began their study in 1993, two years before TV was introduced, and continue their study today.

Aim

To investigate the effects of television on children's behaviour.

Procedure

Charlton and his colleagues began their study of children's behaviour two years before TV was connected to the island. This is a **natural experiment** because the researchers did not have to set up the experiment themselves – the introduction of television was happening naturally. The independent variable was television – before and after its introduction – and the dependent variable was the children's behaviour on the island.

Examiner's tips

You will have already studied independent and dependent variables in Topic A, pages 30–31. A natural experiment also has an independent variable, but this is not manipulated or set up like a field or laboratory experiment. The independent variable in a natural experiment occurs by itself. In this study, the researchers did not introduce TV themselves – it was happening naturally.

Charlton collected data about the children's behaviour using a number of methods:

- The researchers collected information on the children, using questionnaires and asking parents and teachers about the behaviour of children.
- Observations of the children's behaviour were made in the school playground, particularly the level of aggression the children displayed.
- The researchers' content analysed what and how much the children watched on television. They were particularly interested in how much violence children watched and for how long.

- Video cameras were placed in the school classrooms and playgrounds to watch the children and measure the level of aggression.

Quick check

A Name two methods that the researchers used to investigate children's behaviour.

Results

Charlton found very little difference in the children's behaviour before and after the introduction of television. The island had a very low rate of behavioural problems with children before the study, and this did not significantly increase because of watching TV.

Because the population of St Helena was so small, with everyone knowing everyone else, and parents having a high level of control over their children's behaviour, the effect of television was reduced. TV did not have the impact it could have had in a less isolated environment.

Conclusion

This study shows that TV did not have a significant impact on children's behaviour. Even if violence was watched it was not copied. This was due to high levels of community control and surveillance and parents' control over behaviour.

Taking it further

Go to www.heinemann.co.uk/hotlinks (express code 4837P). Click on the *Guardian website* to read an article on the study written by Charlton.

Quick check

B What was the main finding of Charlton's study?

Key definitions

natural experiment: an experiment where the independent variable is naturally occurring and not set up by the researchers.

Evaluation

Strengths:

- This study is a natural experiment, which means it has greater realism than a laboratory or field experiment. This is because the researcher does not set up the situation – it is happening naturally.
- Discreet cameras were used so the children would have acted naturally, because they did not know they were being watched.

Weaknesses:

- Because of the close nature of the community it might be that the children were more aggressive after watching TV, but that parents and teachers were unwilling to report this because of the negative view researchers would have of the Island. Also, if children were aggressive in the classroom or playground this could have been controlled quickly by teachers to prevent a negative perception of the children.
- Other psychologists have reported that the programmes watched by children contained less violence than programmes watched by mainland children. Popular programmes with high violent content, such as 'Mighty Morphin Power Rangers' and 'Teenage Mutant Ninja Turtles', were not broadcast to St Helena children.

Quick check

C Outline one strength or one weakness of a method you named in question A.

D Suggest similarities and differences between the isolated St Helena community and your community.

Questions

1 Outline the aim of Charlton's research.
2 Describe one strength of Charlton's study.
3 Describe one weakness of Charlton's study.

C2c3 Williams et al (1981): does TV affect children's behaviour?

Learn about

- How Williams found out about the influence of TV on children's behaviour
- Whether the introduction of TV was linked to increased aggression
- The strengths and weaknesses of this study

Is TV all that bad? How would we ever find out if it were? Most of us have been exposed to television from a very young age. Its effects would be difficult to measure because we would not be able to tell what we would have been like without television.

Williams et al (1981) study

What if we could prevent children from watching television, then introduce it and measure the effects? Wouldn't it be very difficult to set up an experiment like this? Tannis Williams and her colleagues had just such a unique opportunity when a small, remote town in British Columbia, Canada, applied for a television transmitter to be installed because they had no TV reception. (British Columbia is very mountainous; many remote places find it difficult to pick up a TV signal.)

Does TV affect our behaviour?

Aim

Williams wanted to measure children's behaviour before and after television had been introduced to the town and also to compare the children's behaviour with that in other towns that did have TV.

Procedure

Williams et al carried out a natural experiment. They measured a range of behaviours before and after the town received television:

- aggression of children in the playground and classroom
- leisure activities the community were involved in
- intelligence level (IQ) of children
- creativity and reading ability of children.

To measure aggression, two observers watched children in the school playground and classroom. They only started observing once the children were used to their presence. This was to make sure the children did not behave differently because of the observers watching them. They measured the number of physical acts of aggression (hitting) and verbal aggression (teasing). They called the town 'Notel' (not its real name) and also studied two neighbouring towns with similar population and economy: Unitel and Multitel.

- Notel: had no television.
- Unitel: had one TV channel.
- Multitel: had many TV channels.

All three towns were studied before TV was introduced in Notel, and for two years after.

Quick check

A How did Williams measure the behaviour of the children in this study?

Results after the introduction of TV to Notel

- The most significant finding came from the observations of aggressive behaviour – the children were twice as aggressive after television was introduced.

C2c3 Williams et al (1981): does TV affect children's behaviour?

113

Examiner's tips

The code names of these towns will help you remember them.

- Notel was code named because it had 'No tel'evision.
- Unitel was code because 'Uni' is Latin for 'one', so 'Uni tel'evision.
- Multitel was code because 'Multi' is shorthand for multiple, meaning more than one.

- Children and adults spent less than half the time they had spent previously on other leisure activities.
- Children began to see increased gender differences between boys and girls after watching television. This might be because gender differences that are emphasised on TV would have probably gone unnoticed in children growing up without TV.
- Children became less creative.
- Intelligence (IQ) scores dropped slightly after TV was introduced.
- Although aggression in all towns increased over the two-year study, aggression in Notel children increased far more in comparison. Overall, Unitel and Multitel were quite similar. This suggests that one channel or many channels seem to have a similar effect. The largest difference was found between Notel and the other two towns.

Conclusion

Notel showed increased levels of aggression because of the introduction of television; we know this because aggression increased far more here than in towns that already received television. Television also reduced time spent on leisure activities and lowered creativity and intelligence slightly.

Evaluation

Strengths:

- A strength of this study is that it was done in a real place and television was introduced naturally. This has far greater realism than any other type of experiment.

- Because the same children were followed over a two-year period, their behaviour before and after TV could be directly compared.
- The children were observed in their natural surroundings; at school in the class and playground. The researchers did not make any recordings for a whole week to make sure the children were used to them being around. This was a control for the children behaving differently because they were being watched.

Quick check

B Why do natural experiments have greater realism than other types of experiment?

Weaknesses:

- The researchers did not control what or how much TV the children watched, or the adult supervision and control of viewing.
- Observations might be biased because the researchers see what they want to see. They might have reported higher levels of aggression because they expected it to happen after children started watching TV.

Taking it further

You will need to be able to compare this study with Charlton et al's (2000) study (see page 110). Look up the location of British Columbia and St Helena on a map of the world. This will help you understand the geography of each location and possibly a reason for the different findings.

Questions

1 Why did the researchers spend a whole week in schools before they started their observations?
2 Outline one factor, other than television, that might explain the increased aggression in the children of Notel.
3 Charlton et al (2000) and Williams et al (1981) came up with very different findings. Can you think of a reason for this? (Hint – the key is in their geography.)

C3a1 Comparing Charlton et al (2000) and Williams et al (1981)

Learn about

- The differences and similarities between Charlton's and Williams' studies
- The reasons for the difference between their findings
- Main strengths and weaknesses of both studies

What do these two studies tell us about the effect of TV? Most television programming broadcasts violence – even children's television. Charlton et al's (2000) study suggests that television violence has very little effect on aggression in children, whereas Williams et al's (1981) study tells us that TV almost doubled aggression in children. The differences in findings between these two studies leave us wondering what to think. Is TV bad for children or not?

Making comparisons

There are similarities between these studies that make them comparable, but there are also big differences that can help us to explain why they found what they did.

Similarities between the two studies

- Both studies were natural experiments. The researchers did not control the introduction of TV, it was naturally occurring.
- Both studies were conducted in real-life communities.
- The communities of St Helena and Notel had never had access to broadcast television (as opposed to videos) and were introduced to satellite TV for the first time.
- There were variables outside the control of both studies: other children or parents' behaviour.

- Both Charlton and Williams conducted observations to measure the amount of aggression children displayed.
- Both studies used questionnaires to ask teachers and parents about their children's behaviour and viewing habits.

Differences between the two studies

St Helena is so remote that it had developed a unique culture of parental control. Notel was not unique in this way because it is a mainland town.

On St Helena most people knew each other and their families. Notel was a normal town with inhabitants coming and going; not everyone knew each other well.

Notel was on the mainland, so had access to popular cultural trends, whereas St Helena only had a ferry visit every month to deliver supplies and so was isolated from popular culture.

The adults on St Helena may have been reluctant to admit the children had aggressive behaviour because it might create a negative image of the island. The same reluctance would be unlikely of a mainland town whose name was never disclosed.

Quick check

A Why is it important to try to do real-life research in psychology?

B What are the problems with conducting real-life research?

It is the differences between these two studies that might give us a clue about why the findings are so different. Children on St Helena were monitored by family and friends more closely because of being an isolated community.

This means that the children were unlikely to carry out aggressive acts they watched on TV even if they wanted to. The parents of these children had strict control over their behaviour and guided them more closely.

This means that their behaviour was influenced more by their parents and community than by TV. In Notel, the children were monitored less by parents and the community. Because of this, children could copy what they watched without fear of surveillance.

Summary of the main comparison points between Charlton (2000) and Williams (1981)

Similarities	Differences
They were natural experiments	Remote island versus mainland
They were real communities	Different sense of community
Both communities never had access to television prior to the studies	Different guidance and parental monitoring
Both studies conducted observations and used questionnaires to measure aggression	Cultural differences between the locations

A conclusion

Children are affected by watching TV. But parents and community can lessen the influence of TV by controlling what their children watch and how they behave. Living in smaller neighbourhoods with a strong sense of community helps.

However, we should always remember that, although TV and family are important, aggression occurs for a number of reasons; friendship groups, biological factors and triggers in the environment can also play a part.

Parents can have a strong influence over a child's behaviour.

Examiner's tips

Use the following terms to help you express your comparison points clearly:

- similar to
- unlike
- different from
- whereas
- the same as

Questions

1 How was St Helena different from Notel?
2 How do these differences explain their findings?
3 Can we conclude that TV makes children more aggressive?

C3bl The job of the educational psychologist

An educational psychologist (Ed Psych) works with children and young people in schools to help resolve problems of classroom behaviour or to help with developmental issues such as dyslexia or autism. They work with a wide range of issues and include children, school staff and parents as their clients.

What an educational psychologist does

The job of an educational psychologist is very varied, although the focus is always on children and their learning. The main features of their work are outlined in the table below.

Statutory (legal) duty

Ed Psychs carry out assessments of children with special needs. The Education Act (1996) to Local Authorities (who govern schools apart from independent schools) sets out the relevant Code of Practice. The Code requires that children with special educational needs must achieve their full potential and says that children with severe and complex needs must be assessed so that those needs are met. The Ed Psych carries out this assessment. Children and parents must also be involved in any decision-making, as well as other agency workers, such as health workers.

Consultation

An Ed Psych's role can differ depending on who they work for. Often an Ed Psych is attached to several schools. They visit each school once a term or more, depending on the size of the school. They talk to teachers, head teachers and other staff, such as the special needs co-ordinator (SENCO) and also children and parents, giving support and advice.

What an educational psychologist does		
Statutory duties (legal requirements and code of practice)	Consultation (e.g. giving general support and advice)	Individual assessments (looking at needs of individual children)
Planning interventions (suggesting solutions)	Training (e.g. teachers)	Research (can be commissioned)
Multi-agency working (working together)	System-level work (e.g. advising re school policy)	Keeping up-to-date (e.g. reading journals and new studies)
Multi-professional diagnosis (reporting on a child's needs)	Chartered status and CPD (Continuing Professional Development)	

An Ed Psych has to weigh up the concerns of many groups and individuals in the course of their work. Above all, they must put the child's needs first.

Individual assessments

An Ed Psych carries out assessments and testing, such as IQ testing and other **standardised tests**. Children are tested for literacy and numeracy ability as well as in other developmental areas, such as physical abilities and language. They may test for **dyslexia**, for example. Alongside such tests an Ed Psych makes their own observations and talks to other professionals, and anyone else involved, gathering qualitative and quantitative data from as many sources as possible.

How the questions are asked is very important and needs a lot of skill, for example asking a child how they feel when they wake up rather than asking them why they are causing a problem. Indirect **open questions** are more likely to uncover meaningful information in such cases.

Quick check

A Why would an Ed Psych use different methods when assessing a child's needs?

Sitting a test as part of an assessment

Planning interventions

After gathering the necessary information the Ed Psych plans an **intervention**. This means planning a way to solve a problem. They often work with the child and the teacher, and either or both of these people may need to change in some way, so that behaviour changes.

The Ed Psych does not usually put this plan into action themselves; they leave that to those involved, and then check up on progress and review. These interventions can include suggestions about spotting problems early, communicating more successfully, or acknowledging good behaviour more often.

Training

Planned interventions need training so that the teacher, child or anyone else concerned understands what is required (and why).

Research

An Ed Psych might choose to carry out a research project, such as helping children in Year 7 with social skills when they move to a new school.

Multi-agency working

Multi-agency working means different agencies – such as health workers, social services and education personnel – work together to support a child or family. This is to make sure that no case 'falls between' agencies and gets missed.

System-level work

An Ed Psych may advise on systems in schools, such as bullying policies or policies with regard to support for additional needs.

Keeping up-to-date

The Ed Psych must also keep up-to-date by knowing about new studies and new ways of working (such as new reading schemes).

Multi-professional approach to diagnosis

Although a **psychiatrist** will formally diagnose a disorder such as **ADHD**, an Ed Psych may be involved in an early diagnosis, perhaps by preparing a report or by referring the child to a psychiatrist.

Questions

1 Outline briefly two jobs of an educational psychologist.

2 Choose one of the jobs that an Ed Psych does and explain why you think it is the most useful job. Show that you understand the job when discussing why you chose it.

C3b2 Becoming an educational psychologist

Learn about

- Who an educational psychologist might work for
- Skills required, qualifications required and what it means to be 'chartered'

Who might an educational psychologist work for?

An educational psychologist (Ed Psych) could work in the UK for:

- the local authority responsible for state schools in the area
- an independent (fee-paying) school
- themselves – self-employed.

Alternatively they could work abroad, for example as a school psychologist in Australia or the USA.

Examiner's tips

Practise making three simple bullet points after each section of text below to help you organise the information. Then make your own notes alongside the points so the information will make sense to you and be easier to remember.

Quick check

A Give two ways in which an educational psychologist could be employed.

Skills required

Before thinking about getting qualifications, you need to know you have the right skills to be a good educational psychologist. Communication is the main skill required. You need to be able to listen carefully and also to speak with people comfortably. The Ed Psych training covers communication skills such as **empathic listening**.

Empathic listening is a way of listening to another person so that there is real understanding. It also involves responding in a way that shows that you have listened. Your training would also

Most of an educational psychologist's time is spent working in schools.

do two years' teaching before doing a Masters degree, which is one level above a degree.)

3 Then you have to do a three-year doctorate in educational psychology (a doctorate is one level above a Masters degree).

The changes that have taken place were designed to bring the training in line with clinical psychology (see page 154).

Key definitions

empathic listening: a way of listening to another person so that there is real understanding. It also involves responding in a way that shows that you have listened.

Chartered status

If an Ed Psych is a **chartered** psychologist they have to prove their **Continuing Professional Development (CPD)** in the course of their work.

'Chartered' means you have satisfied the requirements of the BPS (British Psychological Society) and have sufficient qualifications and experience to be called a psychologist. Not all educational psychologists are chartered and not all educational psychologists decide to become members of the BPS, even if they have the appropriate degree. Most psychologists who work on a self-employed basis are chartered, as being in the Directory of Chartered Psychologists is a sign of competence that can help them gain business.

Quick check

B What does it mean to say someone is a chartered psychologist?

Questions

1 List two qualifications required to be an educational psychologist.

2 Explain the skills required to be an educational psychologist.

It is very important for a psychologist to be able to communicate well.

include role play to practise communication skills. You have to be able to talk to a range of different people too because you have to communicate with children from a very young age right up to shy 17-year-olds, for example. You would also need to be able to communicate effectively with parents, teachers and other professionals.

Taking it further

Go to www.heinemann.co.uk/hotlinks (express code 4837P). Look up an educational psychologist and find out what they offer on the *British Psychological Society website*.

Qualifications required

1 First, you need a degree in Psychology – one that is recognised by the British Psychological Society (BPS), which most Psychology degrees are.

2 You need to get some experience that involves education, though you don't need to teach. (Previously you had to train as a teacher and

C3b3 Educational psychology and anger management

Learn about
● Dealing with anger management

Helping a child with anger management problems

An educational psychologist (Ed Psych) can deal with cases that involve anger management. There is often an 'incident' in the classroom that draws in the Ed Psych, or there may have been several incidents before advice is sought. Teachers have many pupils in their classroom and having a very disruptive child can be extremely hard to deal with. The Ed Psych will want to help the child, the teacher and the other children by solving any issues.

Anger refers to an outburst, which could be brief or sustained. The child will not be learning if they are emotionally aroused, and other children, as well as adults in the situation, will be affected, so it is important for the child to be able to control their anger.

Observing the child and the situation
The starting point, as with most individual assessments, is observation. The Ed Psych may go into the classroom to watch the child to see what triggers the behaviour and to look for patterns. The teacher is also asked to observe and keep records – and is often given a form to help them to know what to record. They need to know about the environment and the situation, often before any 'incident'. The aim is to try to find out what causes the anger, and how to identify an 'incident' before it occurs. Often there is no specific trigger for an outburst, so general features of what goes before an incident need to be identified.

An angry child can disrupt a classroom and is also likely to be unhappy and unable to learn.

Gathering as much information as possible
The Ed Psych needs to gather specific information about what happens in the classroom, and also other information, such as whether the child displays the same behaviour at home.

Parents are always invited to the school to discuss issues, and sometimes the Ed Psych will visit the child's home to make observations there. Parents are asked questions such as 'Is the child's behaviour like that of anyone else in the home?' or for other times or occasions when the child displays inappropriate behaviour at home. By gathering information like this, the Ed Psych tries to establish patterns. If the parents say that there are no problems with the child's behaviour at home, the Ed Psych would try to discover what it is about school that triggers the behaviour. It could be, for example, that the child's life at home is very structured and organised, whereas at school they feel 'lost'.

The Ed Psych asks the teacher to note whether there is a particular day, time of day or type of environment when the problems occur. The type of environment could include the classroom set up, whether group work is going on, which lesson it is, whether it is after lunch – all these aspects can trigger inappropriate behaviour. The teacher is also

Quick check

A What is the aim of observation before planning an intervention with regard to anger management?

Children can find the playground a hostile environment.

Taking it further

Go to www.heinemann.co.uk/ hotlinks (express code 4837P). Click on the *BBC website* to find out more information about anger management.

asked whether they can tell straight away what sort of day they will have with the child – and often they say yes they can tell. The Ed Psych can then explore how they know – is it the way the child walks in, or how they slam their bag down on the desk, for example?

The Ed Psych also talks to the child. This might uncover factors such as that the lunch break is too long for them, or that something happens on the way to school that upsets them. Or there might be playground behaviour that is causing a problem.

Quick check

B What sort of information are the teacher and parents asked about when an anger management intervention is being investigated?

Helping to solve the problem

Helping the teacher to identify when an incident is going to happen can be very useful to stop the problem before it starts. By keeping a record of what is happening during the day in relation to that child, the teacher might identify signs before an outburst. For example, if the teacher can tell immediately that it will be a bad day, they can say to the child when they enter the classroom that they will talk to them at break time. Or they can smile to show recognition that they understand the child is feeling bad. If they acknowledge the child and the child feels supported, this may stop an outburst.

Helping the child to identify when an incident is going to happen can also be useful. The child, depending on their age, can learn what feelings come before an outburst, for example, or learn what triggers their anger. Then, armed with this understanding, they can be taught techniques that will help to calm them down. They can learn to identify how their body feels and how to change those feelings. Relaxation techniques can help, such as controlling their breathing or focusing on something else. If they can learn to relax and breathe 'easy', for example, they can use a word like 'easy' to bring back those relaxed feelings when they need them.

Needing further diagnosis

Sometimes the Ed Psych may feel that the child has a more serious mental health problem, such as ADHD. In such cases, they would ensure that the child is referred to another agency or specialist.

Questions

1 What techniques can help a child to manage their anger?

2 What is a teacher asked to do when an educational psychologist is called in to help with a particular child's outbursts?

3 Explain the procedures an educational psychologist is likely to follow to help avoid a child's angry outbursts in the classroom.

C4al Introducing censorship and the 9 o'clock watershed

Learn about

- The role of the 9 p.m. watershed
- What censorship means

In the UK there is a 9 p.m. **watershed** for television programmes, which means that some programmes have to be shown after 9 o'clock in the evening. This is part of the **censorship** that is in place. This section discusses the issues of censorship, including the watershed.

It is not easy to decide what material should be censored. Consider a classic painting or statue of a nude in an art gallery compared with a picture in a 'top shelf' magazine. Why is one seen as artistic and one pornography?

What is censorship?

Censorship means preventing the circulation of information. Information is censored if it is considered by some people to be harmful to others, or too sensitive or private in some way. For example, military information can be censored to prevent information falling into enemy hands, business information can be censored to prevent competitors finding things out, and political information can be censored so it is kept secret.

Censorship can apply to speech, written material and to films and programmes on TV. In your course the focus is on **moral censorship**, which is censoring information for moral and ethical reasons.

Quick check

A Name three types of censorship.

Moral censorship

Material that is thought to be **obscene** or objectionable can be censored. This is known as moral censorship. A decision has to be made about what is morally objectionable, what is obscene, what is pornographic, what is unacceptable violence, for example, and what is suitable for certain age groups. This is the job of the censor.

The role of the film censor

The BBFC (British Board of Film Classification) was set up in 1912 by the film industry to monitor films. The BBFC views films and categorises them to indicate features of the film and what age group the film would be suitable for.

Example of film censorship

A U film has the following censorship guidelines:

- Suitable for children from the age of four
- A moral framework that is reassuring and not frightening
- Handles themes sensitively, without bad language
- Some kissing is acceptable
- Some nudity is acceptable if it does not have a sexual context
- Mild violence is ok – but there must be no emphasis on realistic weapons or any behaviour that might be dangerous for children to copy
- Mild horror with reassuring outcomes is acceptable
- No reference to illegal drugs

This is the symbol for a film with a 'Uc' rating, suitable for even the very young.

Compared to a U rating, a Uc rating would have no violence, nudity and similar topics, as it means the programme is suitable for preschool children.

An 18 categorisation

If a film is given an 18 categorisation then you have to be 18 to see the film in a cinema or rent or buy the video of the film. There are exceptions, for example when sex material is informative and educational, such as explaining about safe sex.

This is the symbol for a film with an '18' certificate.

Quick check

B Give two features of a Uc categorisation with regard to films.

Taking it further

Go to www.heinemann.co.uk/hotlinks (express code 4837P). Click on the *British Board of Film Classification website* for information on film classifications.

The role of the watershed

The 9 o'clock watershed is widely supported by the TV industry in the UK, parents and other adults. It is designed to protect children from viewing unsuitable material, such as acts of sex and/or violence. The watershed does not only mean that fewer violent or sexual acts will be shown before it, but also considers the consequences of such acts. For example, if there is mild violence that has no severe consequences that might mean a programme is allowed before 9 p.m.

The Internet is unregulated and there is a debate about how far this situation should continue.

Censorship and type of government

There are different types of government and some types are more likely to want strong censorship than others. Governments that are

Key definitions

watershed: term used to indicate a turning point. When applied to TV programming it is the 9 p.m. deadline *before* which programmes (including cable and satellite programmes) that contain certain levels of violence and/or sex *cannot* be broadcast.

censorship: preventing information from being circulated in some way.

moral censorship: deciding what material is suitable for broadcasting or publishing and what material is not considered moral or suitable.

authoritarian: a style of government where society's members have little input and have to accept the government's decisions.

paternalistic: a style of government where its decisions are made for the good of everybody else. This rests on the idea of the head of the household knowing what is best for everybody else in the household.

authoritarian or **paternalistic** are more likely to favour censorship. Authoritarian means taking decisions and imposing them and paternalistic means taking a 'father' role and thinking that they know best for members of society. So in both these types of government there will be censorship. In many countries, broadcasting is controlled by the government, and this can result in severe restrictions on freedom of speech, which is considered a basic human right in a democratic society.

Questions

1 What does 'censorship' mean?
2 Explain some issues that are considered by the film censor when deciding what categorisation to give a film.
3 What is the effect of being in a different society on what is censored?

C4a2 For and against censorship and the watershed

Learn about

- The effectiveness of censorship
- Arguments for and against censorship and the watershed

Studying violent acts on television

Guy Cumberbatch is a researcher in the UK who has carried out studies using content analysis to look at how much violence there is on television.

Watch some television just before 9 p.m. Soaps have been said to have too much violence, so perhaps choose a programme like 'EastEnders'. Decide on a way of defining a violent act, such as shouting at someone, pushing them, threatening them, or giving them an aggressive look. Then count the number of violent acts that appear in one episode. Compare your findings with those of Cumberbatch and other researchers.

The general finding of studies is that there are between five and six violent acts per hour on prime-time television in most countries, but findings in the UK suggest that the number is lower here. A problem with comparing studies, however, is that measuring a violent act is likely to be a subjective decision.

Is censorship good or bad?

Effectiveness of the watershed

As there seem to be fewer violent and sexual acts on British TV than elsewhere, this means that the watershed might not be as necessary in the UK as in other countries. However, counting violent acts might not be a good indication of what is suitable for young children and what is not. So perhaps a watershed is necessary after all. There are also questions about the data gathered, as it depends how violent acts were measured.

Quick check

A Outline one reason why content analysis might give unreliable or invalid data.

What people think about regulating TV programmes

Research from 18 workshops carried out by programme makers (ITV and BBC) found that 95 per cent of adults and 72 per cent of children surveyed thought that the watershed should remain in place, to protect children from unsuitable material. According to the study, most people are concerned about children between the age of 8 and 12. Before the age of 8 it is felt that parents are more able to control their children's viewing, and after the age of 12 children are thought more able to make judgements for themselves. The watershed is also useful because it helps to show parents what programmes are suitable for their younger children. The ITC (Independent Television Commission) suggests that a 15-certificate film can be shown after 9 p.m. but an 18-certificate film must be shown after 10 p.m., so the watershed has more than one cut-off point.

Effectiveness of the watershed

Most adults and children agree with having the 9 o'clock watershed. This backs up the idea that censorship and the watershed are there in response to society to protect society.

Freedom to watch anything

Cumberbatch (1999) wrote about attitudes to television viewing and carried out a study, using adults. In general, as with the industry's own findings given above, most people thought the regulation was about right. Having said that, though, 89 per cent said they – not regulators – should decide what they watched, and 82 per cent felt that films should be broadcast in their entirety (that is, not censored at all) if it is later than 10 p.m. His study found that 84 per cent knew about the watershed and that 62 per cent thought that parents should be responsible for what children watch. Note that they were still in favour of the watershed idea.

However, questionnaires may give answers the researcher is looking for if respondents can guess. Or they may give what a respondent feels is a socially acceptable attitude – rather than the truth.

Quick check

B Give two pieces of data (percentages) that give evidence for people being in favour of the watershed and two pieces of data (percentages) that people do not want it.

Arguments for and against censorship, including the watershed

As has been shown, in the UK at least, most adults agree that there should be regulation such as the 9 p.m. watershed, which is a form of censorship. There are arguments for and against this kind of censorship, some of which have been explained already. Mainly the ideas are based on the idea that people, including children, learn from media images and information using learning principles such as **social learning theory**.

Censorship relies on 'proof' of social learning theory

Studies have suggested that children (and adults) learn through observing role models. However, research methods have been criticised and there are many factors affecting behaviour. Role models may be just one factor. So perhaps censorship is not all that effective in preventing violence because observing media role models is only one possible cause of violence.

Taking it further

Go to www.heinemann.co.uk/hotlinks (express code 4837P). Search for news items that connect violence and media on the *Independent website*.

Arguments for censorship

- Censorship protects children from viewing acts they are not ready for. This rests on the idea that children imitate role models and are likely to copy what they see in films or on television. It also rests on the idea that children are not little adults but are different in their abilities and understanding.
- Studies show that the vast majority of people are in favour of the watershed to protect children.

Arguments against censorship

- Censorship restricts people's freedom to choose what they want to watch. In a 'free' country people feel that they should be able to monitor themselves.
- It restricts freedom of speech, which in the UK and USA (and other countries) is a central feature of society. Freedom of speech does not mean that anything can be published or broadcast, but the restrictions on it are extremely limited.
- If in Britain there are fewer violent acts per hour on TV then the watershed might not be necessary. However, any violent acts might be important and also the research method (content analysis) can be criticised.
- Authoritarian and paternalistic types of government are more likely to use censorship and this can be seen as another way of control without reference to members of society, again restricting freedom.

Questions

1 Outline two reasons for having censorship.
2 Outline two reasons for not having censorship.
3 Evaluate methods used to collect data when investigating.

Know Zone - Topic C
Do TV and video games affect young people's behaviour?

You should know...

ANSWERING THE QUESTION

☐ The causes of aggression, including biological and social learning explanations – evaluate and compare them.

☐ Some psychologists believe that aggression can be explained by looking at biological factors.

☐ The nature-nurture debate in relation to biological and social learning explanations of aggressive behaviour – evidence suggests that the limbic system is involved in aggression, and that aggressive behaviour is produced by the amygdala.

☐ Testosterone hormone has also been linked to aggression in males.

☐ Social Learning Theory explains aggression as a form of observational learning.

☐ Whether there are individual differences in aggression – Ramirez et al (2001) and Anderson and Dill (2000).

☐ Content analysis as a research method used to investigate media violence – ethical issue of protection of participants.

☐ A description of the psychological studies by Anderson and Dill, Charlton et al (2000) and Williams (1981).

☐ Anderson and Dill's lab experiment and Williams' natural experiment both support the idea that young people copy aggression from the media (TV and video games).

☐ Charlton et al found that mediating effects, such as family and community, can prevent modelling from happening.

☐ The role of an educational psychologist, including what they do, what skills and qualifications they need, and how they might help to treat a child with anger management problems.

☐ The role and effectiveness of censorship, including the watershed and arguments for and against censorship.

EVALUATING THE ANSWER

☐ Biological research using animals and case studies are problematic, making the link between the brain, hormones and aggression difficult to establish.

☐ Limited case studies of tragic events have linked social learning and aggression, but others might argue that there are more complex reasons for such tragedies.

☐ Social learning of aggression has many problems, including the idea that watching and playing violent media actually lowers aggression and that aggressive young people seek out violent media.

Support activity

Imagine that you aspire to become an educational psychologist. Write a diary entry describing how you intend to fulfil your ambition and what type of activities you will do as part of this occupation. Explain how you plan to deal with children with anger management issues as part of your job.

Stretch activity

Recall your knowledge of Social Learning Theory, biological explanations of aggression, and censorship.

Discuss the arguments for and against censorship, including your knowledge of explanations of aggression, and draw a reasoned conclusion.

The role of an educational psychologist

The effects of media on aggression, including a comparison of Charlton (2000) and Williams (1981)

Censorship and the watershed

KEY QUESTION: Do TV and video games affect young people's behaviour?

Biological causes of aggression

Social Learning Theory

Nature-nurture debate in understanding aggression

Content analysis

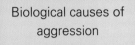
Explaining the question
Investigating the question
Why psychology matters
Exploring the question further

Methods from Unit 1

Ramirez et al (2001 Anderson and Dill (2000) Charlton (2000) William's (1981)

Examiner's tip: Stretch activity

A good answer for this question will only include the arguments for and against censorship. You should then draw upon your knowledge of Social Learning theory and biological explanations of aggression to add to the debate. Try to include relevant evaluation points for each explanation. A reasoned conclusion should not be your own opinion, but a balanced conclusion based on the research, theory and arguments about the effect of media violence on young people's behaviour.

Key terms

- Limbic system
- Amygdala
- Hormones
- Social Learning Theory
- Role model
- Vicarious reinforcement
- Modelling
- Observational learning
- Identification
- Sampling
- Generalisability

Practice Exam Questions

1 Describe the research method content analysis.
2 How is content analysis used to investigate media violence?
3 What are the problems with content analysis?
4 What is meant by protection of participants and how might this issue be dealt with in aggression research?

Topic D
Why do we have phobias?

Introduction

This chapter will help you to explain, investigate and explore why we have phobias.

Do you know anyone who leaps on a chair if they see a mouse on the floor? Or dives into a corner if they see a butterfly? Some people are frightened of animals but others have fears of open spaces or heights. Maybe you know someone who won't look down from a tall building?

What is a phobia?

Some fears make sense. It is useful to be afraid of crocodiles – they are dangerous. When a fear is severe and is focused on a harmless object or situation, it is called a **phobia**. Some people have phobias of social situations, such as crowds. Others are afraid of particular animals like birds or spiders. These fears are real to the person, even though the animal is not dangerous. For example, there is only one poisonous snake in Britain, the adder. Snake bites are very rare, yet many people are still very afraid of them.

A person with a phobia has a strong reaction to the situation or object that they fear. They may:

- feel anxious
- have a racing heart
- sweat
- be short of breath
- suffer intense fear.

Many people have a phobia of snakes.

Explaining the question

The key thing to explain is what causes phobias. The causes include:

- learning – the theory of classical conditioning
- learning by imitating others – **the social learning theory**
- evolution – the theory of preparedness.

Do children learn phobias by copying adults?

You will also explore whether phobias are controlled by our biology or our environment. This is called the **nature-nurture** debate.

Investigating the question

Psychologists investigate phobias using laboratory experiments and questionnaires. You will look at different types of experiments and ways to evaluate them. A key study will show you how a person can develop a phobia and how it can be removed.

Psychologists sometimes use animals instead of people in their experiments and this raises different issues. You will learn about ethical and practical issues in animal research.

To learn how psychologists use questionnaires you will look at another key study. This investigates how people feel about different animals and tells us why some phobias are more common than others.

Why psychology matters

There are two areas of interest here:

- how phobias are treated
- the job of a clinical psychologist.

You will learn about the ethical issues of treating people with phobias and two possible treatments:

- flooding
- systematic desensitisation.

Exploring the question further

Psychologists are still exploring phobias. One recent question is: Do phobias differ between cultures? You will learn about a study to help you to answer this question.

D1a1 Classical conditioning and phobias

130

Learn about

- Classical conditioning
- The terms 'association' and 'generalisation'
- How classical conditioning explains phobias

Pavlov experimenting with his dogs

Pavlov and his dogs

Ivan Pavlov explained **classical conditioning** – a way that animals and people can learn to link two things together. Pavlov was studying eating in dogs by measuring their saliva. Sometimes his dogs started to produce saliva (a response) before their food arrived. He thought this was because they could hear the footsteps (a **stimulus**) of the person carrying the food.

Pavlov tested his idea using a dog that had a tube through its cheek to measure its saliva. First he rang a bell. The dog didn't salivate. Then he rang the bell and gave the dog some food. This was the 'conditioning' process and he repeated it many times. He then just rang the bell and the dog salivated even though there wasn't any food. The dog had learned to associate the bell and the food. It had become *conditioned* to salivate to the bell. This learning process is called classical or Pavlovian conditioning. It works for lots of different behaviours. The general pattern is always the same, and special terms are used (see box below).

Pavlov's dogs: the conditioning process

- the bell has no effect at the start = *neutral stimulus (NS)*
- the food naturally produces salivation = *unconditioned stimulus (UCS)*
- the natural salivation to food = *unconditioned response (UCR)*
- after the association process, the bell = *conditioned stimulus (CS)*
- the effect the bell has is salivation = *conditioned response (CR)*

The pattern of forming links between the stimuli and responses is always the same:

Before conditioning:

neutral stimulus (NS) ⟶ no effect, *unconditioned stimulus (UCS)* ⟶ *unconditioned response (UCR)*

During conditioning:

neutral stimulus (NS) + *unconditioned stimulus (UCS)* ⟶ *unconditioned response (UCR)*

After conditioning:

conditioned stimulus (CS) ⟶ *conditioned response (CR)*

Quick check

A Using the pattern above, rewrite the footsteps and food examples of conditioning in Pavlov's dogs.

In classical conditioning, learning happens because an **association** forms between the neutral stimulus and the unconditioned stimulus. This usually takes many pairings or trials. During these pairings the neutral stimulus becomes a conditioned stimulus which can cause a conditioned response.

Key definitions

classical conditioning: a learning process which builds up an association between two stimuli through repeated pairings.

association: the link between the neutral stimulus and the unconditioned stimulus that makes the neutral stimulus cause the same response.

generalisation: when a conditioned response is produced to stimuli that are similar to the conditioned stimulus.

phobia: an intense fear that prevents 'normal living' in some way.

extinction: the loss of a classically conditioned response when the conditioned stimulus is repeated many times without the unconditioned stimulus.

Classical conditioning and phobias

If a real fear is triggered by something when a harmless stimulus is present, an association may be made between the two things. This can cause a **phobia** to be learned. For example, a little girl is playing on the beach in shallow water. She catches her flip-flop on a stone, trips, and hurts herself. Her dad picks her up but she is wet and frightened.

Before conditioning:
NS (water) ⟶ no effect, UCS (falling over) ⟶ (UCR) fear

During conditioning:
NS (water) + UCS (falling over) ⟶ UCR (fear)

After conditioning:
CS (water) ⟶ CR (fear)

The fear the girl feels when she falls is associated with the sea. When she gets home, she is afraid of having a bath. Even though the accident happened in the sea, her phobia has made her afraid of water in other situations. This is called **generalisation**.

Watson and Rayner (1920) produced a phobia in a little boy called Albert. Each time a white rat was shown to Albert, a loud noise was made with a steel bar behind him. The noise frightened him and he associated his fear with the rat. Albert's fear generalised to other white, fluffy things such as cotton wool and a Father Christmas mask.

Quick check

B Explain Albert's fear of the rat using the correct terms.

Can phobias be changed?
Even in people, conditioned responses often take many trials to learn. If a conditioned stimulus is repeated many times without the unconditioned stimulus, the conditioned response is lost. This is called **extinction**.

However, extinction doesn't happen very easily. Once a phobia has been learned, it is very hard to lose. For example, if a child gets bitten by a dog, they might become afraid of dogs. Even though dogs don't often bite and the child is never bitten again, it may be hard to overcome the fear.

Learning fears in one trial
Classical conditioning usually takes many trials but phobias can be learned from a single event. This is called 'one-trial learning'. A person might learn to be afraid of driving if they have one bad car accident, for example.

Questions

1 What does the neutral stimulus become after classical conditioning?
2 What does 'generalisation' mean?
3 Toby was looking at lizards at the zoo when a friend startled him. Toby was very frightened and since then he has been terrified of lizards. Use classical conditioning to explain why.

D1a2 Social learning theory and phobias

Learn about
- Social learning theory
- Vicarious reinforcement
- How social learning can explain phobias

What is social learning theory?

In Topic C we saw that social learning involves gaining new behaviours by watching and imitating a role model (page 98). Some role models, such as same-sex ones, are more likely to be imitated.

Another factor that affects imitation is the reaction the role model gets to the behaviour. If the role model is rewarded then the observer is more likely to imitate them. This is called **vicarious reinforcement**. For example, Ben is a toddler in a nursery. He bites other children and gets their toys. Other children see Ben getting extra toys and start biting too. This is more likely to happen because they see that Ben gains. If they saw Ben being told off and having the toys taken away, the other children would be less likely to copy his behaviour.

Role models and learning

Some research into social learning uses animals. Birds can learn to eat or avoid foods by observing the behaviour of other birds. For example, you might have seen young birds watching older ones before taking peanuts from a feeder.

In an experiment, Coombes et al (1980) let two rats drink from a spout. One rat had been given an injection to make it sick. Later, both rats avoided the drinking spout. The rat which hadn't been sick learned not to drink from the spout because it had seen the other rat being sick. Learning to avoid something unpleasant is similar to learning a fear.

Key definitions

vicarious reinforcement: learning through the positive consequences of other people's actions rather than firsthand – we are more likely to copy if they are rewarded.

modelling: imitating the behaviour of someone.

Children copy Ben because they see him getting more toys.

Quick check

A Explain how parents might use **modelling** to help children to learn about crossing the road safely.

Social learning and phobias in animals

Social learning applies to emotions as well as behaviours. For example, people will imitate the anger or sadness of a role model. Can fear be learned by observing others?

Mineka et al (1984) found that their laboratory monkeys that had grown up in the wild were afraid of snakes. The ones born in captivity were not afraid. Mineka et al thought that the wild-born monkeys had learned their fear by observing adults in the wild. To test this idea they watched the monkeys' reactions to:

- snakes (real, toys and models)
- other things (black and yellow cord, triangles, etc.)

The wild-born monkeys were only afraid of the snakes. The lab-born monkeys were not afraid of any objects.

The lab-born monkeys then watched a wild-born monkey reacting to each object. They learned to fear snakes but not the other objects. This shows that the monkeys could learn to be afraid of snakes through social learning.

However, snakes really are dangerous to monkeys. Phobias, on the other hand, can be fears of things which are not harmful. Can animals learn through observation to fear things which are not a threat?

When birds such as blackbirds see a predator, they often give a warning call. Curio (1988) showed that social learning explained how blackbirds could learn to give predator alarms to a non-predator.

Curio put two blackbirds (a 'teacher' and a 'learner') in cages so they could not see each other but could each see a stuffed bird. The 'teacher' bird could see a stuffed owl – owls are dangerous to blackbirds. The 'learner' bird could see a harmless stuffed honeyeater. The 'teacher' bird produced an alarm call (even though the owl was stuffed). The 'learner' bird could hear the teacher's alarm but could only see the honeyeater. Later, it imitated the behaviour and produced an alarm call when it saw a honeyeater! This shows that social learning can produce fears in animals even when the object of the fear is not dangerous.

Social learning and phobias in humans

Why do phobias sometimes run in families? Children could be observing and imitating their parents' fears. For example, evidence suggests that one factor affecting children's dental phobia is whether their parents are anxious about the dentist (Townend et al, 2000).

Taking it further

Go to www.heinemann.co.uk/hotlinks and enter express code 4837P. Look at the advice given on the *WebMD website*.

Can you explain the advice in the first paragraph and in points 3 and 4 about what parents should do?

Leib et al (2000) looked at why children have social phobias (like being frightened of new people). They found that children were more likely to have a social phobia if their parents did, so the children may have imitated their behaviour.

Questions

1 Give two reasons why we are likely to imitate a parent.

2 What does 'vicarious reinforcement' mean?

3 Garry, like his dad, is scared of cows. Use social learning theory to explain why.

D1a3 Phobias and preparedness

Learn about
- Evolution and fear
- The theory of preparedness

Evolution and phobias

Imagine two animals living in a forest. There is a forest fire, and one animal runs away while the other shows no fear and sticks its nose in the flames. According to the theory of evolution, the scared one would be more likely to stay alive – because it would be less likely to get trapped and die. This example shows that some behaviours are adaptive, that is, they can help an animal to survive. It also shows that sometimes being afraid is useful. Animals that respond with fear to dangerous situations are less likely to be injured.

This fear makes sense because fire is deadly. However, we often have irrational fears about objects or situations that are not dangerous. We need to be able to explain this too.

Many people in the UK are scared of spiders, even though all UK species are harmless.

Preparedness

We can use evolution to explain irrational phobias. Seligman (1971) suggested that we learn links between some things more easily than between others. For example, we are more likely to fear deep water or thunder than long grass or sunshine. Evolution seems to have 'prepared' us to learn about things that are threatening. This is called **preparedness**. Seligman thought that less input was needed to learn an association to a prepared stimulus than to a non-prepared one. If evolution prepares us to learn to be afraid of fire, we will make an association (see page 131) between fear and fire much more quickly than between fear and a non-prepared stimulus such as a rock.

Seligman believed that prepared stimuli would have been threatening to humans early in their evolution. These things included snakes and spiders, both of which can be poisonous. Situations that can kill or injure people, like fire, deep water and lightning, would also be prepared stimuli. For early humans, fearing these animals and situations would have been adaptive.

People who avoided getting hurt or killed would have had more children. If 'playing safe' was partly controlled by genes, the children would also be more likely to survive. This is an example of 'survival of the fittest'. Early humans who failed to learn to be afraid of danger would be more likely to die, so would have fewer children. The growing population would be made up of more people with genes that helped them to learn to fear, and avoid, danger.

Learning to fear some things and not others
We have already looked at learning phobias through classical conditioning (page 130). Seligman is saying that we have evolved to be conditioned to fear some things more easily than others. The idea of preparedness is useful as it can explain more than simple classical conditioning. If phobias were just caused by conditioning, we would be equally likely to fear any stimulus, but we aren't. For example, we should be as likely to be scared of clothes as of thunder.

We tend to learn to be afraid of things which were dangerous for early humans, rather than modern threats.

However, phobias are not random. Many more people are afraid of thunder and this is because storms would have been risky for early humans. Being struck by lightning can kill. This would have meant that being prepared to learn to fear thunder would help survival but learning to be afraid of clothes wouldn't. The idea of preparedness can therefore explain why some phobias are common and others aren't. So preparedness also explains why we do not easily learn fears of modern things that are potentially dangerous, such as electric sockets or knives.

dangerous immediately. For example, a child who became afraid of wasps the first time they were stung would be unlikely to play with a wasps' nest again. A child who did not learn so quickly might make this mistake and be very badly hurt. So preparedness helps to explain one-trial learning of phobias.

Taking it further

Go to www.heinemann.co.uk/hotlinks and enter express code 4837P. Read about evolution and phobias on the *Psych Web website*.

Quick check

A Should it be easier to learn to fear dogs or guns?

Key definitions

preparedness: the tendency to learn some associations more easily, quickly and permanently than others.

Do you remember one-trial learning from page 131? Early humans would have been more likely to survive if they learnt to be afraid of something

Questions

1 According to the idea of preparedness, would a child be more likely to be afraid of rats or cars?

2 The noise of the wind whistling frightens some people. Think about how the wind could have been dangerous to early humans and explain why this might be a prepared fear.

3 Why must fear be at least partly genetic if preparedness is correct?

D1b1 The nature-nurture debate

Learn about

- Nature and phobias
- Nurture and phobias
- How important nature and nurture are in the development of phobias

You have already learned about the nature-nurture debate on page 101. This says we might be the way we are because we were born like it or because things that have happened to us make us that way. We will now apply this debate to phobias.

What is nature?

Nature is about the biological factors that affect our development. Do genes from our parents make us who we are?

Genes can control some physical features, like eye colour, directly. Control by single genes doesn't happen with psychological characteristics as far as we know. Instead, many genes may act together to affect our development. For example, psychologists know that combinations of genes influence our personality and whether we develop some mental illnesses. If genes, even in combinations, affect our development we would expect children to be like their parents. So parents with phobias may have children with phobias because they pass on genes that make them more 'prepared' to be afraid.

Quick check

A If genes affect the development of social phobias, would you expect to find families with several socially-phobic people in, and families with none?

What is nurture?

Nurture is about the environmental influences on our development. Do our experiences and our opportunities to learn make us who we are?

Social learning says that our behaviour changes because we observe models in our environment, like the children who copied an adult hitting a bobo doll (see page 98). In classical conditioning we learn by associating two stimuli that are repeated together, like the bell and food for Pavlov's dogs.

Both social learning and classical conditioning are examples of the influence of nurture on development.

Quick check

B If the environment affects the development of social phobias, would you expect to find families with several socially-phobic people in, and families with none?

The nature-nurture debate and phobias

Did you notice that the answer to both of the Quick Check questions was 'yes'? This is a problem. Is a family likeness the result of nature or nurture?

A tendency to learn phobias could be genetic. Parents with phobias may have children with phobias because they pass on genes that make their children more likely to learn to be afraid. This tendency could evolve, as people who inherited the ability to learn to avoid danger would be more likely to survive.

Alternatively, social learning would say that, if a parent has a phobia, the child will see the way the parent behaves. As parents are powerful, likeable people, they are important role models. Children could therefore learn the same fears by observing and imitating them when they are showing fear. This is like the argument on page 98 that says aggression can be learned from parents if they are aggressive.

Evidence for the nature argument

The idea of preparedness supports the nature side of the debate. It suggests there is a genetic influence on the kinds of things we learn to fear. Bennett-Levy and Marteau showed that more people are afraid of animals with certain characteristics. These could be the ones that our genes make us likely to fear. So people seem more often to fear stimuli that have been prepared by evolution.

If genes are important in the development of phobias then more closely related people should be more similar in this regard. Slater and Shield (1969) found that identical twins were more similar in their phobias than non-identical ones. This supports the nature side of the debate.

Evidence for the nurture argument

We saw on page 133 that Mineka et al found that monkeys learn fears through social learning. As monkeys and people are very similar, it is likely that we can learn fears too. This is likely as we can learn other responses, like aggression, by observation.

Watson and Rayner (1920) used classical conditioning to make Albert frightened of a white rat (see page 131). This shows that the environment can produce phobias.

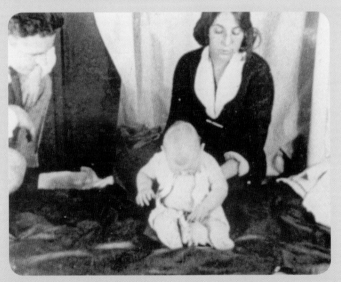

Little Albert was classically conditioned to fear a rat.

What does the evidence tell us?

Both nature and nurture seem to be important. They may even act together. Parents may pass on genes that make their children more likely to learn to be afraid.

Taking it further

Go to www.heinemann.co.uk/hotlinks (express code 4837P). Look at the article on the *Cognitive Behavioural Therapy in Brussels website* and find 'nature' and 'nurture' explanations for phobias.

Quick check

C Several cats live on the same street as Betty and Barney, who are both terrified of cats. If a cat comes near them they scream and run away. Betty and Barney have two children, who are also cat phobic.

  (i) Explain why Betty and Barney's children have a phobia about cats using the nature argument.

  (ii) Explain why Betty and Barney's children have a phobia about cats using the nurture argument.

Questions

1 What do 'nature' and 'nurture' mean?

2 What evidence supports the nurture side of the debate?

3 Is one side of the debate right?

4 How does preparedness support the nature and the nurture side of the debate?

D2a1 Questionnaires

Learn about

- What questionnaires are
- How questionnaires are written

Suppose you want to find out the opinions of students about school meals. How would you find out? You could either ask them directly or write down some questions.

What is a questionnaire?

Look at Bennett-Levy and Marteau's study on page 148. How did they collect their data? They used a **questionnaire**. A questionnaire is a set of questions that are written down and given to participants to answer. They can answer them by ticking boxes or writing in answers. Questionnaires can also be done on computers, with participants checking boxes or typing in responses.

The questions in a questionnaire are usually in a fixed order and everyone answers all the questions. This is called a structured questionnaire.

So that a participant knows what to do with a questionnaire, they are given **standardised instructions**. These help to make sure that all the participants are treated the same. The instructions can either be written on the questionnaire or read to the participants from a script.

Writing different kinds of questions

Questionnaires use different kinds of questions to get different sorts of data.

Closed questions

Closed questions are very simple. They have a fixed number of possible answers and participants often just tick a box. Examples of closed questions are things like:

- Are you afraid of spiders?   Yes / No
- Which animal are you most afraid of: rats / mice / slugs / rabbits
- How old are you?

Closed questions produce numerical data. The answers can be tallied to give totals for each answer. For example, you could count the number of people who said 'yes' or 'no' to a question about whether they would hold a mouse in their hand.

Quick check

A Write two closed questions asking about a person's TV viewing habits.

Open-ended questions

These are sometimes also called 'open questions'. **Open-ended questions** are used when the researcher wants a more detailed answer. The participants are asked for descriptions. For example, an open-ended question might ask:

- How do you feel when you see a spider?
- Describe why you think you became afraid of water.
- What do you do when you are worried about going out of the house?

Open-ended questions produce more in-depth answers than closed questions. People can describe their feelings, opinions or actions. These descriptions can be used to look for patterns, similarities between people, or as examples.

Examiner's tips

If you find it hard to explain the different types of questions, it is often useful to make up an example to help you to gain marks.

Taking it further

Access the link to the *Student Room website* on www.heinemann.co.uk/hotlinks, entering express code 4837P. Read the video games questionnaire and decide which questions are closed and which are open-ended.

Quick check

B Write two open questions asking about opinions on TV violence.

Rank-style questions

A **rank-style question** asks the participant to say how much 'more' or 'less' things are. This can be done in several ways. Participants can be asked to put a list in order, for example:

- Give each animal below a number from 1 (most scary) to 4 (least scary):

  Cat ☐   Fish ☐

  Worm ☐   Hamster ☐

Alternatively, participants can choose one option in a list which is in order, for example:

- Which one best describes how you feel about beetles:

  I like them ☐   I don't really like them ☐

  I don't mind them ☐   I really hate them ☐

Quick check

C Write two rank-style questions about opinions on film or computer game age-certification.

Likert-type scales

A special kind of question is called a Likert-type scale. Participants are asked to judge how much they agree with a statement. These can be used to measure people's attitudes. For example:

- Snakes move suddenly:
  strongly agree, agree, undecided, disagree, strongly disagree
- Robins are slimy:
  strongly agree, agree, undecided, disagree, strongly disagree
- Rats are slow:
  strongly agree, agree, undecided, disagree, strongly disagree
- Slugs are pretty:
  strongly agree, agree, undecided, disagree, strongly disagree

The participant chooses one answer on the scale for each statement. There should be an equal number of statements that express a positive attitude and a negative one.

To work out the results, the answers are given numbers like this:

- Snakes move suddenly:
  strongly agree, agree, undecided, disagree, strongly disagree
  5   4   3   2   1
- Rats are slow:
  strongly agree, agree, undecided, disagree, strongly disagree
  1   2   3   4   5

Note that in the second question, the numbers are in the opposite order. This is so that the more phobic answer still earns 5 points.

Quick check

D Write four **Likert-style questions** to ask about views on the 9 p.m. TV watershed.

Key definitions

questionnaire: a research method using written questions.

open (-ended) question: question that asks for description and detail.

closed question: simple question with few possible answers.

Likert-style question: question using statements with five choices from 'strongly agree' to 'strongly disagree'.

rank-style question: question with points *either* in order that can be chosen *or* that can be put in order.

standardised instructions: guidance for participants that is the same for everyone.

Questions

1 Katya is investigating dreams. Write two:
   a) closed questions she could use
   b) open questions she could use
   c) rank-style questions she could use
   d) Likert-style questions she could use.

2 Explain how you would work out the scores for your questions.

D2b1 Evaluating questionnaires

Learn about

- The strengths of questionnaires
- The weaknesses of questionnaires

140

In your course you have already learned about:

- writing questionnaires
- standardised instructions and controls
- ethical issues.

These will help you to understand how to evaluate questionnaires.

Strengths of questionnaires

Some important strengths of questionnaires are that they:

- can use standardised instructions
- allow for informed consent
- allow for the right to withdraw
- can represent real life.

Standardised instructions

Participants should be given standardised instructions (see page 138) with their questionnaire. These tell participants what to do and are the same for everyone. This is good because what the researcher says might influence how the participant answers.

Standardised instructions also matter in experiments using a questionnaire to measure the dependent variable. They make sure that people in each condition are not treated differently. This is an important control. You have already learned about dependent variables and controls in Topic A, pages 36–39.

Quick check

A If they did not have standardised instructions, how might a researcher introduce a questionnaire about aggression to a group of violent criminals compared to a non-violent group?

Informed consent

Participants need to know what a study is about so they can give their consent (page 44). Questionnaires may ask people personal questions, so ethics are important. As a questionnaire can give information, and ask if people are happy to continue, they are good ethically, as they can easily get informed consent.

Imagine answering a questionnaire giving gruesome details of TV programmes and asking you how you felt. You might not have wanted to read about them at all. The start of the questionnaire should give you enough information to decide not to participate.

Right to withdraw

Ethically, participants should be told they have a right to withdraw. They then know they do not have to answer the whole questionnaire if they don't want to.

Supposing you are filling in a questionnaire that asks you to describe an embarrassing dream. You should be aware that you can leave that question out. In general, questionnaires are good because the right to withdraw can be printed on the front.

Representing real life

Although questionnaires only ask about attitudes, people can describe what they do in everyday situations. This is more realistic than some experiments, for example investigating dreams in a laboratory. This would be an unfamiliar setting and might not produce very valid results. A questionnaire can ask about what dreaming is like at home, so is more life-like.

Weaknesses of questionnaires

Some important weaknesses associated with questionnaires include:

- **response biases**
- **social desirability biases**
- the need to hide the aims.

Response bias

When participants fill in a questionnaire they sometimes fall into patterns of answering. This is called a response bias. Imagine guessing that a questionnaire is about TV violence. If you think TV is damaging, you might keep giving answers expressing this view.

Participants who volunteer for a study are generally helpful. Sometimes this means they give the answers they think the researcher wants. This is another response bias. For example, if a participant believes a questionnaire is about fear of big animals, they may say they are more afraid of cats than worms even if they aren't.

Sometimes participants get into patterns of saying 'yes' to every question or always choosing the middle answer. These are response biases too. One way to reduce responses biases in Likert-style questions is to have some questions stating positive attitudes and others stating negative attitudes.

Do people tell the truth about their behaviour in questionnaires?

Social desirability bias

When participants answer a questionnaire, they know someone will read it. They may want to look good, even if this is unconscious. This can make them give socially acceptable answers rather than what they really believe. This is called a social desirability bias.

> ## Key definitions
>
> **response bias:** the patterns that participants fall into when answering a questionnaire, for example always saying 'yes' or trying to guess the aim.
>
> **social desirability bias:** when participants give the answers they think will be acceptable to other people, to make themselves look better.

Imagine a participant who illegally downloads violent computer games. They probably wouldn't be honest about the games they used. This would be the effect of social desirability. We can reduce this problem by giving participants numbers rather than using their names on questionnaires.

Hiding the aims

Sometimes researchers need to avoid participants knowing the aims of the study as this might bias their responses. Ethically, this is a problem, because it means they cannot give full informed consent.

> ## Questions
>
> 1 Is a response bias in a questionnaire a strength or a weakness?
> 2 What does 'social desirability' mean?
> 3 Describe one strength of Bennett-Levy and Marteau's questionnaire.
> 4 Describe one weakness of Bennett-Levy and Marteau's questionnaire.

> ## Quick check
>
> **B** Think about how a parent might answer the question 'How much TV does your child watch?', if they were:
> - unaware of the aims
> - knew the questionnaire was about the damage done by early TV viewing.

D2c1 Experiments using animals: ethical issues

Learn about
- Ethical issues with laboratory experiments using animals
- Solving these ethical issues

Your course features studies using animals. These have included:

- Hobson and McCarley (dreaming in cats) – page 67
- Pavlov (salivating dogs) – page 130
- Coombes et al (rats watching another rat being sick) – page 132
- Mineka et al (monkeys copying snake alarms) – page 133
- Curio (blackbirds copying alarm calls) – page 133
- Jones (rat and rabbit used with Little Peter) – page 146.

All these will help you to understand how animals are used in laboratory experiments and the ethical issues that surround their use.

Ethical issues with animals

You have already learned about the ethics of using people in experiments. Here we will look at the different ethical issues raised by the use of animals.

There are laws as well as guidelines to help researchers to work ethically with animals. These include:

- minimising the amount of pain and fear caused
- avoiding social isolation
- using the smallest possible number of animals
- using a species that will suffer the least.

Causing pain and fear
Some experiments on animals cause pain or fear. This is only done when it is essential to the experiment. The experimenter has to make sure that only the lowest level of pain or fear possible is used.

For example, in Coombes et al's experiment one rat in each pair was given an injection to make it sick. This was essential to the experiment. They would not have been made more sick than was needed for the other rat to see.

Examiner's tips
It is important that you do not muddle up the ethical issues for people and animals. Students often say that animals cannot be asked for their informed consent. This is irrelevant and does not earn marks.

In Mineka et al's experiment the monkeys were shown snakes, which some were afraid of. This was important as they were looking at how different monkeys reacted. They couldn't just use snake models as the monkeys were afraid of them too. Mineka et al only showed the monkeys the snakes for as long as was needed for them to react and act as role models.

Quick check
A Curio's experiment, like Mineka et al's, exposed animals (blackbirds) to a predator (an owl). What effect would this have had on the blackbirds?

Social isolation
In some experiments it is important to keep an animal on its own. Animals such as dogs, rats and monkeys are social animals. This means that they normally live in a group. For animals like this, being on their own could cause distress so the time alone should be kept to a minimum.

In all the experiments discussed here, the animals would have been on their own for at least part of the time. Often social animals such as rats are kept permanently alone. Sometimes the animals are only separated during the experiment. For example in Curio's experiment, it was important that the birds could hear but not see each other, so they had to be kept apart.

Numbers of animals

It is often important to use several animals to be sure that the result is typical rather than a one-off. However, researchers still have to use as few animals as they can. Mineka et al only tested six laboratory-raised monkeys. This is a small number for an experiment.

Choice of species

Different species of animal find different things distressing. For example, a social animal would find isolation more unpleasant than a species that normally lived alone. Researchers should choose species that will be the least distressed.

Jones chose to use a rabbit to help Peter overcome his phobia. This was a good choice ethically. Rabbits are domesticated animals, so are less frightened by contact with people than a wild species would be.

Quick check

B Which species would be better for an experiment that involved social isolation, hamsters or gerbils?

Taking it further

Go to www.heinemann.co.uk/hotlinks and enter express code 4837P. Click on the *Nobel Prize website* to learn more about Pavlov.

Questions

1 Pavlov had to operate on his dogs to put a tube through their cheek to collect saliva. Which ethical issue would this raise?

2 What does 'social isolation' mean?

3 A researcher is studying social learning in birds. She needs to isolate her animals so they can't learn from one another. Her choices are robins or sparrows. Which should she choose and why?

D2d1 Experiments using animals: practical issues

Learn about
- Practical issues with laboratory experiments using animals
- Solving practical issues

Strengths of animal experiments

There are several reasons, besides ethical ones, for using animals in studies. These include:

- they are similar to humans
- they are simpler than humans
- their environment can be controlled
- they can be used in deprivation experiments
- they are interesting and can benefit.

Humans and animals are similar

On page 134 we looked at evolution. Humans and animals share evolutionary history so they are similar. We are much more similar to some species than others. Animals such as monkeys are more like humans than dogs or cats are, because monkeys are primates. Dogs and cats are more like humans than blackbirds are, because dogs and cats are mammals.

Dogs and cats are more like humans than birds or fish.

Animals that are like us have brains more like ours. This is important because our brains control the way we think and learn. For example, animals and humans both learn through classical conditioning and social learning.

Quick check

A If you wanted to use the results to understand classical conditioning in people, would it be better to do an experiment on rabbits or fish?

Animals are simpler than humans

The behaviour of animals is often simpler than human behaviour. This means they can help us to understand why humans react the way they do, as the behaviour of animals is easier to explain.

Using controls

In laboratory experiments, we want to control variables. Think about controlling variables in an experiment on classical conditioning. The researcher might control:

- where the participant is
- how much they can move around
- the food they can eat.

People are not very likely to volunteer for an experiment like that so it would be done on animals. Other controls that can be used with animals that can't be used with people include access to:

- social companions
- sexual partners
- light and dark.

Controlling these factors improves the experiment as the researcher can be more sure that changes in the dependent variable have been caused by changes in the independent variable. This means that sometimes it is better to use animals than people.

Deprivation

Do you like going without things? How do you feel if you can't watch the television, use your phone or find something to eat? Probably not very happy! People are unwilling to volunteer for experiments that involve deprivation. Instead, animals are generally used.

Depriving animals of food or social companions is often important in experiments on learning. Sometimes experiments involve deprivation of care by parents, sleep or the chance to dream. This is possible on animals but would be unethical to perform on humans as it is potentially very harmful.

Animals are interesting and can benefit

One other practical reason to study animals is to find out about animals! It is interesting to know about the behaviour of animals, regardless of whether it is useful for understanding people. Think about research into whale or bird song. We like to know what animals do.

Humans learn by insight, whereas most animals don't.

People can learn through a process called insight. This is where we have a problem that we can't solve immediately. After a while, the answer comes to us. It seems as though our brains have been using the information to work out the answer. This is very unusual in animals.

This means that the findings from experiments on animals may not always apply to humans. For example, an animal may not be able to solve a problem in an experiment that a human could solve easily.

Taking it further

Go to www.heinemann.co.uk/hotlinks and enter (express code 4837P). Click on the *YouTube website* and watch the video about behavioural enrichment for zoo animals. What benefits does it bring?

Research into animal behaviour can also help animals. By finding out about play or feeding behaviour we can develop ways to stop animals in zoos getting bored. For example, burying food or hanging it from branches keeps animals busy, as they would be in the wild.

Weaknesses of animal experiments

One weakness of animal experiments is that:

• animals are different from humans.

Humans and animals are different

Although humans and animals are similar in some ways, there are also important differences. Humans have bigger brains and they are more complex. We are able to do things that animals can't, such as using language. We can also learn in more complex ways. Animals and humans do learn in similar ways, but humans have extra ways to learn.

Would you get stuck like the dog?

Questions

1 Suggest one thing that can be controlled in an animal's environment that could not be done with a human.

2 Derek wants to apply his findings from a study on animals to humans. Should he use monkeys or mice? Why?

3 Describe an experiment done on animals that could not have been done on humans. Explain why not.

D2el Jones (1924): curing a boy's phobia

Learn about
- What Jones did and found
- The strengths and weaknesses of Jones' study

Can researchers cause and cure phobias?

Watson and Rayner (page 131) planned to remove Albert's phobia of rats using classical conditioning but he was taken away before they could. Before reading on, think about how they could have done it.

Jones' study (1924)

Aim

To investigate whether a phobia in a little boy could be deconditioned and whether this would generalise to other objects.

Procedure

Peter was 2 years, 10 months old when Jones began observing him. She watched Peter playing with beads in his cot as an experimenter showed him a white rat. Peter screamed. He was moved away, leaving his beads behind. When the rat touched Peter's beads he protested but didn't when another child touched them.

The next day Peter's reactions to different objects were observed (see the table below). His fear of the rat generalised to other objects.

Object(s)	Peter's reaction
playroom and cot	chose toys, got into cot
white ball, rolled in	picked it up and held it
fur coat over cot	cried until it was removed
cotton balls	whimpered, cried, withdrew
hat with feathers	cried
blue woolly jumper	looked, turned away, no fear
white cloth rabbit	no fear
wooden doll	no fear

Peter was also shown a rabbit and he was more afraid of this than the rat, so a rabbit was used for deconditioning.

Quick check

A Suggest another object that Peter's fear might have generalised to.

Peter had daily play sessions with three other children and the rabbit, which the other children did not fear. Peter was sometimes observed alone. New situations were used to get Peter closer to the rabbit. Peter's reactions are listed below:

a) rabbit in cage anywhere in room causes fear
b) accepts rabbit in cage 12 feet (4 metres) away
c) accepts rabbit in cage 4 feet (1.3 metres) away
d) accepts rabbit in cage 3 feet (1 metre) away
e) accepts rabbit in cage close by
f) rabbit accepted free in room
g) rabbit touched when experimenter holding it
h) rabbit touched when free in room
i) Peter reacted badly to rabbit, e.g. throwing things at it, but also imitated it
j) rabbit allowed on tray of high-chair
k) squats beside rabbit
l) helps experimenter to carry rabbit to cage
m) holds rabbit on lap
n) alone in room with rabbit
o) in playpen with rabbit
p) fondles rabbit
q) lets rabbit nibble fingers.

Results

The changes above were not continuous or equally spaced in time. Peter's behaviour improved and worsened, for example in session 33 when he was scratched by the rabbit.

Six people were given the descriptions a–q in a random order and asked to put them in order of improvement. The resulting list is called a *tolerance series*.

The chart opposite shows that Peter sometimes got better, sometimes got worse and sometimes stayed the same.

The scale along the x-axis is the session number. Sometimes Peter was observed twice a day (e.g. 11 and 12), sometimes not so often (e.g. two months between 7 and 8). When Peter came back after this break, a big dog jumped at him and his carer, scaring both of them.

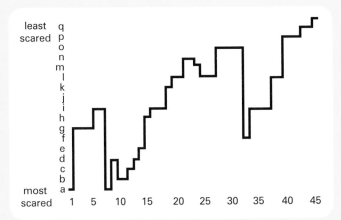

Graph showing Peter's progress.

From session 8 onwards, classical conditioning was used to help Peter. He was given food he liked at the same time as the rabbit's cage was brought closer. It was only moved as close as Peter would allow and still carry on eating (see the box below).

Classical conditioning with food
- Before conditioning: *food → happy*
  rabbit → afraid
- During conditioning: *food+rabbit → happy*
- After conditioning: *rabbit → happy*

The other children acted as role models. In session 9 the rabbit made Peter cry. Another child ran over, saying 'Oh, rabbit', and acted as a role model to help Peter to move closer to the rabbit.

In session 21 the rabbit was put in front of Peter but he cried so another child held it. Peter then wanted the rabbit and held it briefly.

Peter was asked about what he did at the laboratory. At the start he didn't mention the rabbit but later he would say 'I like the rabbit'. He also lost his fear of cotton, the coat and feathers. The reaction to rats and a fur rug improved but he didn't like them as much as the rabbit. He also accepted new animals such as frogs, worms and a mouse.

Conclusions

Both classical conditioning and social learning (see pages 130–133) helped to decondition Peter. The deconditioning also reduced generalised fears and helped Peter to cope with new animals.

Evaluation

Strengths:

- Jones made detailed observations over a long period. These show Peter's progress thoroughly, so the changes can be seen clearly.
- She asked other people to order the tolerance series so avoided being biased herself.
- She used different ways to help Peter. These deconditioned him, and other people have built on her method. Jones was called the 'mother of behavior therapy' by Wolpe, who developed systematic desensitisation (see page 151).

Weaknesses:

- The gaps between sessions were variable, so progress could be due to time rather than the deconditioning.
- Jones used two different techniques (classical conditioning and social learning), as well as other people who made Peter feel confident. This makes it difficult to tell which was most effective.

Taking it further

Go to www.heinemann.co.uk/hotlinks and enter express code 4837P. Click on the *Salve Regina University website* and look at slides 33–38 about Mary Jones and Little Peter.

Questions

1   What were the two methods that Jones used to help Peter?
2   Why was it important that the other children were not afraid of the rabbit?
3   Why did the carer's fear of the dog make such a big difference to Peter?

D2e2 Bennett-Levy and Marteau (1984): fear of animals

Learn about

- What Bennett-Levy and Marteau did and found
- The strengths and weaknesses of Bennett-Levy and Marteau's study

How do we know which animals to fear?

On page 134 we described how evolution prepares us to fear certain stimuli. How do we know which ones to fear? Bennett-Levy and Marteau suggest we have evolved ways to judge which animals are dangerous. Before reading on, think about the animals people are often scared of.

Bennett-Levy & Marteau (1984)

Aim

To see whether we are more afraid of, or avoid, animals that:

- move quickly
- move suddenly
- look very different from people.

Procedure

Bennett-Levy and Marteau used two questionnaires. Both asked questions about the same 29 animals. The participants were told that none of the animals were dangerous.

Questionnaire 1 asked about fear of animals and how close the person would like to get to them:

- Fear scale: 1–3 (1 = not afraid, 3 = very afraid)
- Nearness scale: 1–5 (1 = enjoy picking it up, 5 = move further away than 2 metres)

Questionnaire 2 measured how the participants felt about each animal. They rated each species on a three-point scale (1 = not, 2 = quite, 3 = very) for:

- *ugliness*
- *sliminess*
- how *speedy* they were
- how *suddenly* they moved.

A total of 30 men and 34 women answered questionnaire 1, and 49 different people answered questionnaire 2 (24 men and 25 women). Some participants were also interviewed.

Quick check

A Men and women have different phobias. Do you think Bennett-Levy and Marteau chose a good sample of people to study?

Findings

The animals, in order of the most feared first, were: rat, cockroach, jellyfish, spider, slug, grass snake, beetle, lizard, worm, frog, moth, ant, crow, mouse, grasshopper, squirrel, caterpillar, baby seal, blackbird, hamster, baby chimpanzee, butterfly, spaniel, tortoise, robin, lamb, cat, ladybird, rabbit.

The bar chart below shows that some animals were rated as more ugly. These animals were quite different in structure from humans. For example, cockroaches have six legs, antennae ('feelers') and wings with a hard cover over them. Spiders have eight legs and are hairy all over.

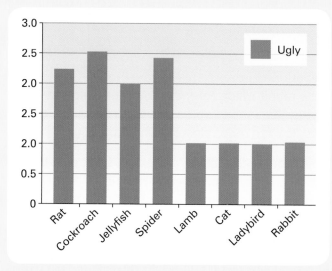

Animals that were very different from people, such as cockroaches, were rated as more ugly than ones like cats that were more similar to people.

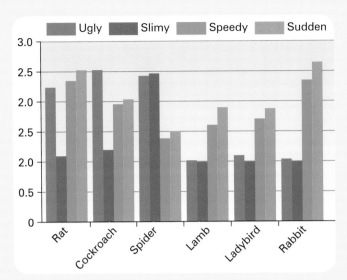

Some species had higher fear ratings and were less likely to be approached.

Bennett-Levy and Marteau found that people were more afraid of some animals and less likely to get near them (see bar chart above). For example, even though the participants were told that the rats and jellyfish were harmless, they were still more likely to be afraid of them and didn't like to get close to them.

When interviewed, participants described ugly animals as slimy, hairy and dirty, with antennae, eyes in odd places and a strange numbers of legs.

Quick check

B Describe three ways that a jellyfish is different from a cat.

Men and women judged ugliness in similar ways. They didn't differ in how ugly, slimy, speedy or suddenly moving they thought animals were. However, women were less likely to approach many of the animals.

Overall, Bennett-Levy and Marteau found some important patterns. People:

- were less likely to approach ugly or slimy, speedy or suddenly moving animals
- were more afraid of ugly, slimy, speedy or suddenly moving animals
- thought that speedy animals moved suddenly.

Conclusions

The features of ugliness, sliminess, speediness and sudden movement all make animals more frightening. Ugliness is judged by how different an animal is from a human. Many animals which cause phobias are ugly, slimy, speedy or sudden movers, which supports the idea that preparedness relates to an animal's features.

Evaluation
Strengths:

- Different participants answered the two questionnaires. This helped to make sure they didn't know what the study was about.
- It was good to use men and women as their phobias are different, so the findings apply to both genders. Also, it was important to see whether men's and women's phobias are different because they judge features differently (which they don't).
- The participants did not need to see the animals, which might have frightened some of them. This avoided ethical problems.
- The findings are useful as they can explain why fears are not always linked to actual experiences with animals. Few people have phobias of rabbits even though they may have been bitten by one as a child. This is because rabbits do not have scary features.

Weaknesses:

- The participants were told the animals were not dangerous but many still thought that rats were harmful, so the instruction was not very successful.
- The questionnaires only asked about six factors. In the interviews, the participants said other things about what makes animals scary. Only a few people were interviewed, so this should have been added to the questionnaire.

Questions

1 What four variables were measured by questionnaire 2?

2 Why would a person be more afraid of a slug than a rabbit?

3 Choose an animal which people found frightening. Explain why.

D3al How to treat phobias

Learn about

- Flooding and systematic desensitisation therapies
- How they are done/carried out

Phobias can be very distressing for people. Some seek help to try and overcome these irrational fears. There are a number of possible therapies for treating phobias (see page 158). Here we look at two of the more traditional therapies:

- flooding
- systematic desensitisation.

Flooding

Flooding is an extreme therapy based on the theory of classical conditioning (see page 130). The therapy involves confronting your fear directly so, if you had a fear of snakes, you would have to deal with being near snakes to overcome it. This might seem cruel but there is a reason for doing this type of therapy.

Classical conditioning is based on the principle of association. We can learn to associate one thing with another. Flooding uses this idea to get people to associate their fear or phobia with relaxation. A phobia normally brings on a response of **anxiety**. This can cause the heart to race, as well as sweating and the desire to run away. If a person can become relaxed around the feared object, then they will lose the anxiety. This is because we cannot be relaxed and anxious at the same time. The aim of the therapy is to substitute the anxiety with relaxation.

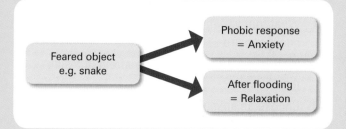

How is flooding done?

The client identifies the feared object or situation. They are then forced into a situation where they are exposed to the fear and cannot escape from it. This is a very stressful process, but after a while the body naturally calms down. You might have heard of the saying 'you cannot scream forever'. Well, this is partly true. Your body will naturally relax because it cannot sustain an anxious state for too long because it harms the body. When we eventually do calm down, we will learn to associate the fear with relaxation.

The South African psychologist Joseph Wolpe demonstrated the effectiveness of flooding. He found a girl who was scared of cars and drove her around for hours. She was panic-stricken to begin with, but after a while she calmed down and learnt very quickly to link cars with relaxation. She overcame her fear of cars.

Case study

In a recent TV programme on fears, a man was exposed to snakes – his ultimate fear. He was harnessed to a chair with his arms strapped to a tabletop. Snakes were put on his arms for over half an hour. He was very frightened to begin with, but after a while he experienced a calming feeling. As this was happening he said it was an odd feeling, but he felt relaxed. He said that the snakes were not as bad as he thought and began to not fear them.

Problem with flooding

The problem with flooding is that it is not always considered a very ethical thing to do and people are not likely to want to be involved in such a treatment. Also, it is not always effective, as far as studies show, and a more ethical and more tested therapy is often preferred (see page 158).

Quick check

A How could flooding be used to treat a phobia of dogs?

Systematic desensitisation

Systematic desensitisation is similar to flooding, but is less stressful for the patient. It still involves being exposed to the feared object, and the principle is still the same: exposure leads to relaxation that can be associated with the feared object. However, it is done in a more gradual way.

How is systematic desensitisation done?

1 The patient identifies the feared object or situation, for example flying in an aeroplane.
2 With the therapist they develop a list of least and most feared situations (see the table below). This is called a **hierarchy of fears**.

Hierarchy of fears for flying	
Situation	**Rating of fear**
Turbulence whilst on a plane	High
Taking off and landing	
Getting on the plane	
Checking in	Moderate
Getting to the airport	
Packing the luggage	
Booking the flight	
Looking at holidays abroad	Low

3 The therapist teaches the patient **relaxation techniques**. These are to help cope with the exposure to situations within the hierarchy of fears.
4 Starting with the lowest fear rating, the therapist introduces them to the situation. The patient uses the relaxation techniques to deal with the situation. Once ready, the patient can move on to the next level.
5 The patient moves up the hierarchy, becoming relaxed each time, until they reach the most feared situation.

Taking it further

Go to www.heinemann.co.uk/hotlinks and enter (express code 4837P). The *Guide to Psychology website* links systematic desensitisation to classical conditioning (page 130).

Gradually the patient confronts their worst fears and associates them with relaxation.

Many people suffer from claustrophobia – a fear of small spaces.

Quick check

B Construct a hierarchy of fear for someone with a phobia of spiders.

Key definitions

anxiety: a state of fear or worry.

hierarchy of fears: a list of fears that are arranged from most to least feared.

Questions

1 Tom has a fear of water. How would flooding be used to treat Tom's phobia?
2 How does flooding work?
3 How might systematic desensitisation be used to treat Tom's phobia of water?

D3b1 The ethics of therapies used to treat phobias

Learn about

- The ethics of flooding and systematic desensitisation
- The ethical guidelines of distress and the right to withdraw

Flooding (see page 150) is the most traumatic of therapies used to treat phobias, because patients are forcibly exposed to their fear. They are not allowed to withdraw from the situation because this could make their phobia worse in the long run.

Flooding can cause distress because patients are confronted with their most feared situation.

Systematic desensitisation (see page 151) is less extreme than flooding because the patient has more control over when they move on to the next level. They decide if they are relaxed enough to be confronted with a more fearful situation. In a sense, they have a right to withdraw from the situation, unlike flooding where they cannot (it would be harmful to) withdraw at all.

Quick check

A Why is it harmful to withdraw from flooding therapy?

Causing distress

Both flooding and systematic desensitisation are therapies that produce distress. Flooding creates an enormous amount of distress. Imagine if you were forced to confront your own fear with no means to escape. Because systematic desensitisation allows some patient control, it does mean that this therapy is less distressing then flooding. If a patient is distressed then they are clearly not relaxed, so they cannot move up the hierarchy of fears.

We can talk about the ethics of therapies such as flooding and systematic desensitisation. But we must also remember that:

- patients are aware of the nature of the therapy they are undertaking
- the therapies are only used for the most serious of phobias
- patients have to be clearly distressed or unable to carry on with normal activities to access these therapies.

It is important to note, in the context of ethics, that patients know what the therapy involves and whether they are able to withdraw or not.

Quick check

B Why is flooding more distressing than systematic desensitisation?

Other phobias

Phobias take many forms – some more unusual than others. Here, for example, are the names of a few relatively common phobias:

- achluophobia – fear of darkness
- algophobia – fear of pain
- altophobia – fear of heights
- astraphobia – fear of thunder and lightning
- ailurophobia – fear of cats
- entomophobia – fear of insects
- ophidiophobia – fear of snakes
- spermatophobia – fear of germs
- xenophobia – fear of strangers
- zoophobia – fear of animals.

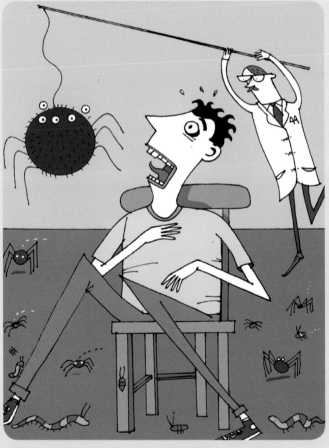

People with phobias need to give their consent before undergoing flooding.

Key definitions

distressing: when a person is suffering physically or psychologically. They may feel harm, embarrassment or pain.

right to withdraw: the ability of a person to remove himself or herself from the situation.

Taking it further

Go to www.heinemann.co.uk/hotlinks and enter express code 4837P. Pick a phobia from the *Phobia List website* and describe how flooding or systematic desensitisation would be used to treat it.

The right to withdraw

Patients who undergo flooding are not permitted to withdraw from the therapy because this could make their phobia worse in the long run. The purpose of the therapy is to associate relaxation with the phobic object, so withdrawing would only serve to reinforce the patient's fear as they will leave more phobic than when they started the flooding session. A patient cannot stop the therapy just because they are very scared as it would be counterproductive.

Systematic desensitisation is different as with this type of therapy a patient can choose to withdraw at any stage. This is because they have much more control over their own progress. A phobic person will not progress up the hierarchy of fears unless they are relaxed, so if they do withdraw at any stage this is not harmful as the patient has already made enough progression to feel less phobic than when they started the therapy. Unlike flooding, withdrawal from systematic desensitisation therapy will not worsen a patient's fear. If a patient withdraws from the therapy before reaching the highest level of their hierarchy of fears, it will not help cure the patient completely but it at least goes some way to helping them cope with the less threatening experiences of their phobia.

Because of the ethical issues of distress and right to withdraw, systematic desensitisation is a much more popular therapy than flooding, which is rarely used today.

Questions

1 Michael was scared of worms. This prevented him from going outside because he would not step on grass. How might a therapist deal with Michael's phobia?

2 Michael was a bit worried about his therapy. Describe the issues with flooding and systematic desensitisation to Michael.

D3cl The job of a clinical psychologist

What the clinical psychologist does

Psychologists in general deal with dysfunction, which means that a family, person or social structure is not functioning appropriately and needs help. A clinical psychologist deals with dysfunction in the sense of mental health problems and works in health settings.

A clinical psychologist can use many different techniques based on different theories, such as psychoanalysis based on Freud's work (see page 54) and counselling based on a holistic view of the person (all about them rather than focusing on one aspect of them such as depression). Some clinical psychologists use **hypnotherapy**, as well as **cognitive behavioural therapy** and systematic desensitisation (page 151).

Quick check

A Explain what it would mean to say a family was dysfunctional.

Working with mental health issues

A clinical psychologist works with people who have mental health problems – or sometimes physical health problems. Examples include people suffering from anxiety, depression, relationship problems, or behavioural disorders. Their clients can be children or adults. Other people they might work with include those who have to adjust to physical illness or learning disabilities. The idea is to help people to cope and to help them make positive changes.

Dealing with anger or withdrawal

A clinical psychologist works with people who are stressed and distressed, who are not going to be easy to deal with. They might be angry or withdrawn, for example. As with other psychology careers, the clinical psychologist solves problems, listening to people and helping them move forward. They must be able to deal with stressful and challenging situations.

Examples of clients' issues

Examples of problems clients go to a clinical psychologist for help with, include difficulties in establishing attachments or building satisfactory adult relationships. Clients may have mood disorders, fears or phobias, or problems in coping with a disability or dealing with death.

A clinical psychologist can provide group therapy or family therapy as well as one-to-one therapy.

What a clinical psychologist does		
Works with those with mental health issues such as depression	Works with people with physical illnesses to help them adjust, cope or make positive changes	Deals with anger and withdrawal in clients, which can be hard to do
Suggests solutions	Training	Research
*Multi-agency working	*Advising regarding policy	*Keeping up-to-date
*Reporting on a client's needs	*Chartered status and CPD (Continuing Professional Development)	

*for more information on these issues check back on the work of the educational psychologist (page 116)

Working in teams and communities

A clinical psychologist is often part of a team focusing on one client. There might be community involvement and other agencies might be part of the team, such as social services, doctors or community health workers. The clinical psychologist will be involved with other professional groups as an adviser perhaps.

How the clinical psychologist works

- Makes an **assessment** of the problem.
- Plans an **intervention** (some way of helping).
- **Evaluates** the intervention.

Assessment of needs

A clinical psychologist starts by assessing a client's needs. They gather as much evidence as they can. This involves listening to their client and discussing issues with them. They are also likely to use observation of the client's behaviour. They might use **psychometric testing** as well, which involves using **standardised tests** (page 117). They could measure stress levels or negative thinking, as well as life pressures, for example.

Taking it further

Go to www.heinemann.co.uk/hotlinks and enter express code 4837P. Click on the *Encyclopedia of Mental Disorders website* for information on Beck's Depression Inventory which is used to test for depression.

Quick check

B Explain what is meant by psychometric testing.

Planning an intervention

After the assessment the clinical psychologist must plan an intervention, which means putting forward a solution. Solutions can involve therapy, counselling or advice. Therapy can be with the client on their own or involving others such as the family. There can also be group therapy, involving others with similar issues perhaps.

Keeping records and evaluation

It is important to keep records of assessment and interventions. Records have to be kept safely to maintain confidentiality. During and after an intervention the psychologist must review the situation to evaluate the success of any programme and to continue to support the client.

Examiner's tips

Psychologists all use assessment, planning, intervention and evaluation in their work. When answering a question about educational, clinical or forensic psychologists, use these elements to explain what they do.

Practical problems

A clinical psychologist might have problems in being under-funded, which makes their working conditions difficult. The NHS has limited funding and different hospitals and institutions have a different focus on a clinical psychology department. This means that there is often not enough opportunity to explore issues with a client because the time of the clinical psychologist is limited (often due to cost).

Training and research

A clinical psychologist is often involved in training others, especially in the NHS where trainees are taken on regularly. A clinical psychologist can also undertake research themselves. They may have a specialism, such as working with adults with head injuries, and they may be involved in research into such issues.

CPD and chartered status

A clinical psychologist usually becomes a chartered psychologist and if they do they have to maintain **Continuing Professional Development (CPD)**. This is done online and their 'CPD' must be kept up-to-date during the year, addressing various issues such as furthering their own training and working ethically. (See page 157 for more about chartered status.)

Questions

1 Why would it be important for a clinical psychologist to maintain a log of their CPD?
2 Describe three types of work a clinical psychologist might undertake.

D3c2 Becoming a clinical psychologist

Learn about

- Who a clinical psychologist might work for
- Skills required
- Qualifications required and what it means to be 'chartered'

Who a clinical psychologist might work for

The job of a clinical psychologist is the most popular career choice for graduates in Psychology – if they plan to be a psychologist.

Most clinical psychologists work for the NHS. You might think that having a problem with relationships or having a fear is not an illness, but in this country we work within a **medical model**, calling problems like these 'illnesses'.

There are also opportunities for clinical psychologists to work in private practice. The **British Psychological Society** has a register of chartered clinical psychologists and they can be contacted about work through the BPS. Some agencies outside the NHS employ clinical psychologists, for example universities. Some clinical psychologists are self-employed. A clinical psychologist tends to work a normal working week from Monday to Friday, though sometimes they work evenings or weekends. Earnings can be from £30,000 to £70,000 and, when working privately, salary varies a lot.

Quick check

A Give two ways in which a clinical psychologist could be employed.

A clinical psychologist works with people who have problems or illnesses – either physical or mental health illnesses – and focuses on problem-solving, support and positive thinking.

Skills required

Apart from qualifications, you need the right skills to be a good clinical psychologist. You should have a strong interest in healthcare and science and be very interested in people. A clinical psychologist needs to be able to:

- listen, understand, reflect on the situation of others
- help with solutions.

There are other skills required as well, such as:

- understanding diversity (that people are different)
- learning to ask open questions
- being able to look at your own experiences and how these affect others.

These can be achieved through training.

In addition to the general skills required by a psychologist, clinical psychologists also need to be prepared to search for solutions that are not at first obvious – for some clients there are no easy answers. Other professionals may disagree with solutions too, which can be hard to deal with, so a clinical psychologist needs to be able to communicate well to clients, their families, and other professionals.

Examiner's tips

When making notes and revising, use bullet points to organise your information. However, in an exam answer, always say exactly what you mean and do not use bullet points or one-word answers (unless the question asks for a one-word answer of course).

Qualifications required

1 You need a degree in Psychology – one that is recognised by the British Psychological Society (BPS), which most Psychology degrees are.
2 To become a qualified clinical psychologist, candidates must also get relevant work experience.
3 You then apply for a place on a **doctorate** course. The doctorate course lasts for three years and is full-time. There is a lot of competition to get onto these courses.

Having completed a doctorate in clinical psychology, most people enter the profession by getting a job as a trainee clinical psychologist in the NHS.

Examiner's tips

A **psychiatrist** is a medical doctor who can prescribe medical treatments. A clinical psychologist is not a doctor and cannot issue prescriptions. Make sure you know the difference between the two.

Chartered status

Most psychologists apply for chartered status with the BPS. This means you have satisfied the requirements of the BPS, have sufficient qualifications and experience to be called a 'psychologist' and have the backing of two people who are already chartered psychologists. It also involves following a Continuing Professional Development (CPD) programme, which requires logging work done, training undertaken, reading done to keep up-to-date and recording other relevant information to show competence.

Taking it further

Go to www.heinemann.co.uk/hotlinks and enter express code 4837P. Click on the *British Psychological Society website* to learn more about clinical psychologists.

Quick check

B Compare the qualifications needed to be a clinical psychologist with the qualifications needed to be an educational psychologist (see page 119).

Questions

1 List two qualifications required to be a clinical psychologist.
2 Explain the skills required to be a clinical psychologist.

D3c3 Clinical psychology and phobias

Learn about

● How clinical psychologists treat phobias

A clinical psychologist deals with many different issues and one of these is helping clients to overcome phobias. There are a number of ways of treating phobias and a clinical psychologist is likely to use a mixture of them, depending on their preference as well as the client's problem(s).

Treating phobias

Some of the treatments for phobias are used more than others. Flooding (see page 150) is not really used much now, although there are examples of its use. Medication is also used, but not frequently as it is only a short-term treatment, and just helps with the associated anxiety.

The main therapies that are used are very similar and rest on two main ideas:

● systematic desensitisation
● cognitive behavioural therapy (CBT).

Exposure therapy, for example, is a mix of these two ideas.

Some people develop a phobia of the dentist. Like many phobias, it can be treated using systematic desensitisation and cognitive behavioural therapy.

Systematic desensitisation

Systematic desensitisation was described on page 151. In this treatment a patient usually imagines the fear-inducing situation (rather than experiencing it) whilst learning to relax. Eventually, if successful, the fear is replaced with a relaxation response.

Cognitive behavioural therapy

Cognitive behavioural therapy (CBT) is a very popular therapy with clinical psychologists. It has had good results in many areas and with many problems, including phobias, and is derived from scientific theories. The therapy uses the twin approach of treating thoughts ('cognition' means thinking) and behaviour. It involves identifying negative automatic thoughts and trying to replace them with less negative thoughts. For example, if someone has a flying phobia, they may be shown figures on plane crashes, which reveal the low level of risk associated with flying.

Quick check

A Briefly outline CBT, including saying what the initials stand for.

Exposure-based CBT

This therapy (sometimes simply called exposure therapy) involves elements of changing the client's thinking patterns as well as systematically lowering the fear response to the situations that are feared. It is very similar to systematic desensitisation.

According to figures from Canada, as many as 90 per cent of patients can overcome their phobias in this way, even in a few short sessions. It works best for **specific phobias**, where the phobia is about something that can be isolated in treatment (for example small spaces, dentists or flying) rather than social phobias, where patients find it difficult to be around other people and avoid public situations.

Taking it further

Go to www.heinemann.co.uk/hotlinks and enter express code 4837P. Click on the *Royal College of Psychiatrists website* for a CBT factsheet.

Some people have a phobia of dogs.

Processes of exposure therapy:

1   Understand exactly what the phobia is about, so it can be focused on. So, for example, knowing whether a phobia of dogs concerns biting or whether it is about catching a disease from a dog.
2   Develop a fear hierarchy (see page 151) by working with the client to find out what they are afraid of and the scale of the fear. So, for a phobia of dogs, the client might be slightly fearful when looking at a photo of a dog, reasonably fearful when seeing someone walking a dog, and very fearful of being in a room with a dog.
3   The next step is to work with the client to overcome each stage of fear, for example sitting for one session with the client looking at photos of dogs. A session typically lasts between one and two hours. The client needs to feel some fear but needs time for that to reduce. Then the next step in the hierarchy is tackled, perhaps taking the client to watch people walking dogs and again waiting until their fear subsides.

Important features of exposure therapy:

• Being systematic and allowing some fear, then for that fear to pass a little. The procedure must be gentle and manageable for the client.
• Allowing enough time for the fear to pass, which is likely to be more than half an hour but within two hours. The client must feel at least some of the fear pass at each stage.
• Sessions must take place often enough that progress is not lost. One or two times a week is best, so that the experience of the lowered fear levels can be brought forward each time.
• During the sessions the client must challenge the thoughts that link to the fears. This is how the therapy links to CBT.

• The client has to face their fear so that they learn to be more confident about their fears.
• They might need skills training as well, such as learning to handle dogs in this case. This, too, links to CBT.

Hypnotherapy

Some clinical psychologists are trained hypnotherapists. **Hypnotherapy** involves helping the client to get into a relaxed state, called an altered state of awareness. In this state they are not focusing on their everyday problems but have a heightened level of awareness where they can accept suggestions from the therapist. In the treatment of phobias, the therapist/psychologist can make suggestions about overcoming the phobia.

Psychodynamic-based therapies

There are psychodynamic-based therapies that focus on understanding the phobia but again these are not often used by clinical psychologists. Many feel that, as psychodynamic theory is not scientifically tested, it should not be used as a therapy.

Questions

1   When carrying out exposure-based cognitive behavioural therapy, what issues would need to be addressed to make the therapy successful?
2   Explain what is meant by hypnotherapy.

D4a1 Heinrichs et al (2005): cultural differences in fears

Learn about
- Cultural issues in the development of phobias
- The study by Heinrichs et al (2005) and what they found out

Does the culture we are raised in affect our fears? We are brought up in a culture that has its own particular **customs**, **traditions** and **social norms**. Social norms are the expected ways of thinking and behaving by people within a culture. These social norms guide our behaviour so we fit in. Think about the social norms in your culture. It might be normal to go to school, have lots of friends, etc. Now think of another culture; what are the social norms for this culture? How do these social norms affect the behaviour of the people within that culture?

Masaai boys have to herd cattle as soon as they can walk.

Individualistic cultures:	Collectivist cultures:
USA	Spain
Australia	Korea
Canada	Japan
The Netherlands	
Germany	

If culture determines how we behave, could it also determine what fears we have? Nina Heinrichs and her colleagues wanted to find out whether there were cultural differences between types of fear. They focused on how culture affects social anxiety.

What is social anxiety?

Social anxiety is a fear someone has of social situations. Someone with social anxiety might worry in these situations:

- meeting new people
- being watched
- being the centre of attention
- public speaking
- using the telephone
- being teased.

In these situations, they might have a racing heart rate, feel light-headed, blush or shake.

The study by Heinrichs et al

Aim
They wanted to see if being brought up in different cultures affected social anxiety and fear of blushing.

Procedure
A total of 909 university students studying psychology were tested. The students were from eight different universities in eight different countries and all volunteered to take part in the study because they were interested in the results.

The students were divided into two groups; **collectivist** or **individualistic** cultures, based on the cultures where they lived. The cultures and relevant countries are shown in the table opposite.

The participants were given a short description of a social situation and asked to say how they would react. For example: 'You are sitting in a maths class. The teacher writes a problem on the board and asks if anyone can solve the problem. The girl next to you has already solved it but does not offer to answer.' If participants said they would speak up or offer an answer to the problem themselves, this would be a low social anxiety answer. However, if they said they would do nothing, it would be a high social anxiety answer.

Quick check

A Using the example given, describe a high and a low social anxiety answer.

The participants were also asked to complete a social anxiety and blushing questionnaire. The social anxiety questionnaire measured their individual fear of social situations and interaction with other people, and the blushing questionnaire measured their fear of embarrassment (blushing is a bodily response to being embarrassed).

Results

Participants from collectivist cultures often responded to the descriptions in a way that showed high social anxiety. They gave answers that avoided public interaction or public speaking. These participants were also more fearful of blushing and scored higher on the social anxiety questionnaire compared with those from individualistic cultures.

Highest social anxiety	Japan
	Korea
	Spain
	USA
	Canada
	Australia
	The Netherlands
Lowest social anxiety	Germany

Conclusion

Collectivist cultures show greater social anxiety and fear of blushing than individualistic cultures. This is because collectivist countries have strict rules about acceptable behaviour. If someone breaks a social norm they will experience a greater punishment, which in turn makes them more anxious. People in collectivist cultures will hold back through fear of letting the group down if they are wrong. These social norms are more important for collectivist cultures as the behaviour of an individual affects the whole group.

This is very different from individualistic cultures where a high value is placed on individuality. It is important to stand out from the crowd and shyness might actually be a burden.

The nature-nurture debate

This study is relevant to the **nature-nurture** debate as it relates to the development of fears and phobias. Although it is clear that phobias of, for example, spiders or snakes probably originate from classical conditioning and evolutionary preparedness, it is interesting to look at social phobias and their link to culture. This study explains that culture determines how we think and act; family and friends teach us these social norms so that we fit in. In this way culture can actually make us anxious or confident in social situations. Because this behaviour is a result of the people around us and the upbringing we have, it supports the nurture side of the debate.

Key definitions

custom: a longstanding practice of a particular group of people.

tradition: a practice that has been handed down through generations.

social norm: a behaviour or belief that is expected and accepted in a particular culture.

collectivist: describes a culture that encourages group dependence, cooperation and group identity, e.g. Japan. People rely on each other to achieve together.

individualistic: describes a culture that encourages independence, personal achievement, competition and individuality, e.g. the USA.

Questions

1 What is meant by the term 'culture'?
2 Outline one social norm from your own culture and describe how it might affect your everyday behaviour.
3 Using Heinrichs' study, explain how culture affects the development of fear.

KnowZone - Topic D
Why do we have phobias

You should know...

ANSWERING THE QUESTION

☐ Causes of phobias – evolutionary explanation of preparedness.

☐ Social Learning Theory – modelling and vicarious reinforcement.

☐ Classical/Pavlovian conditioning – association and generalisation.

☐ The nature-nurture debate in relation to understanding phobias.

EVALUATING THE ANSWER

☐ Jones' study lasted a long period – changes in Peter can be seen over time and confirmed.

☐ Jones used other people in the study to avoid her own bias, and used different ways to help Peter in order to decondition him.

☐ The use of different methods by Jones makes it hard to tell which were effective.

☐ The gaps between sessions in Jones' study were variable – hard to tell whether the changes wouldn't have happened over time anyway.

☐ Bennett-Levy and Marteau's study used a mixture of different participants to ensure they didn't know the aim of the study and a mixture of men and women to see if gender affected the results.

☐ The use of rats in Bennett-Levy and Marteau's study may have made the instructions about animals not being scary less successful, and the questionnaire used did not record all the participants' responses that were identified in the interviews.

Support activity

Dr Grant works at a surgery where they often treat patients with phobias. She decides that it would be helpful to have a poster on display explaining what causes phobias.

Choose one explanation and design a poster that illustrates how someone might develop a phobia.

Stretch activity

Draw a flow chart of what happens during flooding and another for what happens in systematic desensitisation. Look at the ways in which they are similar and different. Make sure that you have included comments on the ethical issues involved with each therapy.

Use your flowchart to help you with the following task:

Write a leaflet for a clinical psychologist that explains about therapy for phobias, including how they deal with ethical issues and what the patient can expect.

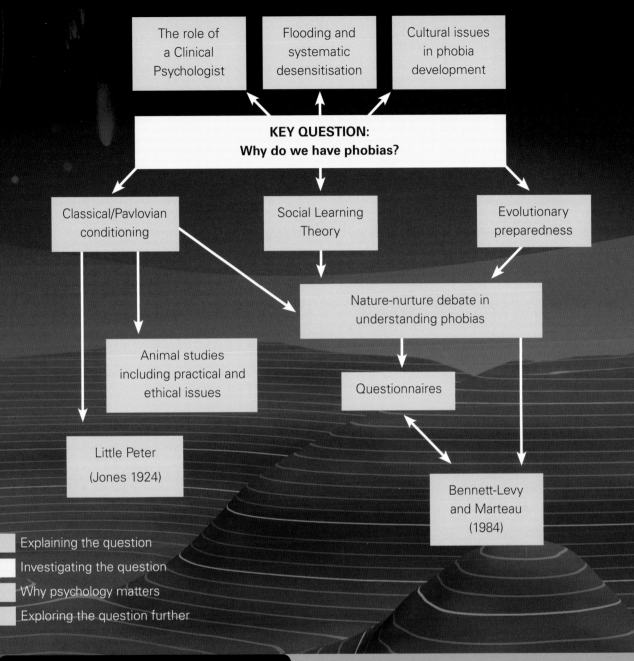

The role of a Clinical Psychologist

Flooding and systematic desensitisation

Cultural issues in phobia development

KEY QUESTION:
Why do we have phobias?

Classical/Pavlovian conditioning

Social Learning Theory

Evolutionary preparedness

Nature-nurture debate in understanding phobias

Animal studies including practical and ethical issues

Questionnaires

Little Peter
(Jones 1924)

Bennett-Levy and Marteau (1984)

Explaining the question
Investigating the question
Why psychology matters
Exploring the question further

Examiner's tip: Stretch activity

A good answer should have a description of what will happen to a client in therapy and explains to them how the clinical psychologist deals with certain issues, such as clients getting distressed or wanting to leave during treatment.

Key terms

- questionnaire
- open-ended question
- closed question
- rank scales
- standardised instructions
- response bias
- social desirability
- social isolation

Practice Exam Questions

1 What do psychologists mean by nature and nurture?

2 Explain the difference between an open and a closed question.

3 What are the weaknesses of animal experiments?

Topic E
Are criminals born or made?

Introduction

Theft, murder, arson, shoplifting, burglary, assault; these are all crimes, but are those who commit them born criminal or is it the way they have been raised? In this chapter we will explain, investigate and explore this question.

Explaining the question

You will explain this topic question by looking into the biological and social causes of criminality. You will be able to explain the genetic causes of criminality and the social reasons for crime, such as family structure, parenting strategies and 'self-fulfilling prophecy'. We will look at whether 'nature' or 'nurture' is responsible for criminal behaviour.

Investigating the question

You will investigate key studies in this topic:

- a study that examines the role of genetics
- a study that looks at the self-fulfilling prophecy
- a study which closely examines what affects a jury's view of a criminal once they are in court.

Research into criminal behaviour comes with its own problems. You will examine these issues and those linked to gathering information from convicted criminals.

Why psychology matters

Psychology has been used to help catch criminals and treat them. You will look at how psychologists profile offenders and examine the case of John Duffy. A forensic psychologist is a trained professional with a background in criminal psychology. You will examine the role of a forensic psychologist, their job and the qualifications needed to become a forensic psychologist.

Exploring the question further

You will explore this topic further by looking into how the court system deals with offenders and how juries can be influenced by how a defendant looks, acts and sounds.

Crime in the UK is a persistent problem. Can we use psychology to explain this?

E1a] Biological explanations for criminality

Learn about

- The genetic basis for criminality
- The link between XYY chromosome abnormality and criminality
- Evidence from studies of twins

Measuring biological links to criminality

There are several ways that we can study whether criminality has a biological basis. Looking at family trees to see how many relatives are criminal can tell us about any genetic link to criminality. We can also examine genes through blood samples to detect any chromosome abnormalities that can be linked to criminality.

Family studies

This involves comparing the family trees of criminals and non-criminals. If many criminals' relatives are also criminals, there could be a biological basis for criminality. If very few relatives are criminals, then the link becomes weaker. Some family studies have shown that a child is more likely to become a criminal if their parents or grandparents are criminal.

Adoption studies

Adoption studies provide even stronger evidence for the biological basis of criminality. They look at relatives, siblings and twins that are adopted at a young age. This means that they share genes, but not the same environment as their parents or grandparents. By taking the environment out of the picture, we can be sure that genetics are the cause of criminality.

Mednick (1984) studied 14,427 adopted children. He looked at how many of the adopted children had criminal records compared to their biological and adoptive parents. He found that adopted children with criminal records for property theft also had biological fathers with criminal convictions, even though their biological fathers did not raise them. This was true even when siblings had been separated and placed in different adoptive homes.

Twin studies

Identical twins.

There are two types of twin:

- identical twins (monozygotic twins)
- non-identical twins (fraternal or dizygotic twins).

Identical twins look the same because they have all of their genes in common. Non-identical twins have half of their genes in common. If both identical twins are criminal this suggests a very strong genetic link to criminality.

Quick check

A What is the difference between identical and non-identical twins?

Christiansen (1977) studied 3586 pairs of twins in Denmark. He found that, if an identical twin was a criminal 52 per cent of the time, the other identical twin was also a criminal. This was only true in 22 per cent of cases with non-identical twins. Christiansen found that the criminal link was for property crime (e.g theft), but not violent crime.

This could be evidence that there is a genetic basis to property crime, because it shows a shared criminal tendency in just over half of the identical twins studied. The decrease to 22 per cent can be explained in non-identical twins because they share only half of their genes in common.

Quick check

B If twins are both criminal, what does this tell us about the cause of criminality?

Understanding genetic inheritance

Family and **twin studies** seem to suggest that we are more likely to turn to crimes such as theft or shoplifting if we have family members who have been convicted of crime.

One argument could be that it is nothing to do with genetics at all. Family members are raised together and treated similarly. Their similar criminal behaviour can be explained by upbringing or observational learning (see Topic C, page 98, for a full discussion of social learning theory). It is also worth considering that the figures used for these studies are only based on criminals that have actually been caught and convicted for their crimes!

Chromosome abnormalities

	Female	Male
Sex Genes	XX	XY

Male and female sex genes

Examiner's tips

Remember XX as female because girls often sign 'XX' (kiss kiss) at the end of a text. Boys may leave girls wondering 'why' (XY)!

Blood samples can be taken from criminals to see if they have any chromosome abnormalities that might cause their criminal behaviour. Normal males have an XY chromosome pattern, but in the 1960s researchers discovered that males with an extra Y chromosome (**XYY** males) are more likely to be violent and criminal. This condition is not inherited, so does not run in families, even though it may be a genetic reason for criminality. XYY is a very rare disorder, however some men who have this disorder have been found to be more aggressive and slower at learning than average.

Another researcher, Theilgaard (1984), also found that XYY males are more masculine and slightly more aggressive. You can read more about this on pages 176–177.

XYY bad guys

The following murderers were found to have the **chromosome abnormality** XYY:

- Richard Speck (murdered 8 student nurses)
- John Wayne Gacy (murdered 33 boys and men)
- Arthur Shawcross (murdered 11 women).

Understanding chromosome abnormality

Chromosome abnormalities, such as XYY, have been linked to violent crime and a handful of murderers have been found to have an XYY gene pattern. However, it is just a handful of murderers and certainly not true of all violent criminals.

XYY is such a rare disorder that we cannot find large enough samples of people with the disorder to be certain of the link to violent crime. As mentioned, it has also been linked to slow learning, so turning to crime might be a result of not succeeding at school rather than a direct biological link to the disorder.

Key definitions

twin studies: research into the similarity of twins, particularly their criminal similarity, to investigate genetic links.

XYY: a rare genetic pattern said to be linked to aggression and slow learning ability.

chromosome abnormality: a mutation of genetic material that results in a change in the number or structure of chromosomes.

Questions

1. Describe two ways of studying whether criminality is biological.
2. What problems might there be with saying criminality is biological?
3. Nathan has a non-identical twin who steals cars. How likely is Nathan to turn to crime?

Ela2 Social explanations for criminality

Learn about

- How divorce affects whether people become criminals
- If we are raised in large families, whether it can affect how likely we are to turn to crime

Made criminal?

If you could describe a perfect childhood, what would it be like? Would your parents/caregivers be wealthy? Would they stay together forever and never argue?

Life is not perfect and psychologists are interested in how childhood experiences can influence the way children turn out. Could it make us criminal?

Family patterns as an explanation for criminality

Family patterns are the experiences children have during their family life. These may include:

- divorce
- separation from main caregiver
- family size.

Let's examine some of these risk factors in detail and explore whether they can cause criminal behaviour. Many of these factors explain how children are affected directly or indirectly by their parents. But it is important to remember that parents are not always directly to blame.

Quick check

A Name two risk factors associated with criminal behaviour.

Divorce

Divorce can lead to single parent households, or so-called 'broken homes'. Some research suggests that children who come from a broken home are twice as likely to become criminal as those from an intact family. Boys can be affected if they have

no father figure as a role model and often become more aggressive. Girls tend to respond differently to boys, becoming depressed rather than aggressive.

This is complicated by the reasons for divorce. There is a higher likelihood that children will suffer negatively if there were serious arguments and disruption before the divorce. Divorce often involves many issues such as moving home and school as well as financial difficulties and maternal deprivation.

Maternal deprivation

John Bowlby linked maternal deprivation to juvenile delinquency.

Is there a link between criminal behaviour and a child's separation from their main caregiver? The main caregiver forms a special bond with the child. The child feels a sense of security with them and can become distressed when they are separated, a situation known as **maternal deprivation**. If this bond is broken through separation, particularly during the first two years of life, the child may suffer lasting effects. They typically lose the sense of having a safe world and feel rejected.

John Bowlby (1946) questioned 44 boy offenders about their crimes and their relationship with their parents. He found that 14 boys felt no guilt about their crimes or victims. When he looked into their family life, Bowlby found that 12 out of the 14 boys had been separated from their primary caregiver before they were two years old. When he explored the background of the other 30 children who did feel guilty about their crimes, he found that only five had been separated from their caregiver before the age of two.

Taking it further

'Child of our Time' is a longitudinal study that started in the year 2000 with 25 'millennium babies'. The aim of the study is to explain whether behaviour is due to nature or nurture over 20 years of development. Profession Robert Winston has explored how many social factors can influence behaviour. Go to www.heinemann.co.uk/hotlinks (express code 4837P) and click on the *BBC website*.

Family size

Farrington (2002) found that families with a lot of children, around six or seven, were more likely to be linked to criminality. This is probably due to the lack of attention that each child can be given and the lack of parental supervision over their behaviour. Larger families are more likely to have lower income, or the income has to stretch further. Families with low income offer fewer educational opportunities for their children and this has been linked to persistent youth offending such as fighting and drug use.

Parental occupation

The job that parents have gives only a slight link to criminal activity in children. An Australian study of youth crime (Western, 2003) showed that the father's occupation was not an indicator of crime, even if the father was unemployed. But the mother's occupation did have an effect. Mothers employed as blue-collar workers, such as factory workers, had children who were more likely to turn to crime. One theory is that the children were

suffering maternal deprivation as a result of their mothers working long hours, rather than the type of occupation itself.

Understanding family patterns

It is very difficult to pin down exactly which social factors influence criminal behaviour because families and their circumstances are so complex. Look at this study to see how difficult this theory is.

David Farrington (2002) studied 411 boys from the East End of London for over 40 years. The boys were aged 8 at the start of the study and were visited every couple of years until they were 46. The boys, their mothers, teachers and friends were interviewed throughout the **longitudinal study**.

The study found that, if the boys turned to crime, it was linked to the following factors:

- low supervision by parents
- poor housing
- parental neglect
- harsh or inconsistent parenting
- separation of parents
- low achievement at school.

Not one of these factors alone determines criminal behaviour, but all are involved in some way in providing negative childhood experiences that could increase a child's vulnerability to criminality. The strongest research suggests that prolonged separation from a caregiver and arguments within the family home are bad childhood experiences that may influence whether or not an individual turns to crime, although they do not in themselves produce criminals.

Quick check

B Explain how divorce can cause criminality.

Questions

1 What is meant by the term 'maternal deprivation'?
2 How might this cause criminal behaviour?
3 Why might a child from a larger family be more likely to become criminal?

E1a3 Childrearing as an explanation for criminality

Learn about
- How different ways of raising children can influence criminality
- Examples of power assertion

Think back to when you have been naughty. How did your parents deal with the situation? Did their reaction change your behaviour or did you continue to behave just as you wanted?

Childrearing strategies

The ways in which parents bring up their children are known as childrearing strategies. Hoffman (1984) identified three different childrearing strategies used when parents were dealing with difficult or naughty children:

- induction
- love withdrawal
- power assertion.

Induction

This childrearing strategy involves explaining to a child what it is they have done wrong and what are the consequences of their actions. It helps a child identify their wrongdoings and see how their behaviour has affected other people. It encourages empathy as the child learns to see from another person's perspective.

Love withdrawal

With this strategy, a parent withdraws their affection for the child to make them feel guilty for their bad behaviour. The parent's disapproval is shown by imposing conditions on their love for the child; saying that they do not love them when they are bad. The child's feelings are manipulated in such a way that they do not develop a clear sense of individuality and independence because they have been rejected.

Power assertion

A parent smacks the child or tells them off. The child may be criticised openly by a parent and is threatened with punishment to make them behave. This can be excessive control through the use of physical punishment or a parent can make fun of them. This childrearing strategy is the one most associated with **delinquency** in childhood. It leads to low **self-esteem** because the child may not feel worthy of love. It can also develop into aggression, particularly if:

- punishment is inconsistent – a child is never sure of the type of punishment they will receive or when they will receive it
- the punishment is lengthy and severe
- verbal threats are not seen through, leaving a child scared
- each parent applies different standards of punishment.

Quick check

A Name the childrearing strategy used in the following examples.
- i) Sharon's caregiver said she was stupid in front of her friends.
- ii) Eulalee's mum made her understand that shouting was not appropriate behaviour in class.
- iii) Sita's dad said he did not like her when she was being difficult.

An example

Marta has a son, Lee, who has hit a child at school. Marta deals with Lee's behaviour by smacking him and shouting at him. Lee is sent to bed and is not allowed to eat with the rest of the family. Marta continues to shout at Lee throughout the evening. Lee's father disagrees with Marta's parenting strategy and argues with her openly. He gives Lee a hug and explains that his mum is wrong to hit him. The next day Lee hits another child. This time

Punishing children by threatening them could influence whether they turn to crime as adults.

Marta refuses to talk to Lee all afternoon and his father smacks him and puts him to bed.

You can see from this example that Lee will be confused and very unsure about whether or not he will be punished, and if he is punished, who will do it and what form the punishment will take. Lee will develop low self-esteem and not feel valued by his parents. He might take out his anger towards his parents on other children or try to gain attention by being naughty.

The link in aggression between an unhappy childhood and childhood delinquency might in turn influence the chances that Lee will adopt criminal behaviour later in life.

Understanding parenting strategies

Although this theory seems to suggest that parents are solely responsible for producing delinquent children, it is clear that there are many factors that contribute to delinquency. It is likely that a childrearing strategy used by a parent is just one factor amongst many.

Taking it further

The government believe strongly that poor parenting can make children anti-social. Go to www.heinemann.co.uk/hotlinks (express code 4837P) and click on the *Home Office website* for an article on parenting.

Questions

1   Look back at the example of Lee hitting children at school.

   a) How might Marta have dealt with Lee using love withdrawal as a childrearing strategy?

   b) How might Marta use induction as a childrearing strategy?

2   Carl has been arrested for a number of crimes, such as joyriding and assault. Using your knowledge of childrearing strategies, explain why Carl might have turned to crime.

Ela4 Self-fulfilling prophecy as an explanation for criminality

Learn about

- What is meant by a self-fulfilling prophecy
- How criminality is caused by the way we are treated by others

Being treated differently

So far we have examined the way that family patterns and childrearing strategies can influence criminal behaviour, but we should also think about how people outside of the family can influence our behaviour. Consider how many people you meet and interact with every day. Teachers, friends, neighbours and even strangers can also impact upon how you feel about yourself and how you make decisions in life.

Make a list of how you think other people see you, for example as a good listener, trustworthy, a bad cook! Do you think that the way you are viewed by others can have an influence on your own behaviour; do you burn toast because you are seen as a bad cook?

Taking it further

Go to www.heinemann.co.uk/hotlinks (express code 4837P). Click on the *Motivation Tools website* to see how self-fulfilling prophecy can affect our behaviour in many different contexts.

Self-fulfilling prophecy

Can criminal behaviour be explained by the way people treat us? It is true that people see us in certain ways. This view affects their expectations of us and our behaviour. One theory of criminal behaviour is that if people expect us to behave badly or in a criminal way, then we will **conform** to that expectation. **Self-fulfilling prophecy** is a theory that simply states that a prediction of our behaviour will come true. If we are seen as or expected to be criminal, then we will behave that way.

The way young people are treated could be self-fulfilling.

Quick check

A Define the term 'self-fulfilling prophecy'.

Quick check

B Explain how someone who is thought to be a criminal might be treated by others.

Key definitions

conform: to adjust to expectations made of us.

self-fulfilling prophecy: when the expectations of others influence our behaviour.

Low expectations

A good example of self-fulfilling prophecy is how we are treated at school. If a teacher thinks that we are not going to do very well, they will not expect a lot from our work. They may not give us the opportunity to extend our knowledge and may give us less attention than high achievers. As a result, we may feel less motivation to do well and work hard. This could lead to poor performance in exams because of not revising enough. We have fulfilled the prophecy that we are not going to do well by doing just that.

Rosenthal and Jacobsen

Rosenthal and Jacobsen (1968) conducted an experiment to test whether achievement could be self-fulfilling. They gave school children an IQ test and then told their teachers which children were going to be average and which were going to be 'bloomers'. However, this was a lie and the teachers were actually just given random lists of children's names. They found that the teachers did not expect too much from the average children and gave all the attention to the 'bloomers'. After about a year they came back and retested the children's intelligence. Astonishingly, the IQ of the 'bloomers' had risen and the IQ of the average children had fallen. The teachers' expectations of the children's ability had altered how they were treated and this had affected their ability.

All in a name

Gustav Jahoda (1954) studied the Ashanti people of Africa. The Ashanti have a custom of naming their children after the day of the week they were born. The Ashanti also believe that the names of boys can be linked to their temperament. For example, boys born on Monday are called Kwadwo and are thought to be calm and peaceful children. Children born on Wednesday are called Kwadku and are believed to be aggressive and angry.

When Jahoda studied arrest records he found that 22 per cent of the boys arrested were born on Wednesday, compared to only 6.9 per cent who had been born on Monday. This finding can be explained by a self-fulfilling prophecy. The Ashanti boys born on Wednesday were expected to be aggressive and behave badly. People around them – parents, family, friends and teachers – would have treated them differently from the children born on Mondays. They would have been expected to behave aggressively and so treated as if they would be impulsive or lash out if confronted.

Understanding self-fulfilling prophecy

Jahoda only found a link between a child's name and criminal behaviour by using a correlation. It would be very unethical to study the self-fulfilling prophecy as a cause of crime by treating someone differently and seeing if it affected their behaviour. This is a problem with the theory, as it cannot be studied in a way that proves it causes criminal behaviour.

Another weakness of the theory is that many of us reject the way we are treated by others and so do not fulfil the prophecy. For example, if a teacher believes that we will not succeed we may work harder to prove them wrong. It doesn't take into account that there are many other reasons for crime, ranging from our biology to the families in which we are raised.

Questions

1 Outline one problem with self-fulfilling prophecy as an explanation of criminal behaviour.

2 Children as young as 11 years old have been given ASBOs (Anti-Social Behaviour Orders). How might these so called 'baby ASBOs' become self-fulfilling?

E1b1 Comparing theories of criminal behaviour

Learn about
- How the biological and social reasons for crime can be compared
- How the reasons for criminality relate to the nature-nurture debate

The biological cause of criminal behaviour focuses on whether it is inherited or runs in the family, and considerable effort has gone into finding the criminal gene – without much success.

This is valuable research, but we must also consider the social causes of crime, as the family we are raised in and how we are raised are also important factors in understanding criminal behaviour.

Comparing biological and social theories of crime

Understanding both the biological causes and social causes of crime is important. We need knowledge of both sides of the issue to be able to understand it better.

The nature-nurture debate

Whether we are born or made criminal is an issue that relates to the nature-nurture debate. This issue has been discussed in Topics C and D (see pages 100, 136), so it would be worth going back to those sections to remind yourself of the essential arguments.

Comparing the biological and social theories of criminality	
Biological causes of crime	Social causes of crime
Focus is on how we are born criminal	Focus on how we are made criminal
We inherit the genes that cause criminal behaviour	Being brought up in a family that makes criminal behaviour more likely
Criminal behaviour runs in some families	The size and structure of our family can cause criminal behaviour
Adoption studies show how crime can be inherited.	Separation from parents can cause distress and mistrust that can affect later development
XYY chromosome abnormality may cause aggression in males, leading to violent crime.	The self-fulfilling prophecy explains how behaviour can be influenced by the way we are treated and expected to behave
This theory is weakened by the confusion between genetics and upbringing in twin and family studies	This theory cannot separate the influence of many social factors that influence criminality, such as peers and other experiences
Chromosome research is limited, as only small samples have been gathered and studied	People often rebel against how they are treated by others; they do not fulfil the prophecies that are made

Nature of criminality

The biological side of the debate argues that criminal behaviour is inherited through our genes. This means that if a family member is criminal we are more likely to be criminal ourselves.

An alternative biological explanation is that criminal behaviour is caused by a chromosome abnormality, the XYY gene pattern. This is a chromosome pattern that affects aggression and comes from within us.

Nurture of criminality

The nurture side of the debate states that it is our upbringing that causes criminal behaviour. This refers to family patterns such as divorce and family size that result in negative childhood experiences or lack of surveillance that can lead to crime.

It also links to how we are raised – what childrearing strategies our parents used, and whether harsh and inconsistent punishment can lead to aggression. The idea of the self-fulfilling prophecy is also a social explanation, because it argues that the way others treat us affects our behaviour.

A conclusion

Both sides of the nature-nurture debate present evidence for a biological or social cause for criminal behaviour. However, whether criminal behaviour is a result of genetics or upbringing is not fully understood. Often research focuses on one aspect and ignores the other; it only looks at one side of the story.

As responsible researchers we should consider both sides of the story and explain criminality as a combination of both biological and social factors. After all, we might have a criminal family history or gene but have been raised in a nurturing and/or privileged environment. We do know that not all people with a criminal family are criminals themselves, and not all criminals came from large families, or were physically punished as children.

It is probably safest to talk about having a biological tendency or social vulnerability to criminal behaviour. That means that we are more likely to turn to crime if criminal behaviour runs in the family or as a result of the way we are raised, but it does not mean that it is inevitable that we will turn to crime.

The nature–nurture debate is important in helping to understand what creates criminal offenders.

Quick check

A How does the social explanation of criminality link to nurture?

Questions

1 State one difference between biological and social explanations of criminal behaviour.
2 Larry is arrested for shoplifting. Use either biological or social factors to explain Larry's behaviour.

E2al Theilgaard (1984): the criminal gene

Learn about
- How Theilgaard conducted her study to search for the criminal gene
- What she found and the usefulness of her findings

In the 1940s, research aimed at finding a criminal gene was begun. It was thought that if a gene for criminality could be isolated it could be treated, or people with the gene could be identified before they committed crimes.

Theilgaard's study

Aim
Alice Theilgaard (1984) wanted to see if criminals had a particular gene that could be responsible for their criminal behaviour.

Procedure
Theilgaard and her colleagues took blood samples from over 30,000 men born in the 1940s. From these initial blood tests two chromosome abnormalities were found; an XXY chromosome pattern and an XYY chromosome pattern.

Quick check

A How did Theilgaard find out which men had a chromosome abnormality?

Out of the 30,000 men tested, 16 had the XXY chromosome abnormality and 12 had the XYY abnormality.

The men were interviewed by a social worker about their backgrounds and criminal history and given intelligence tests. A personality test was used to see if they displayed more aggression than normal XY males.

Interviewing and researcher bias
Theilgaard used a social worker, who didn't know the aim of the study, to interview the men. By using an independent interviewer, Theilgaard was able to avoid the problem of researcher bias. This occurs if the researcher carries out and interprets the findings of a study in such a way as to meet the expectations of the study aim. Put simply, it means that they find out what they want to find out.

Quick check

B What is meant by researcher bias?
C How did Theilgaard prevent researcher bias?

Results
Theilgaard found that the XYY males had slightly lower levels of intelligence than average and tended to be more aggressive towards other people than normal men. This could be evidence for a criminal gene if aggression is a sign for criminality (although not all criminals are aggressive). However, the simple truth about Theilgaard's study is that there were far more similarities between the XXY males and the XYY males than there were differences. No solid evidence of a criminal gene was found.

Conclusion
Theilgaard's study provides limited evidence for XYY males being more aggressive than XXY males. However, they were more similar than they were different.

Evaluation

Strengths
A major strength of this study is that all tests and interviews with the men were conducted by an independent social worker who had no knowledge of the study aim. The social worker would not have been biased in reporting and would not have led the males to answer in a particular way.

Another strength of the study is that Theilgaard used a vast range of tests to measure different aspects of the men's lives, backgrounds and personality.

Weaknesses

A weakness of this study is that there was only a small sample of men used for the investigation. It is hardly surprising as it is estimated that only 1 in 1000 males are born with the XYY chromosome abnormality.

As only 12 XYY males were tested, we cannot be sure that all XYY males are more aggressive or have lower intelligence. The findings cannot be **generalised** to all XYY males with any certainty. This problem is made worse as XYY males are fairly average and cannot be picked out from other males easily. Because the chromosome abnormality is not inherited, they cannot be tracked easily in families either.

Another major problem with this investigation is that the link between XYY males and aggression is only a **correlation**. This means that the XYY chromosome abnormality may not have caused increased aggression at all and there could be many other reasons for aggression in these males.

The most obvious reason for aggression is that the males were of lower intelligence and delayed speech. This could have made school very difficult for them as children. They could have been frustrated because they did not understand as well as other children. This frustration could lead to anger and aggression in childhood that became a pattern in adult life.

The movie Alien 3 *was set in a maximum-security prison of XYY male offenders. This is a common misrepresentation by the world of film and media, as not all violent criminals are XYY.*

A simple fact from many similar studies that have been done is that not all criminals are XYY, and not all XYY males are criminal. This means that we cannot be sure the chromosome abnormality causes criminality at all; otherwise all criminals would be XYY.

A moral dilemma

What would have happened if the XYY chromosome pattern had been identified as the criminal gene? Could this have led to identifying all XYY males through screening?

An important moral question is how results like this would have been used. It is possible that XYY males could have been found and monitored because of the expectation that they would turn to crime. If so, could this have led them to crime as a result of being labelled?

Taking it further

Watch the film *Minority Report*. Consider how knowledge of future behaviour can influence the way society controls such behaviour.

Examiner's tips

You need to remember at least one strength and one weakness of this study, so read through the evaluation and pick out those you understand the best, as these will be the ones you remember.

Key definitions

generalised: whether the results can be applied to other people.

correlation: a measure of an association or relationship between two factors or variables. For example, the factors of family size and crime can be correlated to see if there is a link between the two.

Questions

1 Using your knowledge of social explanations for crime (page 168), give an alternative explanation for the males being more aggressive, other than the XYY chromosome abnormality.

2 Evaluate the usefulness of Theilgaard's study.

E2a2 Sigall and Ostrove (1975): attractiveness and jury decision-making

Learn about

- Why and how Sigall and Ostrove conducted their study, and what they found
- The strengths and weaknesses of the study

There are many ways of studying crime in criminological psychology. Theilgaard looked to see if there was a criminal gene and later you will see how Madon used a questionnaire to study the self-fulfilling prophecy. This study is about a different area of criminological psychology, the way juries make decisions about a defendant.

We often see attractive people as friendly and trustworthy. Are juries equally inclined to rush to the same decision when they see an attractive person accused of a crime?

Sigall and Ostrove's study

Aim

Sigall and Ostrove were looking at two aims:

- whether attractiveness affected jury decision-making
- whether there was a relationship between attractiveness and type of crime committed.

WANTED
Barbara Helms is a con artist who swindled £1000 from a man. She told him it was an investment into a company.

WANTED
Barbara Helms is a thief who stole £1000 worth of belongings from a neighbour's flat. She was caught trying to sell them.

Participants were asked to state how many years Barbara should go to prison for.

They used the two crimes of burglary and fraud in their study. Would an attractive person be more likely to be guilty of swindling someone, or of breaking and entering a house?

Procedure

120 participants were given a piece of card with a crime written on it and a photograph of a woman, known as Barbara Helms.

They were split into six different groups of 20 participants. Each group saw either an attractive or an unattractive photograph of Barbara and read about a fraud or burglary she had committed:

1 attractive photograph of Barbara accused of burglary
2 unattractive photograph of Barbara accused of burglary
3 no photograph with the burglary case (control group)
4 attractive photograph of Barbara accused of fraud
5 unattractive photograph of Barbara accused of fraud
6 no photograph with the fraud case (control group).

Firstly, all participants were asked to rate how attractive Barbara was to make sure that the participants agreed which photographs showed Barbara as attractive or unattractive. Then the researchers asked the individual 'jurors' in each group to give Barbara a prison sentence ranging from one to fifteen years.

Results

The table opposite shows the **mean** average length of prison sentence (years) based on type of crime and attractiveness that Barbara was awarded.

The table shows that a similar length of sentence was awarded for both crimes, with both the unattractive photograph and no photograph. However, the attractive photograph had a big effect on the participant's decision. They thought the 'attractive Barbara' should spend longer in prison for fraud, and less time in prison for burglary.

Attractive people are associated with crimes like fraud because they use their good looks to swindle money out of others. Their victims would see them as trustworthy in order to hand over their money.

	Attractive photo	Unattractive photo	No Photo
Burglary	2.80	5.20	5.10
Fraud	5.45	4.35	4.35

However, we do not associate good-looking people with burglary, as we do not believe a good-looking person could break into a flat to steal.

Conclusion
This experiment highlights the importance that looks have on jury decision-making. Good-looking people do get away with some crimes, but if they have used their looks to commit a crime they are less likely to get away with it.

Evaluation
Strengths:

- The study used good **controls**; participants were all given the same instructions, similar cases to read and a sentence to decide. This means that there are fewer **extraneous variables** that could have affected their decisions. It means that the findings are reliable and the study could be repeated in the same way again.
- The control group was useful to show whether the photographs did affect participants' decisions or not.
- The participants were less likely to guess the aim of the study because they did not know what the other groups were doing (**demand characteristics**).
- The study could be used in real life to inform jurors not to base their decision on what a defendant looks like. They should only use the evidence and testimony presented in the courtroom.

- The participants were asked to rate the attractiveness of the photograph. This was to make sure that the participants agreed that the photograph shown was of an attractive person. As people's views of attractiveness can vary, this was a good control.

Weaknesses:

- This experiment is not realistic as it is not what a jury would normally experience. A jury member would see the defendant in real life, listen to evidence and testimony and decide as a group. Using a photograph and only brief details of a case is not realistic.
- Juries only normally decide whether a defendant is guilty or not. It is the judge that decides the length of prison sentence. In this way also, the study is not realistic.

Quick check

A Outline three key points about Sigall and Ostrove's procedure.

Key definitions

controls: ways to keep variables constant in all conditions of an experiment.

control group: a group that does not receive an experimental condition. This group provides a baseline on which to compare those participants who do experience a condition of the experiment.

extraneous variables: any variables that might affect the results of the study that may not be controlled.

demand characteristics: when we change our behaviour to meet the demands of the situation.

Questions

1 How can the study findings be used in the real world?
2 How does Sigall and Ostrove's study differ from the experience of a real jury?

E2a3 Madon (2004): self-fulfilling prophecy and drinking behaviour

Learn about

- Why and how Madon conducted the study
- The findings in relation to self-fulfilling prophecy
- An evaluation of the study

Quick check

A What was Madon trying to find out?

We discovered on page 172 that sometimes, when you are told something about yourself by others, you might actually start to believe it. This is known as a **self-fulfilling prophecy**.

Madon's study

Aim

The aim of Stephanie Madon's study was to see if a parent's expectation of their child's drinking habits would become a reality. If parents thought their child would drink lots of alcohol, would this lead them to actually drink more?

Procedure

Madon questioned 115 children aged between 12 and 13 years old and their parents. Parents were asked to guess how much alcohol their child regularly drank or would drink over the coming year. A year later, the children were asked to say how much alcohol they actually consumed.

Results

Madon found that the children who drank the most alcohol were the ones whose parents had predicted a greater use of alcohol. It only took one parent to have a negative opinion about their child's drinking habits to show a relationship with high levels of drinking. However, the child seemed at greater risk of higher alcohol use if both parents held negative beliefs.

Conclusion

The study showed that a parent's prediction of their child's alcohol use was very accurate. The parent's expectations were consistent with alcohol use after 12 months. It could be concluded that this is a self-fulfilling prophecy because what the parent expected came true. This study may show that a parent's beliefs can have a massive influence on a child's behaviour.

Britain's binge drinking problem

Taking it further

Britain is reported to have one of the world's highest binge-drinking rates. Can we fully explain increased drinking by looking at parents' expectations of their children? Go to www.heinemann.co.uk/hotlinks (express code 4837P) and click on *The Site website*. Look at the fact sheet on binge drinking statistics and decide for yourself.

Evaluation

Strengths:

- A strength of this study is that there was a large sample of participants, so the results are likely to be more **valid** or true. Smaller samples can produce unreliable results.
- This study does give a strong warning to parents about holding negative beliefs about their children – it could be that they become true even if they were false beliefs in the first place.

Weaknesses:

- Parents may not have influenced their child's behaviour at all – they were just very accurate at judging their child's alcohol use. It may be an accurate prediction rather than a self-fulfilling prophecy.
- Many other people influence children so there could be other explanations. Friends are a strong source of influence for a teenager. It could be that friends had a greater influence over drinking behaviour than the parent's prediction, but this was not studied (social learning theory covered in Topic C page 98 could explain this).
- The study only shows a correlation. Correlations have less **control** than experiments and the researchers cannot be sure of a true link between the **variables** they are measuring. In this study, the researcher could not be 100 per cent certain of a definite link between parents' predictions and a child's alcohol use. Other factors could have influenced the child rather than parental beliefs.
- A questionnaire such as the one used may have **social desirability bias**. Children may say they drink more to look tough, or say they drink less in case their parents find out. Similarly, parents may predict their children drink more because they think it is a badge of honour, or predict they drink less because it is not acceptable.

This kind of research is socially sensitive because it can be viewed as parent-blaming. Parents are often blamed for their child's actions, and this study is no different. We should be careful when interpreting the findings of this study, carefully weighing up the strengths and weaknesses before using the evidence to advise parents.

In the exam you may be asked to apply your knowledge of the self-fulfilling prophecy. Think up some scenarios and practise explaining them using the self-fulfilling prophecy.

Quick check

B This study involved using a questionnaire with parents and their children. Give two reasons why the parents and children might not tell the truth when answering questions about drinking.

Examiner's tips

Try revising key psychological studies by using the prompts:

- Aim (A)
- Procedure (P)
- Results (R)
- Conclusion (C)

APRC – this will help you remember the key points of the study; what the researchers wanted to find out, how they did it, what they found, what it meant.

Questions

1 Explain Madon's findings in terms of the self-fulfilling prophecy.

2 Janek was arrested for being 'drunk and disorderly' after a night out clubbing. His parents were not surprised when the police phoned them. Use Madon's study to explain Janek's behaviour.

E2bl Is criminal research practical and ethical?

Learn about

- The practical problems with research into criminality
- The ethical problems with research into criminality

Practical and ethical issues

Research into criminality is important, but not without its problems. There are practical and ethical problems when researching criminality.

- Practical problems refer to difficulties accessing and researching criminals.
- Ethical problems refer to the moral issues, or rights and wrongs of conducting this research.

Imagine that you are given the opportunity to conduct your own research into what causes criminal behaviour. This would be important research that could really make a contribution to our understanding of criminality. However, there are issues you need to consider before planning your research.

Now look at it from another point of view. Imagine that you are the criminal that a psychologist wants to research. How might you feel as the participant rather than the researcher? When you begin to consider how you might feel as a criminal subject to psychological research you will start to appreciate some of the ethical problems associated with it.

Problems with biological research

Biological research looks at the inheritance of criminality and whether chromosome abnormality is linked to criminal behaviour. This research has not yet yielded direct evidence for a biological basis for crime, and there are also practical and ethical issues associated with such research.

Practical problems

- In a study with thousands of participants, only a handful will have the XYY chromosome abnormality, supposedly linked to criminality. This lowers the validity of such studies because samples are so small.
- Chromosome abnormalities, such as XYY, are very difficult to detect, as there are very few obvious signs that a person has it. This makes the gathering of participants very difficult.
- Although we can find family links to criminality quite easily, there are many different types of crimes and criminals. To say that a father who was convicted of theft has a son who is a murderer is a very weak link. These crimes are very different, so a criminal gene as a general concept is unlikely to be found.
- We should also consider that family, twin and adoption studies often rely upon convictions or arrests. Many criminals are successful, so will not be caught for their crimes and therefore not be included in these studies.

Ethical problems

- It would not be ethical to say that having a specific chromosome pattern caused criminality if the link found is not 100 per cent true. Telling someone with a chromosome abnormality that they are likely to become a criminal could become a self-fulfilling prophecy.
- To tell a criminal that their behaviour was due to a chromosome abnormality might lead them to believe that they were not responsible for their criminal actions; they can blame their genes.
- Studies that have been conducted always maintain the participants' anonymity; they are never named, nor can they be identified from the research.

Quick check

A Why is XYY syndrome difficult to detect?

B How could finding an XYY person become a self-fulfilling prophecy?

- If psychologists found a genetic link to criminal behaviour, this knowledge could be used to control individuals with a chromosome abnormality before they even commit a criminal offence. This would be a very dangerous use of power and prevent people from living a normal life.

Problems with social research

Social research looks at how the environment we are raised in may cause criminality. It examines family relationships and influences in our social environment. As with biological research, there are practical and ethical issues associated with it.

Practical problems

- We cannot carry out an experiment to make someone a criminal, so any social research just examines a link between criminality and social or biological factors. For example, we might find a link between criminal behaviour and family income. However, it is only a link and there may be other causes for criminal behaviour, such as the way that the child has been raised.
- Research often involves examining why people have turned to crime. Criminals and their family are questioned about past events that might have caused them to turn to crime. There are several practical problems associated with this:
  - Memory is not very reliable after many years, and the answers given might not provide an accurate account of what really happened.

  - Asking the criminals themselves might be unreliable because they might blame aspects of their upbringing as a reason for crime, rather than the true reason or reasons.

  - It could be a way for criminals to avoid taking responsibility for their own actions.

Ethical problems

- If there is a link between the family and criminal behaviour it could be used to blame parents for their children's behaviour. Results for these studies should be treated with care and not used to hold parents responsible for their children's actions if this is not a certainty.

- Investigating the self-fulfilling prophecy as an explanation may create or reinforce existing labels and therefore encourage criminal behaviour.

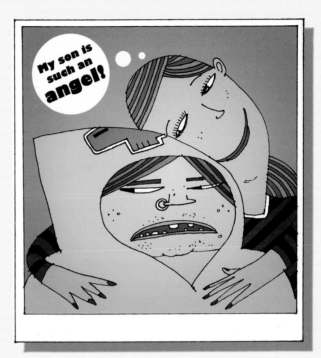

A parent's perception of their child may not be reliable for research.

Quick check

C Why can't we conduct an experiment into the social factors that may cause criminality?

D What could be an issue with social research into criminality if we question parents and family about a criminal?

Questions

1 Before conducting social research into criminality, what ethical problems should you consider?

2 Jonah wanted to see if criminal behaviour was a result of self-fulfilling prophecy. Explain some of the problems he might have to consider when conducting this research.

E2b2 Gathering information from convicted offenders

Learn about

- The practical and ethical problems of gathering information from convicted offenders

Convicted offenders are sometimes used in criminal research. These could include serious offenders – murderers and rapists. We can ask direct questions about their crimes and the social conditions that may have led them to become criminals. We can also ask them about their families, and any other family members who have also been convicted of crimes. This is a valid way of investigating crime, but it does have its problems.

Quick check

A Why might offenders be dishonest when asked about their crimes?

Practical problems

- Convicted offenders may use the research as a way of gaining early release from prison by telling psychologists that they are sorry for their crimes or by underplaying the crimes they have committed. This might lead to results that reflect dishonesty rather than truth.
- Convicted offenders might try to glorify their crimes to make them feel more important than they are. This can lead to useless study findings.
- Offenders might feel guilty about their crimes and feel uncomfortable talking about what they have done.
- Criminals may believe that the information they give could be used to convict another criminal. They may fear that the other criminal might get back at them. This could lead to distress.
- They might withhold certain information to protect themselves, their families or their criminal group.

Convicted criminals can be interviewed about their background.

Ted Bundy, a notorious American serial killer, was imprisoned and later interviewed by the FBI. He did not disclose all of his murders but was said to have glamourised the 30 murders he was convicted of.

Taking it further

Go to www.heinemann.co.uk/hotlinks (express code 4837P). Click on the *All About Forensic Psychology website* to learn about criminal profiling.

Ethical problems

Criminals are often used in psychological research and asked directly for insight into their own behaviour. This process can be therapeutic for some criminals as they can talk about their crimes and 'get it off their chest'. But others may feel intimidated and threatened by being asked personal questions. There are ethical problems to consider when gathering information from convicted offenders:

- Criminals who are used in psychological research should not be treated any differently from non-criminal participants, just because they are criminals and are in prison.
- Criminals, ex-criminals and prisoners have the same human rights as any other member of society.
- Like all participants of psychological research, convicted offenders should have the right to give consent, be able to withdraw from the study, have their privacy respected and be debriefed. No humans should be put at risk of harm or distress.
- Criminals might feel guilt about their crimes and feel uncomfortable talking about them.
- Criminals may believe that the information they give could be used to convict another criminal. They may fear that the other criminal might look for revenge. This could lead to distress.

Examiner's tips

You have already studied ethical guidelines used for human research on pages 44, 106, 142, 152. Refer back to these sections, because they are relevant to all participants in psychological studies, including convicted offenders.

Quick check

B Can we expect to be able to use criminals as we want to when conducting research? Explain your answer.

Questions

1 Emma wanted to interview convicted criminals to see if their crimes could be linked to how they were raised by their parents. Outline one practical and one ethical issue that Emma might have to consider.

E3al Offender profiling

Learn about

- The purpose, process and effectiveness of offender profiling

LL Cool J in Mindhunters *(2004), a film dramatising the role of profiling.*

What is offender profiling?

Offender profiling is the name of a process used to help police catch criminals. It does not produce the name of a criminal, as some films and TV programmes would lead you to believe, but does help narrow the number of **suspects** that police should investigate. This might seem a little weak, but when a police force has many thousands of suspects, narrowing this to a few thousand is very useful.

Examiner's tips

A common misconception of offender profilers is that they are telepathic. They do not possess psychic powers that can find the criminal. They are scientists with an enormous amount of experience of criminal behaviour.

Traditional policing involves the analysis of physical evidence, such as fingerprints, bloodstains, shoe prints and DNA evidence. But police and psychologists have long believed that the way in which a crime is committed gives additional clues about the criminal.

A criminal will leave clues at the crime scene such as:

- the type of victim
- the type of crime
- the location
- the time of day or night
- specific features of a crime
- what is taken or left behind.

All of these features can tell us more about the type of person who committed the crime.

The underlying ideas behind profiling

- There are often similarities between crimes committed by the same person that can be picked out. Even if the crimes develop and change over time, they still have similarities that show it is the same offender who commits them.
- The way in which an offender commits a crime is a reflection of their self. We all have habits and likes or dislikes. We prefer to act in certain ways. A criminal is no different and they will not change their normal behaviour when they commit a crime. This is known as **criminal consistency**.
- We can track a criminal over many crimes, as each time the criminal leaves behind a trace of him or herself.

The aims of offender profiling

As well as helping the police narrow down the number of suspects, the profile can help the police predict the type of future victims and offences. The **profile** can give clues about evidence that might be found on the criminal, such as **souvenirs** taken from the crime scene. It can also suggest very useful interview techniques for the police to use on the criminal.

For example, a clever criminal will not talk if they are interviewed in a severe way. The police may be advised to use a softer interview strategy and let the criminal take control of the interview until they slip up and give too much away.

Quick check

A List four aims of offender profiling.

186

Creating a profile

Creating a profile involves:

1   analysis of the crime – the police make detailed records of the victim, place, photographs, DNA evidence and time of day.
2   building a profile – a criminal profiler uses this information to construct a list of probable features of a criminal.

A typical profile has a number of key bits of information:

- sex of offender
- race
- age
- marital status
- occupation
- intellectual ability
- possible criminal history
- area where criminal lives.

These details would make it much easier to narrow down a list of suspects.

Taking it further

Go to www.heinemann.co.uk/hotlinks (express code 4837P) and click on the *Criminal Profiling Research website* to find out more.

Does offender profiling work?

There are a handful of profiles that have been successful; you will read about David Canter's profile later (see page 188). But there are also profiles that have led to the **victimisation** and **entrapment** of innocent people.

Colin Stagg was arrested for the murder of Rachel Nickell (1992) based on the profile developed by an experienced profiler, Paul Brittan. Brittan and the police could not get any physical evidence to arrest Stagg, so they got an undercover policewoman to date him. They wanted him to give away his crimes to her. Stagg never did, but was arrested because the police felt he was the right man. Although he was taken to court, the case was eventually thrown out by the judge. However, Stagg was followed by the media and the police and made an outcast because of a profile that seemed to point to him.

In 2008 Robert Napper, a convicted killer held at Broadmoor hospital, pleaded guilty to the manslaughter of Rachel Nickell. Colin Stagg received a public apology from the police.

Guesswork?

Many people argue that offender profiling is nothing better than experienced guesswork. More serious critics of offender profiling say that it is about as accurate as horoscopes are. This is a little unfair, as successful profiles have been quite specific and much less general than newspaper horoscopes.

The problem with measuring the success of a profile is that it is just one of the many links in the chain when police try to catch a criminal. From the witnesses, evidence and police analysis, to the profile and follow-up enquiries, there are many factors that could affect the successful arrest of a criminal. It is a little unfair to blame the profile for a failure to catch a criminal. But a profile does guide the police. If the profile is wrong, the criminal could slip through the net unnoticed.

Most police officers believe that profiles are useful, but that they do not always help solve the crime. It seems that traditional policing is still the most effective way of catching criminals.

Key definitions

criminal consistency: the idea that a person will commit a crime in a way that mirrors his or her own personality and ability. An organised person will commit an organised crime.

profile: a list of predicted abilities, personality characteristics, occupation, marital status, etc., that can be used to narrow down a list of suspects for a crime.

Questions

1   How is offender profiling different from traditional policing?
2   Is offender profiling effective?

E3bl The case of John Duffy

Learn about
- John Duffy's crimes
- The profile of John Duffy

The case

David Canter is one of Britain's leading offender profilers. He was asked to profile a case in London, code-named 'Project Hart'. It involved a series of sex attacks and murders that the police believed were carried out by the same man.

The facts
- Twenty-six sex attacks between 1982 and 1986.
- Three murders between 1985 and 1986.
- All the offences were committed against young women.
- All the offences were committed in and around London, near railway stations.

Witness reports
- The women victims were approached near railway stations.
- The man attempted to talk to the women before attacking them.
- They were then forced to a side street, track or alley where the public could not see them.
- Most of the women reported that the man used a knife and their hands were restrained with a rope tie or an article of clothing worn by the victim.
- The attacker still talked to the women throughout the attack in an attempt to form a relationship.
- After the attack the man cleaned the victim to try to remove any physical evidence.

Murder victim details

Victim 1

On 29 December 1985, Alison Day was going to where her boyfriend worked. She was attacked near Hackney Wick railway station. Her hands were tied and there was evidence that she was strangled. She was knocked unconscious before the attack. She was found 17 days after the attack in the canal that ran beside the station. Her pockets were filled with stones.

Victim 2

Maartje Tamboezer was attacked and murdered on 17 April 1986. She had been riding her bike to a sweet shop in Surrey. She was knocked off the bike and dragged to a side road. A length of fishing wire was found tied between two bushes near her body, which could have been used to knock her from her bike. She had been tied and strangled. Her hands were tied behind her back. The attacker attempted to burn her body.

Victim 3

On 18 May 1986, Anne Lock was attacked after she had finished her working day at Weekend Television in London. Her attacker approached her after she left the train station, as she was unlocking her bike. Her hands were tied behind her back and she was suffocated.

Offender profiler David Canter

The profile

David Canter developed a profile of the attacker based on the evidence. He reasoned that Duffy

John Duffy, known as the 'Railway Killer'.

tied up his victims for the simple reason that he was not a strong man. He was small and unable to restrain them during the attack. Because he was small, he was able to approach his victims without them seeing him as a threat. If you were approached by a tall, strong man, you would be less likely to trust them.

Was Canter's profile of Duffy accurate? Looking at the profile and the man John Duffy (see the table below), we can safely say that the profile was accurate. Canter used the criminal consistency hypothesis to good effect,

John Duffy was found and arrested on 7 November 1986. He was finally convicted of three murders and seven counts of rape and sentenced to three life sentences. He also revealed an accomplice David Mulcahy, John Duffy's school friend, who had committed some of the crimes with him.

David Canter's profile of John Duffy

David Canter's profile	Facts about John Duffy
• Lived in London • Was married with no children • Had problems with his marriage • Was a small man • Physically unattractive • Had an interest in martial arts • Was a semi-skilled carpenter • Link to British Rail • Aged 20–30 years	• Lived in Kilburn, London • Married with no children (infertile) • Separated • 5 feet 4 inches tall • Unattractive • Member of martial arts club • Trained carpenter with British Rail • Ex-British Rail employee • 28 when arrested

Questions

1 Describe the crimes of John Duffy.
2 Outline the profile created by David Canter.
3 Assess whether the profile was accurate.

E3cl The job of the forensic psychologist

Learn about
- The work of a forensic psychologist

In your course you will look at the work of a **clinical psychologist** (page 154), an **educational psychologist** (page 116) and a **forensic psychologist** as well as others who work in areas of psychology such as a **psychoanalyst** (page 82). Within this topic you will look at the work of a forensic psychologist.

Forensic psychology is a fairly new 'type' of psychology and there are fewer than 1000 **chartered** forensic psychologists in the UK.

Examiner's tips

Be ready to answer 'role of the psychologist' questions based on:
- who they might work for
- what they do
- skills and qualifications required
- chartered status
- treatments they offer.

This applies to the three 'role of the psychologist' sections in the course (educational, clinical and forensic psychologists).

What a forensic psychologist does

In general, a forensic psychologist:
- works in the courts to uncover psychological issues
- looks at psychological aspects of criminal activity
- looks at psychological issues to do with treating criminals.

Taking it further

Go to www.heinemann.co.uk/hotlinks (express code 4837P). Click on the *NHS website* to read about the job of a forensic psychologist.

Summary of the main tasks

A forensic psychologist sets up treatment programmes and evaluates them as well. They also work with offender behaviour to look at the needs of the prisoner as well as staff. There is also a research role, as with other psychologists. When prisoners are profiled, the forensic psychologist might gather data for a review. They may give evidence in court and advise parole boards, as well as be involved in analysing crime. As with other psychologists, forensic psychologists work with other agencies, assessing problems and coming up with interventions. They also help to develop policy.

Quick check

A List three tasks of a forensic psychologist.

Who the forensic psychologist works with

They work with offenders and prison staff to reduce and manage stress. They may look at coping with bullying if this is appropriate in a particular setting such as in prisons, and other similar issues depending on need. Forensic psychologists might also work with victims and witnesses to support them and help them to overcome problems. Other work might involve judges and juries in the courts.

Key definitions

psychopath: person suffering from a chronic mental disorder with abnormal or violent social behaviour.

A forensic psychologist may have to attend court as part of their job.

Some examples of what a forensic psychologist does

- Advising prison governors about prisoners, staff, implementing change or other organisational issues.
- Carrying out one-to-one assessments and treatments of prisoners as appropriate. Such an assessment may be requested by the court or by a prison governor.
- Assessing the risk of re-offending (often using one-to-one assessments and psychometric testing).
- Presenting assessment findings to others in multi-agency working.
- Carrying out research projects, for example looking at drop-out rates for probation or evaluating group programmes, such as anger management programmes in prisons.
- Doing crime analysis, such as using offender profiling. This is likely to be carried out to assist the police.

There are three hospitals in the UK for prisoners where the mentally ill can be treated, one of which is Broadmoor (pictured here). The others are Rampton and Ashworth.

- Training prison staff and others, for example with regard to managing behaviour or understanding mental health issues if they are relevant.
- Evaluating and monitoring treatments.
- Writing up notes and attending meetings.

The problem of psychopathic disorders

One problem that has been highlighted by forensic psychologists is that of offenders who have a **psychopathic** disorder. This is defined as 'having no guilt or conscience and showing behaviour that is very aggressive or violent'. The person does not function normally with regard to social norms and rules.

Psychopathic disorder is the subject of debate with regard to 'treatability'. Those who have psychopathic disorder are detained in secure hospitals to protect the public but they are not always on a treatment programme. This raises the question of whether they should be in a secure hospital or in a main prison.

To be treatable, for example, a prisoner must show progress, which many with psychopathic disorder are not able to do. Psychologists aim to provide treatment and prefer not to consider a disorder as untreatable. If one disorder, such as psychopathic disorder, is not considered suitable for treatment, it is argued that this would mean little research would be carried out, and little progress would be made in treating the disorder.

A related problem is the diagnosis of psychopathic disorder, which might be a label given to those with a personality disorder who are also offenders, and as such it may not be a 'real' disorder that has one set of symptoms or one cause. This makes such a 'disorder' hard to treat.

Questions

1. Explain some examples of what a forensic psychologist might do.
2. Who might a forensic psychologist work with?

E3c2 Becoming a forensic psychologist

Learn about

192

- Who a forensic psychologist might work for
- Skills required, qualifications required and what it means to be 'chartered'

The work of a forensic psychologist covers a wide range of criminality issues, but most often they deal with prisons and prisoners.

Who might a forensic psychologist work for?

A forensic psychologist works mainly for HM Prison Service. They can also be employed by the NHS because they work in secure hospitals. Social services can also employ a forensic psychologist, for example in young offender units or the probation service. They might work on a self-employed basis as consultants or they can work in university departments doing research and teaching.

Quick check

A Give two ways in which a forensic psychologist could be employed.

Skills required

You need the right skills to be a good forensic psychologist. Communication is the main skill required. You need to be able to listen carefully and to speak comfortably with people. You also need to be able to be write well, as you will have to produce concise reports.

In the same way as other psychologists do, the forensic psychologist observes a lot to gather information, so they need to notice body language as well as what people say. They also need to have problem-solving skills when they put a programme together, either for an individual or for an institution.

Rampton is one of three high-security hospitals for mentally-ill offenders in the UK.

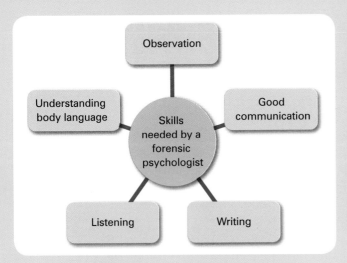

Qualifications required

Firstly, you need a degree in Psychology that is recognised by the British Psychological Society (BPS) – which most Psychology degrees are. When a degree matches BPS requirements, this is called having graduate basis for registration (GBR).

Work experience is preferred before applying for a Masters in Forensic Psychology (a Masters Degree is one step above a degree). This Masters is Stage 1 of the Diploma in Forensic Psychology. Stage 2 is next, and this consists of two years of supervised practice.

The salary for a forensic psychologist is quite high, ranging from £20,000 at the start to £60,000 when fully qualified and experienced. It is one of the fastest-growing areas of psychology.

The three psychologists covered in the course have similar roles. They:

- carry out assessments, interventions and evaluations of their interventions
- all use treatment to help manage behaviour
- mainly work for a government department such as the NHS, Prison Service or Local Education Authority
- need to have a degree in psychology as well as a specialist degree
- tend to be chartered
- all have similar skills such as listening, writing and problem-solving skills
- carry out research and extend psychological understanding in their field.

Most importantly, all psychologists have to work with clear ethical guidelines, focusing in particular on competency, confidentiality and privacy.

The differences are in the actual job that each psychologist does:

- educational psychologists work with children and focus on their development and learning
- clinical psychologists work with those who are mentally ill and focus on helping them to get better or manage their illness
- forensic psychologists work with criminals themselves, as well as people working with criminals such as the police.

Chartered status

'Chartered' means you have satisfied requirements of the BPS (British Psychological Society) and have sufficient qualifications and experience to be called a 'psychologist'. There is a directory of chartered psychologists, maintained by the British Psychological Society, and it is useful, especially for a self-employed psychologist, to be on the list as it gives credibility.

Taking it further

Access the link to the *British Psychological Society website* on www.heinemann.co.uk/hotlinks, entering express code 4837P. Use the 'Find a psychologist' search engine to look at the different services that psychologists offer.

Questions

1 List two qualifications required to be a forensic psychologist.
2 Explain the skills required to be a forensic psychologist.
3 Compare the job of a forensic psychologist with one of the other psychologists you have studied.

E3c3 How a forensic psychologist might help treat offenders

Learn about

- How a forensic psychologist might treat offenders
- The treatment of sexual offenders, as an example

Treatment of offenders

It is the forensic psychologist who is likely to develop **rehabilitation** programmes. They may use anger management, skills training such as learning to interact well with others or using appropriate body language depending on a situation, or treatments for addiction.

They might develop one-to-one programmes or group therapies. The aim of the treatment is to address both the behaviour of the person and their psychological needs, such as anxiety, depression or stress, to make them feel better and manage their own behaviour more successfully.

A forensic psychologist often focuses on working with offenders to reduce the risk of them re-offending, as this is important both for society and for the individual.

An example of therapy: personal construct therapy

Personal construct therapy is an example of the sort of therapy that can be used by forensic psychologists. This might involve the following:

1 Thinking of three people you know.
2 Writing down one way in which two of them are the same and one is different.
3 Repeating steps 1 and 2 a number of times, so that you come up with more people.

The person ends up with a list of their personal constructs. For example, think of two friends and your mother. How are two of them the same and one different? Are two generous and one less generous? If so, one of your constructs would be 'generous or not'.

Personal construct therapy is based on the idea that an individual sets their own **constructs** of how they see other people. Then they judge people, based on these criteria.

In this therapy, the psychologist helps the person to understand their own constructs and then repeats the task later to help them to see how they have changed.

After some intervention by the psychologist, such as social skills training, the individual judges people on their own constructs again to see what changes have been made by the treatment.

Treating drug abuse

Drug abuse links to crime, such as stealing and crimes against the person. Offenders who are drug addicts, if treated, would probably not re-offend. Many crimes are committed by drug addicts who need money to fund their habit.

Treatment to help someone to stop abusing drugs tends to involve prescribing substitute drugs (if appropriate), monitoring the addict's progress closely and providing support and counselling. The probation service can be very involved in such treatment when the offender is being released, providing support and making sure that they have adequate housing and funding to help prevent them returning to drug abuse.

The UK Drug Policy Commission has said that there is not enough evidence of effective treatments for drug abuse. This may be because abusers return to their community, where they mix with other abusers. Another factor can be life pressures that led to the drug abuse in the first place, as well as new pressures associated with being an ex-prisoner.

There is current focus on these issues to explore what can be done to aid the effectiveness of treatment for drug abuse. Reinforcing treatment through therapy is one way of trying to overcome the problem.

Quick check

A List two ways of treating drug abuse.

Treating sexual offenders

It is **mandatory** that sex offenders attend a treatment programme. This means that their progress on such a programme affects their release.

One issue with treating sex offenders is the question of what 'causes' sex offending. If it is thought to have a biological basis, such as inherited tendencies and desires or certain brain structures and functioning, then biological treatments are likely to be thought appropriate.

Medication can be prescribed to reduce the sex drive. In the past, surgery was even used to remove sexual organs. However, medication is not considered effective, partly because the underlying causes may be non-sexual. Some offenders are given further medication to treat anxiety about the treatment.

One difficulty in planning treatment for sex offenders is that the offenders themselves vary in temperament, reasons why they offend, and in the types of sex crimes committed. This means treatment required also needs to vary. **Cognitive behavioural therapy** (see page 154) is now thought to be more helpful than drug therapy.

Sex offender problems that may need treating

- Intimacy problems: poor childhood relationships with parents or other significant people can lead to loneliness and a lack of skills when it comes to intimacy. This can cause relationship difficulties. The offender may also have distorted views of what is appropriate behaviour towards other people.
- Social skills problems: child molesters tend to lack confidence and to have difficulty mixing socially. There is a general idea that sex offenders are thought to misinterpret signals from women, thinking that women are showing positive interest when they are not. Some offenders may also see aggression as socially acceptable.

- Problems with empathy: empathy means being able to take the view of someone else and to have compassion. These skills are often missing in sex offenders, especially rapists and child abusers. Sex offenders have been shown to confuse fear, anger and disgust, finding it hard to separate these emotions. If someone misinterprets signals, then they are likely to find empathy difficult.
- Cognitive distortions: if the sex offender has distorted thinking, they can justify their behaviour to themselves.

Cognitive behavioural therapy and behaviour modification

Treatment for sex offending often involves group therapy, using cognitive behavioural principles. The list of issues above mainly relates to inappropriate thinking or difficulty with social skills. Cognitive behavioural therapy involves helping someone to change how they think about something and therefore behave differently.

Behaviour modification is also used to correct sex offender behaviour. It is focused on helping someone to change their behaviour, not their thinking. Behaviour modification can involve reinforcing required behaviour and removing reinforcement of unwanted behaviour.

Cognitive behavioural therapy is explained in more detail in the context of clinical psychology, so check back to find out more (page 154).

Key definitions

mandatory: has to be done.

personal construct therapy: a therapy where someone finds their own way of looking at people (their personal constructs) and uses those constructs, not only to see how they judge the people they know but also to measure change after therapy.

Questions

1 Describe how cognitive behavioural therapy is used to treat sex offenders.
2 What is meant by personal construct therapy?
3 Discuss problems with treating offenders.

E4al How defendant characteristics affect jury decision-making

Learn about

● How psychology investigates jury decision-making

● How defendant characteristics affect jury decision-making

It is unlikely that you have ever seen inside a courtroom. Most of us believe that it is where justice takes place. However, psychologists have looked at how juries make their decisions and believe that it might not be as fair as we think.

What happens in a courtroom?

Serious criminal offences are dealt with in a court of law, with a judge and a jury. The jury is a group of twelve people who have been randomly selected from the local area. During the trial, the jury listens to all the evidence and **testimony** presented by the defence (those who are supporting the **defendant's** innocence) and the prosecution (those who are trying to prove that the defendant is guilty).

The jurors then talk to each other in private before they make a decision. If the jury comes to a guilty **verdict**, the judge then decides on a sentence. However, the system is not perfect and sometimes innocent people are sent to prison or guilty people are released. Psychologists try to find out why this happens.

Key definitions

defendant: a person who has been accused of a crime and is now in court.

verdict: a decision made by a jury. The verdict can be guilty or innocent.

testimony: the evidence given by a witness, expert, or a person the defendant knows well.

stereotype: a general view of a person based on little or no factual information.

Can juries make mistakes?

A jury should base their decision only on what they see and hear in the courtroom – the evidence and the testimony of witnesses. This ought to be a fair process. However, jurors might be affected by other factors. In everyday life we make decisions about people by the way they look and sound. Jurors also use this information to decide upon a person's guilt, even if it is not important to the case and without even realising they are doing it.

Examiner's tips

Don't worry, this is not GCSE Law, so you will not be expected to remember all these legal processes. You will have to know what a jury is to be able to understand how their decision-making is influenced. You will also need to be familiar with the terms:

● defendant   ● testimony

● jury   ● evidence.

Quick check

A Who is the defendant?

Juries can make incorrect decisions based on information not related to the case.

Defendant characteristics

How a defendant looks, acts or sounds affect how they are viewed by a jury. When we meet someone new, we often base our decision of them on a few features that are **stereotypical**. If we met someone with a shaven head, we might view them as aggressive because we have a stereotyped view of them as a football hooligan or gang member. Psychologists have investigated factors like accent, race and attractiveness, to see how it affects jury decision-making.

Race

There is a higher proportion of ethnic minorities in prison (15 per cent) than in the UK general population (8 per cent). Is this because ethnic minorities commit more crime? Or are there other factors to consider?

Which man is more likely to be guilty?

Psychologists have researched how a defendant's race affects jury decision-making. If we have a stereotypical view of black men as more likely to commit a crime, then we are more likely to find them guilty. This might explain the higher proportion of ethnic minorities in prison.

Some studies with mock juries have found that white jurors are more likely to find a black defendant guilty compared to a white defendant. It has also been found that a black defendant might receive harsher sentences than a white defendant for the same crime.

However, Skolnick and Shaw (1997) looked at the relationship between the race of jurors and the race of defendants and found that both were important in the decision-making process. They found that both black and white jurors were less likely to find a black defendant guilty (this goes against other studies), and that black jurors were more likely to find a white defendant guilty than a black defendant.

Attractiveness

We often view attractive people as more intelligent, friendly and honest. This means that we are less likely to judge an attractive person guilty of a crime. Taylor and Butcher (2007) conducted a mock jury study. They found that more attractive people were judged as less guilty of a crime and given lower sentences than unattractive people. So beautiful people do get away with murder! Examine this in more detail on page 178, where we look at Sigall and Ostrove's study of attractiveness.

Accent

A jury can be influenced by how a defendant speaks. If a defendant is well-spoken ('posh') we might find them 'not guilty' of robbery. For a defendant with a strong regional or 'rough' accent, the reverse might be true because we might see them as needing more money than the 'posh' defendant.

Mahoney and Dixon (2002) conducted an experiment into accents and found that 'Brummies' (people from Birmingham) were more likely to be found guilty of armed robbery than cheque fraud compared to a defendant with a posh accent.

Taking it further

Go to www.heinemann.co.uk/hotlinks (express code 4837P). Click on the *Lancaster University website* to read the Mahoney and Dixon study.

Questions

1 Outline two defendant characteristics that might affect jury decision-making.

2 Michaela is a jury member. She is watching a burglary case. When talking to other jury members she discovers that some of them are not basing their decision on the evidence presented in court. Explain Michaela's experience of the other jury members.

Know Zone - Topic E
Are criminals born or made?

You should know...

ANSWERING THE QUESTION

☐ The causes of criminal behaviour, including biological and social explanations – evaluate and compare them.

☐ The nature-nurture debate in relation to biological and social explanations of criminal behaviour.

☐ A description of the psychological studies by Theilgaard (1984), Madon (2004) and Sigall and Ostove (1975), including evaluation points for each.

☐ The practical and ethical problems that are found when researching criminal behaviour, particularly with convicted offenders.

☐ The purpose of offender profiling as a method to catch criminals such as John Duffy – how it is done and whether or not it is effective.

☐ The role of a forensic psychologist – what they do, what skills and qualifications they need, and how they might help to treat an offender.

☐ How defendant characteristics such as appearance might influence decisions made by a jury.

EVALUATING THE ANSWER

☐ Genetic research suggests a potential link between genes and criminal behaviour, although only really in property crime. A general link to a criminal gene has not been found.

☐ People with the XYY chromosome abnormality might be more likely to turn to crime if they have lower intelligence – frustrated at school and have fewer chances for good careers.

☐ Theilgaard's genetics study only found a weak link and cannot be trusted because of its small sample size.

☐ Social research offers strong evidence for criminal behaviour developing from the way we are raised and how others treat us.

☐ The social explanation offers many ideas, but it is more likely to be a combination of various bad experiences as we grow up that could contribute to following a criminal path.

☐ Neither the biological or social explanations offer a complete explanation for criminal behaviour. Not all criminals show a genetic link and not all children raised under poor social circumstances turn to crime.

Support activity

Summarise the purpose and process of offender profiling as a poster for your classroom. You might wish to use the case of John Duffy as an example of how a profile is drawn up. You can compare David Canter's profile with the characteristics of John Duffy to examine the effectiveness of profiling.

Stretch activity

Use what you have learned about the biological and social explanations of criminality and put the main points from each explanation into a table. To understand the explanations in relation to the nature-nurture debate, colour code each main point as either nature or nurture. Now answer the question:

Compare the biological and social explanations of criminal behaviour and explain how they relate to the nature-nurture debate.

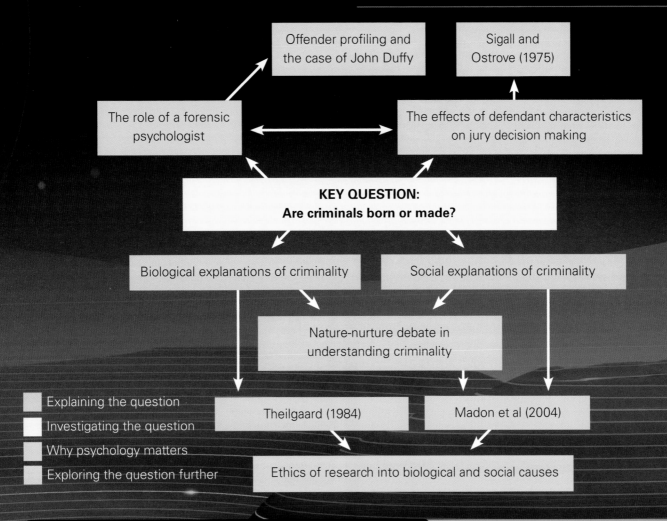

Offender profiling and the case of John Duffy

Sigall and Ostrove (1975)

The role of a forensic psychologist

The effects of defendant characteristics on jury decision making

KEY QUESTION:
Are criminals born or made?

Biological explanations of criminality

Social explanations of criminality

Nature-nurture debate in understanding criminality

Theilgaard (1984)

Madon et al (2004)

Ethics of research into biological and social causes

Explaining the question
Investigating the question
Why psychology matters
Exploring the question further

Examiner's tip: Stretch activity

A good answer for the first part of the question on the left hand page will include differences and similarities between the biological and social explanations of criminality. Use phrases such as 'similar to', 'different from' or 'in contrast to' to ensure you are comparing and not just describing.

The second part of the question asks you to relate each explanation to the nature-nurture debate. A good answer will make a point and then offer a theory which is backed up by evidence. The evidence can draw on research that you have studied during your course to show the examiner that you can support the point you are trying to make.

Key terms

- Genetics
- XYY
- Chromosome
- Twin studies
- Family patterns
- Childrearing strategies
- Self-fulfilling prophecy
- Offender profiling
- Forensic psychologist
- Defendant characteristics

Practice Exam Questions

1   Describe one biological explanation for criminality.

2   Describe one social explanation for criminality.

3   Outline the aim of one study you have learnt when discussing whether criminals are born or made.

4   Describe the purpose of offender profiling.

5   Explain how one characteristic of a defendant may influence jury decision-making.

welcome to examzone

You're almost at the end of your psychology course and it will soon be time to show your knowledge and understanding in the exam. In this section we'll show you how to make the most of your revision, using techniques to achieve your potential and how to get the best grade you can.

Zone In!

During your course, you've learnt about schemas – the way previous knowledge influences how we see our world. Use this knowledge and understanding to develop your own 'exam-passing' schema. Focus on what you need to achieve and how you're going to prepare for the exam to put you in the right frame of mind for revision.

UNDERSTAND IT

The television programme Big Brother makes no sense to someone who has never watched it. To be able to understand something, it needs to have meaning to you. Psychology tells us that the more you understand something, the easier it is to remember. Get down to revision and increase your understanding!

FOCUS

With so many other things going on in your life, you might find it difficult to focus on revision. Switch your attention away from all other issues and focus only on your work when you're revising – this will help you block out any distractions. It will also mean you can focus on having fun and relaxing during your breaks.

DIET AND EXERCISE

Keep active and be healthy when you are revising. Maintain a regular amount of exercise, as revision is an immobile activity and can make you feel lethargic.
We know from studying sleep disorders that poor diet and inactivity can disrupt sleep patterns and make you lose concentration. Make sure you build 'healthy time' into your revision plan.

FRIENDS AND FAMILY

If revising quietly on your own is a good strategy for you, make sure you tell your friends and family when you plan to revise so they can give you some space.

Alternatively, if it works for you, get your friends and family involved in your revision. You could ask your family to quiz you on topics, or you could take turns explaining topics with friends. You could even get a revision group together with others in your class, but make sure you plan your sessions so you don't slip into gossip mode!

REWARD YOURSELF

Remember when you studied reinforcement and learning? Well, learning works better when you receive a reward as reinforcement! Set yourself small goals to aim for and when you have achieved a goal, reward yourself with something nice. This could be a break, shopping trip or treat – but watch out for too many chocolate biscuits!

BE GOAL MOTIVATED

Set yourself a goal to keep motivation high. Motivation is the key to successful revision. Would anyone run a marathon unless they really wanted to? Remind yourself of your goals for each session and why you want to do well in the exams.

Planning Zone

The first step in planning your revision is to take a good look at your specification. You can get a copy from your teacher, or from the Edexcel website. This document tells you what you need to know for the exam.

Colour code each section in the specification using coloured pencils:

Green means 'good to go – I know this'

Yellow means 'I'm not quite sure – this needs checking'

Red means 'stop… I don't know this!'

This will help you to form a visual picture of the areas where you're strong and those you need to spend longer looking at.

Now draw up a revision timetable

Give yourself at least four weeks to revise, so work back from your exam date and plan to study about five times a week. Revise little and often, around 30 minutes each session, so that you don't become exhausted and de-motivated.

Don't believe those who claim that they crammed the night before the exam and achieved a good grade – this is very unlikely! In fact, psychology tells us that cramming even for a few nights impairs memory and performance in exams. Cramming achieves nothing but exhaustion and panic.

Once you've identified the days you'll spend revising, plan the topics you are going to cover in time slots. Plan ahead so you can stay calm and alert for your exam.

The worst feeling is coming out of an exam having not understood a question, so begin with your 'red' areas first and then move on to 'yellow'. This will allow you to read up on bits you may have missed or get help from your teacher in good time. The 'green' areas can be recapped nearer the exam.

Always focus on what you have learned in your revision sessions, not on what you don't know very well yet. Keep noting every bit you learn. Soon these bits will add up and you will gain confidence daily.

MAY

SUNDAY | MONDAY | TUES

Aim high and ignore criticism or doubt from others – you can do it!

Find your **exam dates, specification** and specimen **exam paper**s on the Edexcel website.

Focus on what you have learnt and avoid panicking about what you don't know. Being stressed will affect your performance on what you do know.

Factor all your subjects into your revision plan – Remember that you have many subjects to revise.

Be motivated – if you are feeling low, renew your motivation by visualising yourself on results day holding your exam slip and celebrating.

Use different strategies to revise – Try note-taking, mind maps, flashcards, pictures, colour-coding, making up questions and explaining to others. Variety will spice up your revision and keep you focused.

Stick to your revision plan and don't worry about what your friends are doing. Comparing yourself to others might boost your confidence but it might also stress you out.

20   21
28   29

Don't Panic Zone

ANXIETY

It's normal to get anxious about exams but anxiety tends to get in the way of learning. It's a good idea to learn to overcome any anxiety by making sure you relax.

RELAXATION

Find somewhere comfortable and lie down or sit comfortably. Starting from your feet, tense them and relax them, then work up all the way to your shoulders and head. As you relax each set of muscles, leave them relaxed for a few minutes. Once you are totally relaxed, breathe slowly and deeply. Finally, think of a memory or a place that makes you feel happy. Keep that memory in your mind and it will help you to stay relaxed and happy. You should then feel more ready to learn again. If you feel anxious again, think of that same memory and you should feel more relaxed.

THOUGHTS, FEELINGS, BEHAVIOUR AND CONSEQUENCES

One way of dealing with panic and anxiety is to examine your thinking processes. You feel a certain way because of what you are thinking, and you behave according to how you feel. Your behaviour has consequences. But you can change things anywhere in this cycle – change your thoughts, feelings, behaviour or the consequences. Here is an example:

DON'T BE NEGATIVE!

One negative automatic thought might be 'I'm rubbish at exams'.

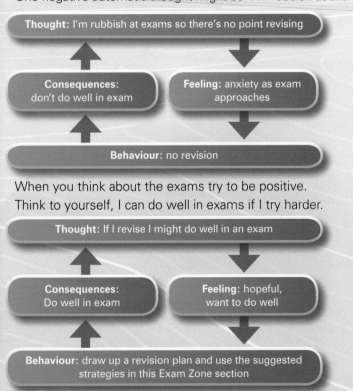

Thought: I'm rubbish at exams so there's no point revising

Consequences: don't do well in exam

Feeling: anxiety as exam approaches

Behaviour: no revision

When you think about the exams try to be positive.
Think to yourself, I can do well in exams if I try harder.

Thought: If I revise I might do well in an exam

Consequences: Do well in exam

Feeling: hopeful, want to do well

Behaviour: draw up a revision plan and use the suggested strategies in this Exam Zone section

What to expect in the exam papers

Let's have a look at each type of skill question in more detail:

All of these questions are in the specimen papers on the Edexcel website, so you can go and find them to see how they can be answered.

KNOWLEDGE RECALL QUESTIONS

For example: *Describe the activation-synthesis theory of dreaming.*

These types of question ask you to recall what you remember about a theory, study or issue. During the course, you have learnt about:

- psychological theories and studies
- key terms
- methodological issues
- ethical issues
- debates
- careers in psychology.

Any of these areas can be asked in a knowledge recall question. You will need to be ready to explain them or apply your knowledge of them.

EXPLANATION QUESTIONS

For example: *Explain why it might be difficult to find a link between genes and criminality.*

Rather than just remembering information about genes and criminality, this question asks you to use this knowledge to explain why it might be difficult to find a definite link between genes and criminality. Explaining involves justifying something. The exam paper will often set the scene for these types of questions with a short introductory passage about the topic.

'APPLYING' QUESTIONS

For example: *Sally has very disturbed nights during which she has vivid dreams. She is so tired she cannot concentrate properly at work. Explain how a sleep disorder clinic can help someone like Sally.*

Psychology is about real people, so being able to apply your knowledge to real situations is a key skill. You will find many applying questions throughout the exam and these can be MCQ, short or long answer questions.

The exam paper will often describe a situation or person to indicate that it is an applying question and encourage you to use your applying skills. A key point to remember is that simply recalling knowledge will not be enough for most applying questions. You must link your answer to the situation to gain marks.

MULTIPLE CHOICE QUESTIONS (MCQS)

MCQs might seem easy, but it is really important that you read the question carefully. MCQs can ask for knowledge, explanation or get you to apply your knowledge to a situation. You will be given a list of optional answers from which you need to select the right answer(s). You may have to pick one, two or more from the options, so make sure you read the instructions carefully.

THE EXAMS

You will sit **two exams**. Unit One is 40 per cent of the whole GCSE and Unit Two is worth 60 per cent as it is longer and has extended writing. Each exam paper covers the key topic questions one-by-one in the order they are in the specification, so you know what to expect.

In both exams the exam questions can draw on specific skills of knowledge recall, recognition and understanding as well as explaining, evaluating and applying your knowledge.

UNIT ONE

The Unit One exam is based on key topic questions A and B, looking at perception and dreaming. The exam is a mixture of multiple choice questions (MCQs) and short answer questions. Unit One has 60 marks and you have 75 minutes for the paper, so you should aim for one mark a minute plus some reading time.

UNIT TWO

The Unit Two exam is based on key topic questions C–E drawing on your knowledge of social and biological psychology (about violence, phobias and criminality).

The Unit Two exam is a little longer with some MCQs and short answer questions. You will find that some of the questions need a more detailed answer of up to around 10 marks (extended writing). Unit Two has 80 marks and you have 105 minutes, so again you should aim for a mark a minute plus some reading time.

Meet the exam paper

Below you can see the front cover of the exam paper. The instructions you can see will always appear on the front, but it is worth reading them carefully now to make sure you understand it.

Print your surname here and other names afterwards. This is used along with your candidate number to make sure you get all the marks you are entitled to.

Write the school's exam number in this box.

Make sure you understand how long the examination will last and allocate your time during the exam. Write down the time when you should be moving on to another section.

Write your personal exam number in this box. It is important to get it right so that the exam board knows who you are.

This box will be used by the examiner to write the total marks you get in the paper.

Read the instructions on which questions to answer very carefully. For psychology you will need to answer **ALL** questions.

Don't feel that you have to fill the answer space provided. Everybody's handwriting varies.

Write your name here
Surname   Other names

Centre Number   Candidate Number

Edexcel GCSE

Psychology
Unit 1: Perception and Dreaming

Sample Assessment Material
Time: 1 hour 15 minutes

Paper Reference
5PS01/01

You do not need any other materials.

Total Marks

Instructions

- Use **black** ink or ball-point pen.
- **Fill in the boxes** at the top of this page with your name, centre number and candidate number.
- Answer **all** questions.
- Answer the questions in the spaces provided
  – there may be more space than you need.

Information

- The total mark for this paper is 60.
- The marks for **each** question are shown in brackets
  – use this as a guide as to how much time to spend on each question.

Advice

- Read each question carefully before you start to answer it.
- Keep an eye on the time.
- Try to answer every question.
- Check your answers if you have time at the end.

Turn over ▶

N35617A
©2008 Edexcel Limited.
3/2

N 3 5 6 1 7 A 0 1 2 4

edexcel :::
advancing learning, changing lives

Edexcel GCSE in Psychology   Sample Assessment Materials   © Edexcel Limited 2008   3

This section provides answers to the most common questions students have about what happens after they complete their exams. For much more information, visit www.examzone.co.uk

What do I do after the exam?

It is tempting to talk to your friends after the exam and compare what you answered on different questions, but remember that once the session is over you can't change anything. Focus on any remaining exams you have to take and wait to see what results you get.

When will I get my results?

Results for January exams are available in March and results for May/June exams are available in August.

How will I receive my results?

Traditionally you will receive your results at school on a piece of paper or in an envelope. You might be able to access your results electronically, if so your school will inform you in advance.

What is ResultsPlus and how do I compare to others?

Results Plus is an Edexcel provision where you can compare your results with others and see how close you were to a different grade and how well you did on certain questions compared to everyone else taking the exam.

Visit **www.resultsplus.co.uk** for more information.

You can compare your results with those of others in the UK who have completed the same examination using the information on the Edexcel website at: **http://www.edexcel.org.uk/sfc/feschools/stats/**

What if I didn't do as well as I hoped?

First of all, talk to your teacher. They are the person who best knows what grade you are capable of achieving. Go through the information on your results slip in detail. If you both think that there is something wrong with the result, the school or college can apply to see your completed examination paper and then ask for a re-mark. The original mark can be confirmed or lowered, as well as raised, as a result of a re-mark.

I achieved a higher mark for the same unit last time. Can I use that result?

Yes. The higher score is the one that goes towards your overall grade. Even if you sat a unit more than twice,

the best result will be used automatically when the overall grade is calculated.

What happens if I was ill over the period of my examinations?

If you become ill before or during the examination period you are eligible for special consideration. This also applies if you have been affected by an accident, bereavement or serious disturbance during an examination.

Can I have a re-mark of my examination paper?

Yes, this is possible, but remember that only your school or college can apply for a re-mark, not you or your parents/carers. You should remember that very few re-marks result in a change to a grade - not because Edexcel is embarrassed that a change of marks has been made, but simply because a re-mark request has shown that the original marking was accurate. Check the closing date for re-marking requests with your Examinations Officer. There is no guarantee that your grades will go up if your papers are re-marked. They can also go down or stay the same. After a re-mark, the only way to improve your grade is to take the examination again. Your school or college Examinations Officer can tell you when you can do that.

Where can I find more information about my exams

For much more information, visit **www.examzone.co.uk**

Answers

Topic A

A1a1 How do we see?

Quick check questions

A Vision is the biological process of seeing. Perception is the psychological process of making sense of the visual image.

Summary questions

1 on the retina

2 nerve impulses (from the rods and cones)

3 (a) rods (b) cones

A1a2 The optic nerve and the brain

Quick check questions

A Because they are falling on the blind spot in your left eye

B Back (because that is where the visual cortex is)

Summary questions

1 cones (and rods)

2 the retina

3 (a) it disappears (b) they look complete (c) the brain

A1b1 Seeing depth

Quick check questions

A Binocular

B Monocular

Summary questions

1 binocular

2 monocular

3 (a) hitting a ball (b) both

A1b2 Depth and size

Quick check questions

A (i) The one in your hand would take up more space (ii) No (because of size constancy)

B You need surroundings to provide depth cues so that you can judge distance.

Summary questions

1 beside it

2 a) near b) scaled up because it will make a small image on the retina (because it is in the distance).

3 the image of her flake will be scaled down because it is near and will make a big image on the retina (so will be scaled down to make it look normal). The image of the boy's flake will be scaled up because it is in the distance and will make a small image on the retina (so will be scaled up to make it look normal).

A1b3 Monocular depth cues 1

Quick check questions

A The cars at the far side of the track should be smaller.

B The children who were closest would look higher.

C Lower (because it is closer to the horizon)

Summary questions

1 bigger

2 at the near end they would be clear and detailed. At the far end they would be less clear and less detailed.

3 a) they are further away (or smaller) b) they are little rabbits c) you would be able to see individual blades at your feet but not in the distance d) the ones furthest away.

A1b4 Monocular depth cues 2

Quick check questions

A The dog

B Narrower towards the house

Summary questions

1 linear perspective

2 superimposition

3
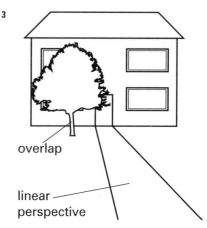
overlap

linear perspective

4 It is impossible because the depth cues contradict each other, e.g. the ladder overlaps the building at the top, so it ought to be at the front, but at the bottom the ladder is overlapped by the post so it must be at the back. It can't be both at the front and at the back.

A1b5 Stereopsis: seeing in stereo

Quick check questions

A Right

B The dolls' house

Summary questions

1 no

2 right-eye dominant

3 the cat

A1c1 Gestalt laws 1

Quick check questions

A The letters

B All the same kind

Summary questions

1 the dog

2 the ground

3 if they were all the same colour (or size or shape)

A1c2 Gestalt laws 2

Quick check questions

A The ones in a 'crocodile' would be grouped by continuity; the ones in clusters would be grouped by proximity

Summary questions

1 continuity

2 the piled-up ones (because of proximity)

3 an oval (because it is a regular, symmetrical figure)

A1d1 What are illusions?

Quick check questions

A A hexagon

B Red replaces green and green replaces red

Summary questions

1 fictions/ambiguous figures/distortions (or paradoxical figures)

2 a conflict between reality and what we perceive

3 a) green b) blue

4 answers will vary

A1d2 More illusions

Quick check questions

A

young woman	old woman
necklace	mouth
chin	nose
nose	wart on nose
right ear	left eye
neck	**chin**

B ambiguous figure

Summary questions

1 ambiguous figure

2 distortion illusion

3 having two possible interpretations

4 the ones shown pictures of animals

A1e1 The Gestalt theory of illusions

Quick check questions

A • figure/ground

• figure/ground

• closure

Summary questions

1 closure

2 it says we complete the edges to make a 'whole' – a regular or familiar shape

3 it says there are two possible ways the stimulus can be understood, as it can be organised into a figure in different ways (and/or because two parts of the stimulus can both be seen as either figure or ground).

A1e2 Gregory's perspective theory of illusions

Summary questions

1 It could be either. Gregory would say that the angled lines are interpreted as a three dimensional figure. The angled lines could point forwards or backwards.

2 It suggests that perception is learned (as the Zulu people have no experience of lines in order to learn linear perspective).

A1f1 Schemas and perception

Summary questions

1 a schema is a framework of knowledge about an object, event or group of people that can affect our perception and help us to organise information and recall what we have seen.

2 they would remember the calculator but not the apple (because you would expect to see a calculator in an office, but not an apple).

3 a kitchen schema (because saucepans belong in kitchens, so participants would have a framework in which to put the information).

4 a band (or orchestra)

A1f2 Bartlett (1932): schemas and remembering stories

Quick check questions

A All reproductions should be done after the same time delay.

Summary questions

1 a) form/detail/simplified/addition (accept 'stereotyped') b) form: once a story had a particular outline it sticks. Details: details change or are lost, e.g. names and numbers. If details are remembered, they become stereotyped. Over a very long time they are remembered if they fit with the participant's interests or expectations. Simplification: events are simplified and details are left out or made more familiar. This can change the meaning of the story. Addition: inaccurate details are added.

2 a task where the participant is given a story or picture to remember. They then recall it several times after time delays. Differences between each version are measured.

3 it could end up looking more like an owl/cat (accept any plausible suggestion). This would happen because it has: a face like an owl/a body like a cat.

A1f3 Carmichael et al (1932): do words affect recall?

Quick check questions

A For example, any one of the following:

• with snow on the top

• with grass at the bottom

• with jagged sides

Summary questions

1 the label 'flower' made their flower schema reconstruct their memory of the picture as a flower, so they drew it with petals. The label 'cup' made their cup schema reconstruct their memory of the picture as a cup, so they drew it with a saucer and handle.

2 answers will vary

3 any one of the following:

• Carmichael et al used a control group who did not hear any words so they could be sure that people's drawings weren't always distorted in the same way.

• They used two different lists, so it had to be the verbal labels that affected people's drawings.

• They had 12 pictures, lots of participants and two word lists, so they could be sure that the findings were not just a fluke.

• Recent evidence supports the idea that verbal labels affect memory (Lupyan, 2008).

A2a1 Designing and understanding experiments

Quick check questions

A His independent variable is whether they see duck ponds or fields of rabbits first; his dependent variable is whether they see a duck or a rabbit in the illusion.

B independent groups (because once they have seen the illusion it won't work again)

Summary questions

1 a) the size of the blind spot b) repeated measures

A2a2 More about experiments

Quick check questions

A The independent variable is whether they saw a priming picture of an old or a young woman. The dependent variable is whether they saw the young or old woman in the ambiguous figure.

B Similarity is more important than continuity (so participants will see one blue and one green line) or Continuity is more important than similarity (so participants will see a straight line and a wavy line).

C For example (one of):

• all the objects should be about the same size

• all the objects should be similar in shape, e.g. rectangular

• all the objects should be familiar (not unusual)

Summary questions

1 possible controls are: making the young and old woman equally clear/showing the priming pictures for the same length of time (accept not showing any priming pictures).

2 the independent variables are: context appropriate, inappropriate, similar object, inappropriate, different object or no context (accept matched context and object/unmatched context and object or kitchen scene/not kitchen scene). The dependent variables are: correct identification of the object (accept whether they recalled seeing the object). Objects are more likely to be correctly identified in an appropriate context than in an inappropriate one.

3 a) scenes – supermarket and classroom b) number of items of fruit and vegetables people can remember c) people will remember more items of fruit and vegetables if the context is a supermarket than if it is a classroom (accept reverse or two tailed). d) the scenes should be equally complex; there should be as many matching as unmatching items.

A2a3 Dealing with results: descriptive statistics

Quick check questions

A The mode is A.

B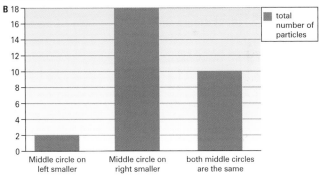

Summary questions

1 they are ways of summarising results from a study. They can show a typical or average score or how spread out the results are.

2 An average is a typical score or one that shows the middle of a set or scores

3 6

A2a4 Dealing with results: more descriptive statistics

Quick check questions

A • 122346678 The median is 4

• 1223456778 The median is 4+5/2= 4.5

B 7/10=0.7 so the mean is 0.7 seconds

C Biggest score =1.5, smallest score = 0.2, so the range is 1.5-0.2 seconds.

Summary questions

1 mode, median, mean

2 to see the spread of results

3 mode

A2b1 Ethics in psychology experiments

Quick check questions

A Right to withdraw

B Informed consent

C (i) an ethical committee at his place of work or, if there is not one, then his peers and colleagues (ii) because they have the right to know what they will have to do and what the results will be used for (iii) that they have the right to withdraw at any time (even if they have been paid to participate); that they will not be identified as individuals in the results.

Summary questions

1 a) informed consent, right to withdraw (accept confidentiality, conduct etc.)
  b) • informed consent: give full information, ask participants and/or their guardians
     • right to withdraw: make sure people know they can leave, offer them the chance to withdraw their data if they choose to leave.

2 Paid participants might feel that they have to participate even if they don't want to. The researcher should make very clear that they have the right to withdraw.

A2c1 Evaluating experiments

Summary questions

1 a) a strength b) yes

2 One of:
  • Palmer controlled how long participants saw the context and the object for, so the differences in accuracy were not caused by having longer to remember some objects.
  • it was good that the participants were given instructions so they knew exactly what they would be doing.

3 Any one of the following:
  • in real life, objects are not confusing – verbal clues generally match objects so the study was not very lifelike
  • verbal labels only seem to apply to recall not recognition, so the findings do not apply widely.

A3a1 Schemas and eyewitness memory

Quick check questions

A Because shouting fits the expectation/schema of being strict

Summary questions

1 someone who sees a crime or aspects of a crime scene, who then helps the police to find out what has happened in order to catch whoever was responsible.

2 stealing (because he has a schema for old people that includes information about them being crafty)

3 if the witness thought bikers were violent he or she might think the biker was joining in rather than trying to stop the fight.

Topic B

B1a1 Freud's (1900) dream theory

Quick check questions

A Because a patient could not remember the session and could not bring into consciousness what happened under hypnosis

B (i) the analyst (ii) Omar

C Displacement

Summary questions

1 condensation, displacement, secondary revision or secondary elaboration

2 • manifest content is the dreamwork – the story of the dream that the dreamer can tell.
  • latent content is the underlying meaning of the dream – hidden as symbols in the manifest content, showing unconscious wishes and desires.

3 The 'true' meaning of a dream is hard to uncover because of dreamwork. Condensation means more than one idea in the latent content shows up as one idea in the manifest content, hindering analysis. Secondary elaboration means things are added by the dreamer, hiding any latent content and adding 'irrelevant' material. Displacement means the analyst has to work hard to find the real focus.

B1a2 Symbols in dreams

Quick check questions

A Dreams often do not make sense so the person relating them has to add bits to the 'story' in order to be able to describe the dream.

B Because each dreamer's unconscious holds personal experiences and thoughts that are unique to themselves.

Summary questions

1 the manifest content is not what it seems but acts as symbols for the unconscious material. Things and people, including actions and emotions, are carefully considered to see what they may represent. Dream analysis involves decoding such signals. For example, falling down stairs may represent fear of succeeding in a job.

2 each person's unconscious is unique and their dreamwork is unique, so their symbols will mean different things. Common symbols are unlikely to be found.

3 once symbols are analysed and discussed with the patient then analysis becomes part of them and therefore part of their analysis and recovery. Analysis cannot be undone only to be done again.

B1a3 Analysing dreams

Quick check questions

A The patient talks freely to the analyst, either about dreams or other aspects of their life. What they say is analysed to reveal and release unconscious desires, hence the term 'talking cure'.

B Dream analysis, free association, slips of the tongue (Freudian slips).

Summary questions

1 psychoanalysis is the therapy Freud developed to help cure neuroses by using methods such as dream analysis to reveal harmful unconscious wishes.

2 to uncover unconscious wishes is difficult and needs careful analysis. This analysis is individual to the client so a thorough understanding is needed. To get a thorough understanding and a careful analysis, it is best to use more than one method of uncovering data.

3 free association can start from a symbol in the dream to uncover more about what it might mean.

B1a4 Evaluating Freud's dream theory

Quick check questions

A Qualitative data are detailed, in-depth and valid. They are detailed and in-depth because they are about stories, opinions and attitudes, rather than numbers. Valid means that they are about what they say they are about; in this case, the patient's real experiences, fears and desires.

B Subjective refers to research methods where the researcher is somehow affecting the results, perhaps by their interpretation. Objective means there is no bias, for example the researcher's own views have not affected the findings

Summary questions

1 (i) Freud developed unique research methods to uncover hard-to-reach material in the unconscious, using dream analysis as one of those methods. Other research methods would not have uncovered such data, so Freud's methods were necessary and useful. (ii) Freud used qualitative data and over time gathered a lot of detailed information from each patient. When he drew conclusions they were based on real-life data and so were valid.

2 (i) Freud studied middle-class Viennese women, so this was a specific sample and findings should not be generalised (said to be true of) everyone else. (ii) The unconscious cannot be tested directly, so Freud's theory about the unconscious cannot be tested scientifically or proven to be true.

3 Freud's theory of dreaming is unscientific because it is not generalisable. This means that the theory cannot easily be applied to everyone, as Freud mainly used middle-class Viennese women and could not say the findings were true of any other group of people. Freud had to interpret his information, meaning that his results were subjective, whereas science has to be objective. Freud's ideas were hard to test as the unconscious is not measurable and dreams are not testable, so it is hard to repeat his work to see if the findings were the same a second time. This means his findings could not be tested for reliability, so his view of dreaming as having meaning is not a scientific one.

B1b1 How the brain sends signals

Quick check questions

A Dendrites, cell body, axon, terminal branches, synaptic gap

Summary questions

1 any two from: axon, dendrites, terminal buttons, neurotransmitter, impulse, cell, or any other suitable feature or term including gap
or synapse

2 a) 3 b) 2 c) 1

B1c1 A biological theory of dreaming

Quick check questions

A Psychological is to do with the brain when thinking, showing emotions, being involved in perception (which includes biology). Biological is to do with physical aspects (which includes the brain). Showing emotions includes biological aspects, such as particular neurotransmitters, parts of the brain, hormones and so on, so there are often both biological and psychological aspects of the same issue.

B Sensory blockade means in REM sleep no information is coming into the brain from the outside world. Movement inhibition means in REM sleep muscles are paralysed and the body cannot move.

Summary questions

1 during REM sleep there is no information coming in from the senses (sensory blockade) and the body is paralysed and cannot move (movement inhibition). There is rapid eye movement where the eyelids can be seen to flicker very quickly. REM sleep occurs five or more times each night.

2 in REM sleep, dreaming takes place. There is no incoming information and the body cannot move. However, in the brain neurons are still randomly activated. The sleeping brain makes sense of the random fragments of thoughts and synthesizes them into a dream.

3 The activation-synthesis theory of dreaming suggests that dreaming is purely biological and relates to how the brain works, whereas Freud's theory of dreaming is psychological because it looks at wishes and desires and how dreams can reveal such desires.

B1c2 Evaluating activation-synthesis theory

Quick check questions

A If everyone has experienced dreaming then a biological explanation seems likely. This is because nature (biology) is similar for everyone, whereas nurture (social conditioning) differs. So when something happens to everyone, it is likely to have a biological (nature) explanation.

B The theory says that there is no physical movement during REM sleep which helps to explain random activation of thoughts and the synthesis of these thoughts. So, if those parts of the brain are working at the time there is evidence for the theory.

Summary questions

1 cats were studied and showed activity in areas of the brain that would shut down physical movements, which Hobson and McCarley linked with their theory, saying that there was muscle paralysis during REM sleep. Another reason is that when neurons activated during dreaming were in the area where movement would be found, the dream was about movement such as falling.

2 in REM sleep there is muscle paralysis (movement inhibition) and sense data does not arrive at the brain (sensory blockade). The brain is not actively working as when the person is awake, but neurons are still active and the brain makes sense of this activity as it would during the day. Areas activated during REM sleep include the pons and the reticular activating system, which are to do with shutting down physical movements, linking to the idea of movement inhibition.

3 Hobson and McCarley found a way of explaining why everyone dreams by using evidence from animals to support their ideas about which parts of the brain are activated during REM sleep. However, animals (e.g. cats) are not exactly the same as humans so their evidence cannot be generalised. They offer an alternative to Freud's ideas about the meaning of dreams.

B1d1 Comparing dream theories

Quick check questions

A Freud's methods are more subjective as they involve interpretation but Hobson and McCarley use more objective methods as Freud used case studies and Hobson and McCarley used animal experiments.

B Nature refers to biological aspects of the person and nurture refers to environmental effects. The debate concerns whether nature or nurture affects human development.

Summary questions

1 activation-synthesis theory

2 Hobson and McCarley's theory is biological and says that dreaming is part of sleeping, relating to brain activity during REM sleep. This is about nature and what people are born like. Freud's theory has an element of nature because he says that a large part of everyone's mind is unconscious and hard to uncover. However, Freud's theory is also about nurture because experiences in the environment that are hard to deal with are what are in the unconscious, and make up the content of a dream.

3 Freud's theory uses dream analysis and free association whereas Hobson and McCarley's theory uses scanning and experiments. Hobson and McCarley's theory is objective and scientific because of the methodology and the biological concepts. Freud's theory is not scientific because the concepts are not measurable (e.g. the unconscious) and also because there is a lack of objectivity. Freud's theory lacks credibility compared with the activation-synthesis theory.

B2a1 Using case studies

Quick check questions

A Case studies are about gathering in-depth detailed data, so they have to cover a lot of ground. One way to do this is to use different research methods, e.g. interviews for depth and questionnaires for quantity of information. Other statistics can add to the information, such as exam results or IQ test results.

B Qualitative data are obtained by using open questions, so they involve opinions or attitudes. Quantitative data are gathered by asking closed questions, where the answers are limited and can only generate numbers or statistics.

Summary questions

1 case studies usually involve one unique individual as a participant. They involve gathering in-depth and detailed data, often using more than one research method. In-depth detail means from many different aspects and more than one research method means interviews, observation and case history, for example.

2 qualitative data are about quality and unique detail whereas quantitative data are about quantity and numbers, not individual detail.

3 an aim is an idea of what is hoped to be achieved from research in answer to a general question; a hypothesis is a statement of what is expected to be found.

B2a2 Weaknesses of case studies

Quick check questions

A To build a body of knowledge it is important to have data that are going to occur more than once and can be relied upon. If a study has flaws then the results will not be reliable.

B a) reliability   b) generalisability   c) objectivity

Summary questions

1 generalisability means that results from a study can be said to apply to other people as well as those involved in the study. Reliability means that if a study is done again the same results are found. Subjectivity means that the researcher has affected the results because of their own opinions.

2 • lacks generalisability because it is a study of one unique individual (or small group), so the information gathered from one situation might not apply to others.
  • might not be reliable. It is hard to repeat a case study to see if the same information is found.
  • can be subjective, because the researcher needs to carry out interpretation of data.

B2a3 Designing case studies

Quick check questions

A Because dreams cannot be measured, so experiments cannot be done. Dreaming is also personal and subjective, so case studies can uncover valid information.

Summary questions

1 • Research methods used, to ensure data are detailed an in-depth.
  • How to avoid subjectivity. If there is bias then the findings are not scientific.
  • How to find the participant and how to get their permission.

2 validity is when data are real life and not artificial

3 case studies are rich and detailed and gather a lot of data for analysis. They are also a good way of uncovering personal and subjective information which is hard to gather any other way.

B2b1 Ethics and case studies

Quick check questions

A To maintain confidentiality and privacy

Summary questions

1 privacy is a guideline so people are not identified. Confidentiality (keeping names and places secret) is part of privacy.

2 participants must be protected, partly to make sure psychological studies do not get a bad name otherwise people would refuse to take part, and partly because being tested about personal issues can be upsetting. Participants' privacy must be protected to ensure that people's views remain private. Confidentiality is essential to ensure that the participant's identity remains concealed.

3 Genie's father had committed suicide but her mother and the rest of the family could have been identified and affected by the study and the situation.

B2d1 Freud's case study of Little Hans

Quick check questions

A The conscious is the part of the mind that is known about and can be accessed. The unconscious part of the mind is hidden and not directly accessible, but it plays an important part in what we think and do.

B The Oedipus complex is about a little boy wanting to possess his mother and transferring sexual attention to her. He feels guilt at wanting to take his father's place and so identifies with (becomes) his father to solve the complex (problem).

Summary questions

1 Little Hans's identity was protected, as was his family's, by giving him a false name.

2 Freud had letters and conversations with Little Hans's father as well as comments the father passed on from Little Hans himself.

3 the giraffe dream was where Little Hans saw a big giraffe and a crumpled giraffe. The big giraffe was shouting at Little Hans for taking the crumpled giraffe away.

4 Freud thought that the big giraffe represented Little Hans's father and was shouting because in real life Little Hans's father shouted at Little Hans for getting into his parent's bed in the mornings. The crumpled giraffe was Little Hans's mother. Freud also thought that the big giraffe was a penis. The analysis showed that Little Hans desired his mother sexually, feared his father, and to overcome his fears and guilt became his father so that he could possess his mother without fear.

B2d2 Evaluating dream analysis

Quick check questions

A Unconscious thoughts are hard to reach because they are inaccessible and hidden deliberately

B Objectivity

C False memory is a memory that is not true and can be given by someone 'remembering' an event and then telling another person, who then 'remembers' it as true.

Summary questions

1 a strength of dream analysis is that it is a unique way of uncovering unconscious desires that 'leak out' during dreaming. However, dream analysis is not a good method because there is a lot of interpretation involved. Someone else might interpret dreams in a different way so the results are not really reliable.

B3a1 The job of a psychoanalyst

Quick check questions

A Listens and observes carefully to gather information. Uses both verbal and non-verbal communication to gain insight into emotions, then offers suggestions to help explain to the client what they have observed.

B The client talks about themselves, their dreams and their concerns, with the psychoanalyst observing and listening. At some stage the analyst will suggest explanations and interpretations.

C In general dream analysis is used in psychotherapy in approximately 50% of cases, though not all the time in those cases. 17% never use dream analysis and only 9% use it often, according to a recent survey.

Summary questions

1 the client discusses dreams with the psychoanalyst, who then interprets the manifest content to find the latent content and unconscious thoughts. The manifest content is symbolic and the symbols must be decoded to uncover meaning, which is what the psychoanalyst does.

2 dream analysis is not used by every psychoanalyst with every client. The client is more likely to bring their dreams into the analysis than the psychoanalyst is to ask about their dreams.

3 clients need to accept the analysis offered to them because they have to make unconscious thoughts conscious in order to release them. If they do not accept the suggestions about the content of their unconscious, this material will not be released into the conscious.

B3a2 Becoming a psychoanalyst

Quick check questions

A Skills needed would include:

- good listening skills so that the client is heard without interpretation
- recording information in detail including evidence of emotions
- ability to remain detached to be able to analyse without their own emotions affecting the analysis.

B There is no regulation to stop someone calling themselves a psychoanalyst. In practice clients should ask about qualifications to check on an analysts's credentials.

Summary questions

1 evidence of continuing professional development is required to show ethical procedures are being followed and that the psychoanalyst is keeping up with new developments in the field.

2 a psychoanalyst should be fully trained through a recognized course and should have undergone the required amount of psychoanalysis themselves. The training lasts four years. Usually only someone with previous academic qualifications or experience would be accepted onto a course.

3 a good psychoanalyst would be a good listener with problem-solving skills. They would be patient and able to work with powerful emotional problems whilst dealing with transference and counter-transference, for example. They would also be able to be open to the views or data coming from the client and the analysis.

B3b1 Psychological sleep disorders

Quick check questions

A Primary sleep disorders are problems in themselves and not related to any other problem, such as problems going to sleep. Secondary sleep disorders are problems with sleeping that are caused by some other problem, such as pain or stress.

B The sleep-wake cycle is over 24 hours and around 8 hours will involve sleep. The sleep cycle is the approximate 8 hours of sleep and refers to the different stages of sleep over that period.

Summary questions

1 hypersomnia and circadian rhythm disorders

2 insomnia means not getting to sleep or not being able to stay asleep. Parasomnia means a problem whilst asleep, for example nightmares or sleepwalking.

3 a psychological sleep disorder involves the brain and mind and not just physical issues such as snoring. Problems during the sleep cycle are psychological ones, such as REM sleep behaviour disorder (RBD) or narcolepsy.

B3b2 Sleep disorder clinics

Quick check questions

A A sleep disorder clinic assesses the problem and then treats it

B Hypnotherapy, acupuncture, cognitive behavioural therapy, medication

Summary questions

1 an automatic negative thought could be 'I don't get enough sleep at night'.

2 cognitive behavioural therapy involves changing thinking patterns. The idea is that negative thinking is the reason for a problem such as a sleep disorder, so by changing the way a patient thinks the problem can be alleviated. For example, if a patient thinks they need eight hours sleep a night but only get six hours, they will think they have a sleep problem. But if they think that six hours is enough the problem is erased.

3 a sleep disorder clinic can observe periods of rapid eye movement and take temperatures and other measures so that a picture can be built up of the individual's 'problem'. Then treatment can be planned such as medication (for narcolepsy, perhaps) or CBT (for insomnia if caused by anxiety or depression).

4 hypnotherapy involves hypnosis, which can be seen as very deep relaxation. In this state suggestions can be made to the client to solve problems, and issues can be raised to see if anxiety or stress is causing the problem in the first place.

Topic C

C1a1 The role of the brain and aggression

Quick check questions

A The role of the limbic system is to produce and control aggression to aid survival

B The amygdala recognises emotion and produces emotional responses. It is also involved in aggression as an emotional response.

C Charles Whitman or King's (1961) study of a woman who had her amgydala stimulated during an operation.

D Animals are different to humans, so research into animals may not apply in the same way to humans.

Summary questions

1 the limbic system contains a number of structures that control and produce emotion. The amygdala is said to produce aggression.

2 animal studies, for example, suggest that damage to the amygdala lowers aggression. Human studies show that damage or stimulation of the amygdala produces aggression.

3 animal studies may not apply to humans. Human studies are one-off cases. These might not apply to everyone.

C1a2 The role of hormones and aggression

Quick check questions

A A hormone is a chemical produced by the body that sends messages to organs around the body via the bloodstream.

B Testosterone is responsible for producing male features and the development of the male reproductive system.

C In human studies, psychologists have measured levels of testosterone and asked the participants how aggressive they are in a questionnaire. In animals, psychologists have lowered testosterone through castration and/or given animals injections of the hormone.

Summary questions

1 high levels of male testosterone has been linked to self-reported levels of aggression in boys. Animals that have been castrated show reduced signs of aggression. But if given testosterone injections, these animals show increased aggression once again.

2 the biggest problem in human research is that we cannot be sure whether testosterone causes aggression or aggression causes increased testosterone. Psychologists cannot directly manipulate the level of testosterone in males and study its effects, so they rely on animal studies that may not apply to humans, or correlation studies which may not be proof of a link between testosterone and aggression.

C1a3 Social learning theory

Quick check questions

A Identification is when we adopt the values and behaviour of a role model that we see as similar to ourselves. We believe we can be like them.

B Vicarious reinforcement is when we observe others being rewarded for their behaviour. It motivates us to copy the role model so we believe we will get the same rewards.

Summary questions

1 Alex watched his favourite superheroes on TV. He liked the way they behaved and remembered their special moves. He dressed up like his heroes because he identified with being strong and saving people. He wanted to be a hero himself. He copied their moves and ran around the house imitating their behaviour from TV. This is known as observational learning, as Alex modelled the behaviour of cartoon characters.

2 it offers an explanation for real-life tragedies such as high-school shootings.

3 an alternative explanation is that aggressive children seek out aggressive TV, so TV is not the cause of aggression itself.

C1b1 Comparing theories of aggression

Quick check questions

A Nature is how behaviour is determined by what we inherit – our biology.

B Nurture is how behaviour is determined by how we are raised – our family, environment and upbringing.

Summary questions

1 biological explanations are on the nature side of the nature-nurture debate because they say that aggression comes from within the person. Social learning theory is on the nurture side of the debate because it says that aggression is learnt from the environment around us – the programmes and games we watch and play.

2 one difference between the two theories is that the biological theory focuses on a physical cause and the social learning theory focuses of an external/environmental cause.

3 one similarity between the theories is that it is difficult to prove each one. The human brain is difficult or unethical to study for aggression centres, and the social learning theory is difficult to measure because of a time lapse between observation and learning.

C1b2 Ramirez et al (2001): culture and aggression

Quick check questions

A Likert-style questions

Summary questions

1 to see if there were gender and cultural differences in aggression

2 this study tells us that men are more aggressive than females in both cultures.

3 Spanish people are more verbally aggressive and Japanese more physically aggressive (despite the stereotype!)

C2a1 Content analysis as a research method

Quick check questions

A Content analysis is a research method used to measure the number of times something comes up in a book, newspaper article, television programme etc.

B (i) a) hitting over the head with a hammer, dynamite exploding, being run over. Answers will vary.
b) kicking, punching, tripping, shouting. Answers will vary.

(ii)

Aggressive act	Tally for each time it is seen
kicking	
punching	
tripping	

C Reliability refers to the consistency of the findings of a study. Can it be trusted to happen the same way again?

Summary questions

1 make a list of stereotyped and non-stereotyped behaviours that a teenager would display. Decide what was stereotypical of teenagers. Select a good range of newspapers. Construct a tally chart of the different categories of behaviour. Read the newspapers and tally each time a teenager fitted into one of the behaviour categories on the tally chart. Count up the number of tallies and draw a conclusion.

2 girls' toys would be dolls, household items such as a cooker, iron and vacuum cleaner, picnic sets. Boys' toys would be soldiers, cars, trucks and tools.

3 each researcher has a different viewpoint about boys and girls toys and therefore might come to different conclusions from their tallies.

C2b1 The ethics of psychological research

Quick check questions

A Sometimes it is not possible to inform participants because telling them the whole truth may affect their behaviour. They may not act naturally and the findings of the study would then be useless.

B Participants should give their permission to take part in the study and, where possible, be informed of the true aim of the study. Participants should not be lied to about any part of the study unless absolutely necessary, as it means they cannot give informed consent and do not really know what they are taking part in.

C Informed consent; deception; protection of participants.

Summary questions

1 ethical guidelines are important to protect participants from being harmed, humiliated, lied to or constrained by being part of a study.

2 protection of participants means that psychological research must not physically or psychologically harm a participant as part of a study.

3 participants could be better protected by asking professional advice from other people to get their opinion about the ethics of the study and the impact upon the participants involved.

C2c1 Anderson and Dill (2000): video games and aggression

Quick check questions

A The *independent variable* was the type of game played. The researchers controlled this by getting some participants to play either a violent or non-violent game – specifically Myst or Wolfenstein 3D.

B The *dependent variable* was the level of aggression. This was recorded by the loudness and length of noise blast that participants gave to their opponent after winning a reaction test.

C Video games have become increasingly more realistic, graphic and interactive. Players become more involved in gaming and are able to personalise characters. This may lead to increased levels of aggression as players are less able to distinguish fantasy from reality, or it could lower aggressions as players are able to act out during the game rather than in reality.

Summary questions

1 Participants did not know that they were giving blasts of noise to an opponent that did not really exist. They were also deceived to believe that the study was a measure of reaction time when it was really a study of aggression.

2 If participants were told the true study aim they may have behaved differently. They could have given louder blasts of noise as they would know they were not really harming someone, or give lower blasts of noise because they would not wish to appear aggressive.

3 One weakness of this study is that people do not normally play video games in a cubicle; they play at home and know they are not being watched. This study lacks realism.

C2c2 Charlton (2000): St Helena study

Quick check questions

A questionnaire/content analysis/observation (discreet cameras and observations in a playground)

B Charlton found that television aggression did not make the children more aggressive.

C • *questionnaire strength* – you can uncover people's views about how aggressive children have become and how much children they watch
- *questionnaire weakness* – respondents may lie
- *content analysis strength* – good for finding out how much aggression children watch by analysing content of TV programmes – this can be correlated with children's behaviour
- *content analysis weakness* – the researchers can chose a biased sample making the findings unrepresentative of all programmes a children might have watched
- *observation strength* – children's behaviour can be directly measured without relying on other people's views, and they are usually done in a child's natural environment
- *observation weakness* – children may change their behaviour if they know they are being watched (secret cameras are good for controlling this but it might be considered unethical to watch someone without their permission)

D St Helena was very remote, whereas your community is likely to be very well connected to others. The St Helena community watched over their children very closely but in your community you probably do not know everyone who lives there.

Summary questions

1 Charlton wanted to find out if television had an impact on children's behaviour; whether it would make them more aggressive.

2 it was conducted in a real place under real conditions and not in a laboratory. This means the findings are realistic.

3 the children may have been more aggressive, but parents and teachers did not report this because they did not want to portray a negative image of the island.

C2c3 Williams et al (1981): does TV affect children's behaviour?

Quick check questions

A Observations of children's behaviour, questionnaires, intelligence, reading and creativity tests

B They are more realistic because the experimenter has not set up the independent variable, it is naturally occurring. This means that it is not artificial to the participants of the study.

Summary questions

1 so the children were familiar with their presence in the classroom and would begin to behave more naturally than if they had started recording on the first day

2 Notel was on the mainland and not isolated from popular culture – this change in culture could explain increased aggression

3 the study findings could be explained by the location of each study. St Helena is remote and isolated from popular culture with a very close-knit community, unlike Notel. The parents and residents of Notel were less likely to be under constant supervision of their children. This could explain why the children of Notel were influenced by television and the children of St Helena were not (because they were not allowed).

C3a1 Comparing Charlton et al (2000) and Williams et al (1981)

Quick check questions

A Real-life research is important because it shows us how people behave normally. In a natural environment they behave naturally, so the findings of the study are real.

B In natural settings, psychologists cannot control every factor. They might not measure things that are important. They could miss something crucial, such as the influence of other children on the aggression displayed by a child.

C a prime minister may suggest local community programmes such as youth clubs, sports and arts so that community adults get to know and can monitor the children's behaviour and reduce aggression.

Answers

Summary questions

1 St Helena was cut off from the mainland and Notel was not. Notel was a small community, still influenced by mainland culture. St Helena had developed a very isolated and close community.

2 St Helena watched and controlled the children of the island more closely than Notel. The island children were not able to develop aggression because they knew they would be watched.

3 no, we cannot be sure TV makes children aggressive. The children of Notel could have become aggressive for many other reasons. The children of St Helena might have been more aggressive but parents and teachers did not report this. There are many other factors that affect aggression. Biological factors like testosterone and the amygdala could make someone aggressive. Life experiences and other people might also play a role. We cannot be sure that TV is entirely responsible.

C3b1 The job of the educational psychologist

Quick check questions

A They use different methods to get an overall picture of the child and the situation. This is important as many factors are likely to be involved, and the Ed Psych needs to address the whole situation.

Summary questions

1 an Ed Psych could undertake research in a school such as to look at how special needs children are treated by other children. Or they may be involved in diagnosing a problem (such as disruptive behaviour) and planning an intervention.

2 Planning an intervention (for example): interventions are important because diagnosing a problem does not help the situation or the child, whereas planning a solution is useful and more likely to lead to a successful outcome for the child and teacher (or others involved). This is an interesting part of the job as it is solution focused and would be why someone became an educational psychologist – to help children to reach their potential. Also a teacher involved in an intervention might then treat the child and other children using that plan as well, which might help the other children if they are having problems too.

C3b2 Becoming an educational psychologist

Quick check questions

A Working for a local authority in a full-time job; working for an independent school in the role of special needs co-ordinator

B It means they have satisfied the requirements of the BPS (British Psychological Society).

Summary questions

1 psychology degree and doctorate in Educational Psychology

2 communication is the main skill required, as listening is very important. The Ed Psych has to be able to communicate with children of all ages including lively five-year-olds and shy seventeen-year-olds. He or she also has to be able to communicate well with parents, teachers and other professionals. There needs to be trust, which requires good communication skills, and empathic listening.

C3b3 Educational psychology and anger management

Quick check questions

A The observation helps to gather first hand information on which to base an intervention and means valid data

B The Ed Psych wants to know all the background detail because he or she is looking to see what triggers any angry outburst and the trigger could be in any part of the child's eye. So the Ed Psych asks about the family, home life, the child's likes and dislikes, for example.

Summary questions

1 • identifying how their body feels before an outburst
  • looking at what makes them angry so that they can avoid such situations or learn to deal with them using relaxation techniques to calm them down before an outburst occurs

2 they are asked to keep a detailed record, not of the incident itself so much as of what happened during the day. They are also asked to talk about their views of the child, such as whether they can tell straight away if it is going to be a bad day with that child.

3 the Ed Psych will start by observing the child and the classroom behaviour. They will ask the teacher to keep detailed records as well using a form to ask about environment and other issues. They will ask the child's parents to come into the school for a meeting so that they can find out the parents' views and find out background information such as what the child is like at home. They might make a home visit so that parents are on their own territory, for example, and to observe what happens in the home and what the child is like there. They might refer the child for further diagnosis, depending on what the initial information suggests.

C4a1 Introducing censorship and the 9 o'clock watershed

Quick check questions

A • military censorship
  • moral censorship
  • political censorship

B There has to be no bad language and nudity must not be in a sexual context. Other possible answers include that there is not much kissing and if there is mild violence there is no emphasis on realistic weapons or dangerous behaviour.

Summary questions

1 censorship means information is not allowed to be communicated in some form or for some reason, which can be moral, political, or military, for example.

2 a film censor would not only consider how much violence is in a film but what type of violence and, importantly, what the consequences of the violence are for the person carrying it out. For example, U categorisation means any consequences are satisfactory and pleasant. The amount of sex from kissing to more intimate detail is also considered.

3 Different cultures will censor different things depending on cultural norms. For example, displays of nudity might be considered totally unacceptable in one country but acceptable in another country. Censorship creates problems with freedom of speech as governments in many countries censor what is broadcast. North Korea is one country where censorship is strictly in force. There are no independent journalists there as the government controls all media in order to dictate what is communicated.

C4a2 For and against censorship and the watershed

Quick check questions

A Content analysis involves counting whilst observing and what is counted is going to be very important. Often acts that are observed are hard to define, for example, deciding what would count as a violent act. So one person might count a different number of acts than another person. So the data would be unreliable. If what is observed is not violence in some way, then the data would also not be valid.

B • in favour: 95% of adults and 72% of children said there should be a watershed to protect children from seeing certain acts on TV.
  • against: 89% said they should have the freedom to choose what to watch and 82% wanted to watch the whole film as long as it was later than 10 p.m.

Summary questions

1 • to protect children so that they do not see violent or sexual acts that they might copy
  • most people (adults and children) want there to be a watershed so it is by public demand

2 • it restricts freedom of speech, which is a valued part of many societies
  • it restricts people's right to do what they want to do in society, which means there is government control, which could work against society's members

3 content analysis is one method but setting up the categories can be subjective. Also, two people may not count the same behaviours so the method can be both unreliable and not valid. Questionnaires can lead to people saying what they think they should say (social desirability) and also what they say one day may be different another day (which means the method is unreliable). Experiments like Bandura's can lack validity because they are controlled and the behaviour is set up (unnatural).

Topic D

D1a1 Classical conditioning and phobias

Quick check questions

A Before conditioning:
  • *NS* footsteps → no effect
  • *UCS* food → *UCR* salivate
  During conditioning:
  • *NS* footsteps + *UCS* food → *UCR* salivate
  After conditioning:
  • *CS* footsteps → *CR* salivate

B Albert wasn't afraid of the rat (NS) but was afraid of the noise (UCR). When the noise was paired with the rat, an association was formed and he learned to be afraid (CR) of the rat (CS).

Summary questions

1 conditioned stimulus (CS)

2 when a conditioned response is produced to stimuli that are similar to the conditioned stimulus

3 Before conditioning:
  • *NS* lizard → no effect
  • *UCS* startle → *UCR* fear
  During conditioning:
  • *NS* lizard + *UCS* startle → *UCR* fear
  After conditioning:
  • *CS* lizard → *CR* fear

D1a2 Social learning theory and phobias

Quick check questions

A • Always stop at the curb when they are with the child (so the child can observe the parent stopping). Always look for traffic and then when it is clear walk across (so the child can observe the parent walking not running). Then the child will copy and learn to stop and walk across the road.

Summary questions

1 • if they are the same sex (e.g. boy imitating dad), because they are powerful/high status
 • because they are liked

2 when a role model is observed to be rewarded for a behaviour, the observer is more likely to imitate them

3 Garry will observe his dad's reaction and imitate it. His dad is the same sex as Garry/ powerful/liked so is likely to be imitated. Garry may be vicariously reinforced if his dad is relieved/satisfied if he waves his arms or shouts and the cows go away.

D1a3 Phobias and preparedness

Quick check questions

A dogs

Summary questions

1 rats

2 wind might cause a lot of damage (especially to early human's houses or food supply) and people could be harmed, e.g. by falling trees.

3 because it must have been possible for early humans who were more likely to learn to get scared of dangerous things to pass on their fear to their children. (This is how natural selection works; the ones that didn't pass on the genes must die out. If it was learned socially, the non-related ones, who didn't have the genes, would also learn to be afraid and survive. This isn't what has happened.)

D1b1 The nature-nurture debate

Quick check questions

A Yes

B Yes

C (i) Betty and Barney's children may have inherited a tendency to be scared from their parents
 (ii) Betty and Barney's children may have learned to fear cats by observing and imitating their parents' behaviour.

Summary questions

1 nature = biological factors, such as genes, that affect our development
 nurture = environmental factors, such as observing models, that affect our development

2 Curio showed that monkeys learn to fear harmless birds through social learning. Monkeys are like people so we probably learn like this too. (Accept Bandura if used to say children can pick up other responses through observation). Watson and Rayner (1920) made Albert scared of a rat using classical conditioning.

3 no

4 nature – because evolution has selected people who can learn fears
 nurture – because it has made us more able to learn

D2a1 Questionnaires

Quick check questions

A Examples:
 – Do you watch TV every night? yes/no
 – How many hours of TV do you watch a night: 0–1, 2–3, 4 or more?

B Examples:
 – Describe a violent TV programme you have enjoyed.
 – Explain why you think violence on TV is a bad thing.

C Examples:
 – Please give each of the video games below a number from 1 to 3 to say which you think is most violent (1 = least violent, 3 = most violent)
 'Chop Till You Drop' ☐
 'MadWorld' ☐
 'Manhunt' ☐
 – Please say which view best expresses your view about age certificates on films
 • I think they should be abandoned ☐
 • I think they should be raised so younger children can view more ☐
 • I think they are about right ☐
 • I think the ages should be raised so only older children can see most films ☐

D Examples:
 • The watershed should start at 10pm: strongly agree agree undecided disagree strongly disagree
 • The watershed is unnecessary: strongly agree agree undecided disagree strongly disagree
 • The watershed protects children: strongly agree agree undecided disagree strongly disagree
 • Parents should monitor viewing, not the state: strongly agree agree undecided disagree strongly disagree

Summary questions

1 Examples:
 a i) Did you dream last night? ii) How many times do you dream a night on average?
 b i) Describe a dream you have had recently

ii) How do you feel when you have had a nice dream?
 c i) Would you say your dreams were generally: wonderful / very nice / okay / a bit unpleasant / very unpleasant.
 ii) Rate your most recent dream on a scale of 1–10 for excitement (10 = most exciting).
 d i) Dreams are important to me:
 • strongly agree, agree, undecided, disagree, strongly disagree
 ii) Dreaming is a waste of time:
 • strongly agree, agree, undecided, disagree, strongly disagree

2 a) i) Count up the number of 'yes' and 'no' answers. (Work out a mode.)
 ii) Count up the number of people who said 0/1/2/3/4 etc. (Work out a mode/ put them in order and find median/ calculate mean.)
 b) i) and ii) Look for patterns or similarities between people's descriptions / find a typical example.
 c) i) Count up the number of wonderful / very nice / okay / a bit unpleasant / very unpleasant answers. (Work out a mode.)
 ii) Count up the number of people saying 1/2/3 etc. (Work out a mode/put them in order and find the median/calculate the mean.)
 d) i) Count up the number of people saying strongly agree/agree etc. Give them a number, e.g. strongly agree = 5, agree = 4. Use the numbers the other way round for the second question, i.e. strongly disagree = 5, disagree = 4. Work out a total for each person (Put the totals in order and find median/ calculate mean).

D2b1 Evaluating questionnaires

Quick check questions

A Any difference, for example more worried about mentioning/not mentioning violence

B If unaware of the aims a parent might give a more accurate answer than if they knew what the questionnaire was about (because of social desirability).

Summary questions

1 weakness

2 when participants give the answers they think will be acceptable to people to make themselves look better

3 the participants only saw either questionnaire 1 or questionnaire 2, so they were less likely to guess the aims so this couldn't have affected their answers.

4 they only asked about six features and other things such as hairiness also made animals seem scary.

D2c1 Experiments using animals: ethical issues

Quick check questions

A Made them afraid

B Hamsters – because they are solitary

Summary questions

1 minimising the amount of pain and fear

2 keeping an animal on its own

3 robins, as they are solitary most of the year anyway so will suffer less than sparrows, which are social

D2d1 Experiments using animals: practical issues

Quick check questions

A Rabbits (because they are mammals like us)

Summary questions

1 Examples: where the participant is/how much they can move around/food/social partners/sexual partners/light

2 Monkeys – because they are more like humans than mice (primates/closer in evolutionary terms)

3 Coombes et al – injecting a drug that makes you sick should not be done on people because it would be unpleasant

D2e1 Jones (1924): curing a boy's phobia

Quick check questions

A Any one of: fur coat/fur rug/cotton/feathers

Summary questions

1 conditioning (accept systematic desensitisation) and social learning/modelling

2 that they were good models (for not being afraid)/because they were the same age as Peter so were good role models

3 Because adults are powerful models (so seeing and imitating her behaviour would have made him more scared)

D2e2 Bennett-Levy and Marteau (1984): fear of animals

Quick check questions

A Yes (because there were about the same number of each sex)

B Any three from: a jellyfish has tentacles, a cat doesn't/a cat has legs, a jellyfish doesn't/a cat has eyes, a jellyfish doesn't/a cat has ears, a jellyfish doesn't/a cat has bones (so is solid), a jellyfish isn't

Answers

Summary questions
1 • ugliness
  • sliminess
  • how speedy they were
  • how suddenly they moved
2 because they: are more different from humans/have no legs/have no head-neck-body/ are slimy/are ugly
3 e.g. spider: more legs than a person, ugly, speedy, moves suddenly. Answers will vary.

D3a1 How to treat phobias
Quick check questions

A Flooding involves the client being immersed in their phobia, for example someone with a phobia of spiders being in a room full of spiders. The idea is that the patient's arousal levels will be very high but the energy in their body will gradually go, so they feel calmer. They then should associate calm with the phobic object instead of fear. So someone with a phobia of dogs could be left in a room with a dog until the person's fear subsides and they start to feel safe.

B A patient could learn to feel comfortable looking at a picture of a small spider, then a larger picture. Then a small real spider could be placed in the room but not close to the patient, then once the patient was comfortable the spider could be brought closer. A larger spider could then be placed in the room and moved nearer once the patient became comfortable with it, eventually even ending up on the person's hand.

Summary questions
1 after learning some relaxation techniques he could be exposed to low anxiety situations with water, building up to high anxiety situations. Tom might be anxious to begin with but would calm down.
2 flooding works by getting the patient to confront their fear directly and getting them to associate their fear or phobia with relaxation. If a person can become relaxed around the feared object then they will lose their anxiety, as we cannot be relaxed and anxious at the same time.
3 systematic desensitisation also involves being exposed to the feared object but it is done in a more gradual way than flooding. Tom would develop a hierarchy of fears with a therapist, listing his least and most feared situations associated with water. The therapist would introduce the lowest level of fear and Tom would use the relaxation techniques he had been taught to deal with the situation. Tom would move up his hierarchy of fears once he felt relaxed at each level, until he reached and overcame his most feared situation.

D3b1 The ethics of therapies used to treat phobias
Quick check questions

A It can be harmful to withdraw from flooding if the person has not reached the stage of relaxation because they would still be extremely distressed, so their learning would be that their phobic situation or object is very distressing.

B Systematic desensitisation is more ethical than flooding because the client has more control over the process. They set up the hierarchy themselves and control their relaxation.

Summary questions
1 the therapist might use systematic desensitisation. Michael would be helped to relax and first be shown a small picture of a worm, then a bigger picture, then a worm the other side of the room. At each stage the therapist would help Michael to stay relaxed. Eventually the worm would be placed close to him, then in his hand. These are the stages on the anxiety hierarchy. Alternatively, the therapist might use flooding which would involve exposing Michael to worms close-up straight away and keeping him in that situation until he had stopped being scared.
2 systematic desensitisation might be easier for Michael as the hierarchy will be agreed between him and the therapist, so he has more control. Also the therapy will be progressive so is less frightening and he can choose to stop at any time without risking making his phobia worse. Michael might find flooding very frightening and could end up more scared if he abandoned the treatment before his fear had subsided.

D3c1 The job of a clinical psychologist
Quick check questions

A Dysfunctional means not functioning properly. A family might be dysfunctional if one family member is made a scapegoat, which means they are blamed for any arguments or problems, whereas, often, it is the interactions that are to blame rather than just one person.

B With regards to tests, saying they are standardised means they have been used often enough to find out what the results mean and to make sure they are measuring what they claim to measure reliably. If the test was done again the same results are likely to be found. There are published data because the tests will have been used enough, so someone can measure 'their' results against the published data and draw a conclusion (such as how 'good' a reading score is for a child's age). Psychometric testing means testing someone's mental abilities or reactions in some way.

Summary questions
1 it is important that professionals like clinical psychologists keep up-to-date with theories and ideas so that they can use research findings in their work and keep reviewing their procedures, assessments and interventions. Also a clinical psychologist has to act ethically at all times and the CPD is a way of the BPS checking up on what a psychologist is doing to ensure that 'psychology' maintains its good standing and that clients of psychologists are protected.
2 i) family therapy – because the person presenting the problem may not be the actual problem, it may be to do with interactions within the family structure
   ii) working through anger and withdrawal to help the individual to understand what is causing the emotional responses
   iii) helping someone to adjust to a physical change and to come to terms perhaps with reduced physical functioning

D3c2 Becoming a clinical psychologist
Quick check questions

A A clinical psychologist is usually employed by the NHS to help patients with physical and mental illnesses. They can also be employed by private companies like charities, to do the same sort of work.

B The routes into being a clinical or educational psychologist are the same. For both you need a degree in psychology that is recognised by the BPS (British Psychological Society) and then some relevant work experience. Here the two qualifications differ because you would need work experience related to health issues to be a clinical psychologist and related to education issues for an educational psychologist. However, in practice, at this stage there is not that much difference as both require experience in helping and dealing with people. Then for both qualifications you have to get on to a doctorate degree that gives you the training. This degree lasts three years and is full time.

Summary questions
1 A clinical psychologist needs to have a degree in psychology and then a doctorate in clinical psychology
2 A clinical psychologist needs to be able to listen carefully and in an objective way. They also need to be able to reflect on what they hear and then come up with a solution. They have to be ready to deal with a client's anger or withdrawal and yet still uncover issues and propose and implement solutions. They have to be able to study effectively, considering the level of qualifications they have to get. They also have to work well with other professionals.

D3c3 Clinical psychology and phobias
Quick check questions

A CBT stands for cognitive behavioural therapy. The main point is to find out what is causing the phobia in the way of how the person thinks about it. Then the psychologist has to address those thought patterns to help the person see whatever is causing the fear in a different way. This would stop the phobia.

Summary questions
1 the therapy must be systematic and manageable for the client, as they need time for the fear to reduce before moving on to the next step. Sessions cannot be too far apart otherwise the reduction of the fear in response to one step in the fear hierarchy would not be remembered/retained. As well as facing the fear hierarchy and learning to manage the fear the client must also look at their thought processes to change them, to stop the fear from continuing.
2 hypnotherapy is a form of therapy where the client is relaxed into an altered state of awareness. When the client is hypnotized the therapist can make suggestions to remove the phobia.

D4a1 Heinrich et al (2005): cultural differences in fears
Quick check questions

A High social anxiety answer: I would not say anything about the girl with the right answer, and I would not speak up and offer a solution to the problem myself. Low social anxiety answer: I might speak up and say the girl next to me had the right answer or prompt her to speak up. I would work out the answer for myself and offer the solution to the teacher.

Summary questions
1 culture is a set of beliefs, customs and social norms that affect how we feel, think and act.
2 in my culture it is important to get a job and succeed in life. This means that I should achieve good qualifications at school, college and maybe university. I work hard to complete my homework, revise for exams and stand out from the crowd. I take pride in my work and put in 100%. (Answers will vary.)
2 social fear is affected by the way we are brought up. Culture affects the way we are raised as people around us teach us how to behave and what is not acceptable. If we are brought up in an individualistic culture we have to be independent and assertive so we speak out and are confident in social situations. This means that we are not

socially anxious. If we are brought up in a collectivist culture it is more important to be part of the group and not stand out as an individual. This means that we are shy and not assertive. Collectivist cultures are stricter and have punishments for people who break social norms. This means that they are less likely to put themselves in a situation where they could be wrong or go against the group. Collectivist cultures are more socially anxious than individualistic cultures because of their social norms and beliefs.

Topic E

E1a1 Biological explanations of criminality

Quick check questions

A Identical twins have all their genes in common, whilst non-identical twins, like siblings, only share half of their genes.

B If both twins are criminal and both share the same genes, it could be that criminality has a genetic basis (although another factor to consider is the influence of upbringing – to be discussed later).

Summary questions

1 you could use family studies that look at how many relatives are criminal. This will show a genetic link to criminality that has been inherited. Twin studies look for genetic similarity or chromosome abnormality.

2 it might be due to upbringing, similar backgrounds and experiences that could explain the fact that criminality seems to run in families.

3 Nathan is not very likely to turn to crime because he only shares half of his genes with his brother. Studies suggest around a quarter of twins will both be criminal if one is.

E1a2 Social explanations for criminality

Quick check questions

A Divorce, maternal deprivation/separation from caregiver, being in a large family.

B Divorce can cause separation from the main caregiver and often involves many disruptions, such as changing homes and financial difficulties. Arguments cause stress and mistrust in families. These are all linked to criminal patterns.

Summary questions

1 A loss of attachment/bond broken between caregiver and child.

2 It can cause a child to become less trusting and distressed. This could have lasting effects and cause a child to turn to crime.

3 Larger families mean that it is difficult for parents to track the behaviour of all the children. They are less closely monitored and can get away with criminal behaviour more easily than children from smaller families.

E1a3 Childrearing as an explanation for criminality

Quick check questions

A i) power assertion ii) induction iii) love withdrawal

Summary questions

1 a) Marta might tell Lee that she does not love him when he hits other children and will only love him again when he behaves well.

b) Marta would explain to Lee that hitting other children is not nice and that they are hurt when he hits them.

2 Carl's parents may have a strict way of disciplining their children, including the use of physical punishment and verbal attack. Carl might take out his anger on other people to get back at his parents. He might have low self-esteem because his parents ridiculed him. He gains confidence by committing crime.

E1a4 Self-fulfilling prophecy as an explanation for criminality

Quick check questions

A When a belief about yourself becomes true because of the way others treat you.

B Someone thought to be a criminal might be treated with suspicion and not trusted. They will not be given as much attention because they are believed to be going nowhere and not making anything of themselves.

Summary questions

1 people often reject rather than follow others' expectations about their behaviour.

2 ASBOs place a label on a person that could be self-fulfilling. If people in a neighbourhood know that a person has an ASBO, they might be more wary of them and suspicious of their behaviour. School teachers might treat them as criminals too and expect very little of them academically. In this way ASBOs can be self-fulfilling, as the person might feel as though they are criminal and have very few opportunities other than crime open to them.

E1b1 Comparing theories of criminal behaviour

Quick check questions

A Nurture is about how we are raised and how this affects how we turn out. The social explanations of criminality focus on how we are raised in terms of our childhood experiences. This makes it a nurture explanation.

Summary questions

1 the biological theory states that criminality is due to what comes from within us – our genes – whereas the social theories explain criminality as coming from external factors, such as other people and our families.

2 Larry could have a genetic reason for his criminal behaviour. His father or mother might be criminal too. He would have inherited this gene from one or both of his parents. Alternatively, Larry could have been treated like a criminal by his parents, friends or teachers. He might have been caught stealing at school. People would then be suspicious that he might do it again and watch him more closely. He might begin to believe that he is a thief and continue to steal.

E2a1 Theilgaard (1984): the criminal gene

Quick check questions

A She did blood tests.

B It is when a researcher finds what they expect to because of that expectation.

C She used a social worker to interview the men and conduct the tests so she did not influence the findings.

Summary questions

1 being in a large family would result in less monitoring by parents. Children could display more aggression due to a lack of attention and would not be picked up and punished for this aggression because their parents had more children to deal with. You may also use genetic inheritance, self-fulfilling prophecy and childhood experiences as alternative explanations of aggression.

2 Theilgaard's study does suggest a link between XYY males and aggression, but because of the low numbers of XYY males in the study the findings cannot be concrete evidence for a criminal gene. The link between aggression and XYY chromosome pattern is only a correlation – there could be other reasons for their aggression. It could be an indirect result of their lower levels of intelligence, if for example they struggled at school and experienced difficulties with their peers.

E2a2 Sigall and Ostrove (1975): attractiveness and jury decision-making

Quick check questions

A i) Participants were given pictures of an attractive person or an unattractive person.

ii) They were told the person had committed the crime of burglary or fraud.

iii) They were asked to give a length of sentence.

Summary questions

1 in the real world jurors should be made aware of stereotypes we hold of attractive people and unattractive people. Lawyers could use this information to make their clients less likely to be linked to the crime!

2 participants did not see the court case and were not allowed to talk to each other to come to a decision. This means that they did not have the same experience as a real jury. Also, juries only decide upon guilt and not length of sentence.

E2a3 Madon (2004): self-fulfilling prophecy and drinking behaviour

Quick check questions

A Madon was trying to see if parent's expectations affected their children's drinking behaviour.

B Some children may think it is cool to say they drink more alcohol than they actually do. Other children might think their parents will find out, so they say they drink less than they actually do. Some parents might say their child does not drink because it is not an acceptable thing to say, even though they know their child does drink. It might also be the case that some parents believe that drinking in young adulthood is a grown-up thing for their children to do. There are many ways of answering these questions and many reasons why parents and children might not tell the truth.

Summary questions

1 Madon's finding that children whose parents expected them to drink alcohol actually did drink more can be explained in terms of the self-fulfilling prophecy. The children believed that they were expected to drink more alcohol, so they did to confirm this expectation.

2 Janek drank alcohol because his parents expected it of him. They were not surprised by his alcohol use. This parental expectation may have led to a self-fulfilling prophecy. Janek drank more because his parents expected it of him.

E2b1 Is criminal research practical and ethical?

Quick check questions

A Because there are so few XYY males and the abnormality has no obvious physical signs.

B If a person finds out they are XYY and others do too, they might be expected to be aggressive and this could lead to them behaving in an aggressive way.

C We cannot set up a social condition to cause criminality as this would be ethically and morally objectionable.

D Parents and friends will have to rely on their memory from the past, and this may be affected by the person's current behaviour. Memory is not very reliable.

Summary questions

1 researching the self-fulfilling prophecy can in itself highlight or reinforce existing labels. You should always be careful what participants are told to ensure this does not happen. You should also be careful when presenting your findings; if they seem to blame the parents, you would have to be sure this is the case or not publish the results/explain them carefully.

2 Jonah could not conduct an experiment that looks at whether calling someone a criminal leads them to criminal behaviour. It would be immoral to make someone a criminal. If Jonah decided to see if there was a link between expectations and later criminal behaviour he would have to rely on interviews. Interviews are not very reliable because people would have to try and remember how the person was viewed earlier on in their life. This type of study might link expectations of others to later criminal behaviour, when in fact there may be other reasons why a person becomes a criminal.

E2b2 Gathering information from convicted offenders

Quick check questions

A • they might want early release from prison
 • they might want to feel important so exaggerate their crimes
 • they may fear other criminals finding out so do not tell the truth
 • they may want to protect their family and friends from the truth.

B No – just because they have their civil liberties removed does not mean that their human rights are removed too. We should treat them exactly like any other participant of psychological research.

Summary questions

1 Emma would have to consider that convicted criminals need to give their consent to take part in the study. They have the same humans rights as all participants, so would need to know the aims of the study before they agreed to take part. Emma would also have to consider that the convicts might lie about their upbringing as they could blame their parents for their crime rather than take responsibility themselves.

E3a1 Offender profiling

Quick check questions

A • to reduce the list of suspects to investigate
 • to suggest interviewing techniques
 • to help police identify clues that the criminal might possess
 • to help predict future offences.

Summary questions

1 Traditional policing relies upon physical evidence such as blood and fingerprints to link a crime to a suspect. Offender profiling looks for invisible or psychological clues, such as the choice of victim or choice of location, which can be used to link the criminal to that crime.

2 There are some who say that profiling is effective and some that say it is not. There are as many successes as failures – often the failures get more media coverage. It could just be guesswork, but profiles can be very specific. If a profile is wrong it can have disastrous effects, either by leading police officers to the wrong person, or trying to frame a person who is innocent.

E3b1 The case of John Duffy

Quick check questions

A The victims were at or near a railway track or station.
B The victims had their hands bound during the attack.

Summary questions

1 John Duffy committed 26 rapes and 3 murders within a 4-year time span. He attacked young women, often using ties. The attacks were all committed near railway stations and the women were lured away to side streets and alleys.

2 the profile said that the attacker was a young male who was married. He enjoyed martial arts and aggressive hobbies. He lived in London and worked with British Rail.

3 the profile was very accurate. The most specific links made were about his hobbies, physical build and marital status. The other parts of the profile were fairly obvious based on the case evidence.

E3c1 The job of the forensic psychologist

Quick check questions

A Treatment programmes; gathering data; advising parole boards; analysing crime. (Answers will vary)

Summary questions

1 a forensic psychologist may plan programmes with a prison governor to help with individual prisoners. They may carry out research projects or assess the risk of re-offending. They may carry out and evaluate treatment programmes.

2 prisoners, prison officers, court officers, probation officers, family, witnesses, victims.

E3c2 Becoming a forensic psychologist

Quick check questions

A The forensic psychologist might be employed by HM Prison Service to plan rehabilitation programmes and work with prison staff as well as prisoners, such as to reduce stress. Another way a forensic psychologist might work is in a young offender's unit where they are employed by the social services.

Summary questions

1 a Master's is needed in forensic psychology, which is Stage 1 of the Diploma in Forensic Psychology. Another qualification is Stage 2, which is the two years of supervised practice that is required.

2 skills needed are good communication, ability to write clearly and concisely, interest in people, ability to focus on issues such as body language, and problem solving skills.

3 all the psychologists carry out assessments and interventions. All need good communication skills and all work with people to help them, often focusing on managing behaviour. But they work in different fields of behaviour, such as education, child development, mental health and criminality.

E3c3 How a forensic psychologist might help to treat offenders

Quick check questions

A A forensic psychologist might use anger management, group therapy or skills training.

Summary questions

1 Cognitive behavioural therapy is used with sex offenders to help to change their thinking as well as their behaviour. This will help an offender to deal with being in prison and might also help with rehabilitation. For example, if an offender can change the way they think about being in prison or can change the way they think about their sex offences, then this can be a successful therapy. The individual is listened to in a non-judgemental way and with empathy. Their thought patterns are addressed for them to look at other ways of seeing issues and problems.

2 It is a way of finding someone's own ways of thinking about people so they can see how they view others and, after some intervention, can see how or if their thinking has changed.

3 A problem in treating offenders is that offenders may renew old habits when they return to their own environment. If the cause of offending is not understood it is hard to be sure of the correct treatment.

E4a1 How defendant characteristics affect jury decision-making

Quick check questions

A The defendant is the person convicted of a crime who is on trial.

Summary questions

1 Attractiveness: people who are attractive are seen as more trustworthy and honest and therefore unlikely to commit a crime. Accent: people with regional accents are stereotyped as being more likely to commit crime because posh accents are held by people who do not need to commit crime because they have money.

2 Michaela is experiencing the influences on jury decision making. It is supposed to be a fair system to judge a person, but people will bring their own stereotypes and prejudices with them to the jury room. The other jury members are not just using the evidence presented in court, but are also basing their decision on their view of the defendant – the way they look and sound, and their race. This means that the decision the jury members reach will not be objective.

Answers to Practice Exam Questions

Know Zone: Topic A Exam Question Answers

1 Part of the retina has no light detecting cells so if an image falls on that part we can't see it.
2 They would get a group of people who would all do each of the conditions in the experiment.
3 People's memory for objects is different in various contexts. It is better in a matching context.

Know Zone: Topic B Exam Question Answers

1 The activation-synthesis theory suggests that during REM sleep there is activation of neurons, sensory blockade (no information from the senses comes into the brain) and movement inhibition (which means the body cannot move). The activation of neurones is internally generated, as if information was coming in through the senses. The brain tries to make sense of the information and 'synthesises' it into a story as best it can. The activation of neurons is the 'activation' part of the theory and the story (the dream) is the 'synthesis' part of the theory.
2 'Little Hans', was a study of a little boy Freud called Hans (though it was not the boy's real name). Freud analysed the boy's behaviour, and what he said, over a long period of time. Along with the information given to him by Hans's father, Freud's observations allowed him to analyse Hans's dreams. One dream involved giraffes. Hans had dreamt that a big giraffe was shouting because Hans had taken a crumpled giraffe away from the big giraffe. Freud analysed the dream as representing the fact that Hans liked to be in his parents' bed in the mornings. The crumpled giraffe represented Hans's mother whilst the big giraffe represented Hans's father. The big giraffe was shouting because Hans had taken his mother (the crumpled giraffe) away from his father. Freud interpreted this as being about Hans's desire for his mother and his fear of his father, who he thought would be angry with him for taking away his mother.
3 Dreamwork is the process of disguising unconscious wishes that tend to 'leak out' during sleep. The manifest content (the 'story' of the dream) disguises the latent content (the hidden content) by using symbols and other means. Dreamwork includes condensation, which means using one symbol in the manifest content but for two or more unconscious thoughts. Dreamwork also includes displacement, which means the focus in the manifest content is on something or someone other than the 'real' (unconscious) focus. There is also secondary elaboration, where the manifest content is made to make sense by changing things into a story, otherwise the manifest content would be very hard to relate to.
4 One similarity between Freud's theory and Hobson and McCarley's theory of dreaming is that they both involve an element of nature. The activation-synthesis theory is a biological theory and suggests everyone dreams for the same reason due to our nature, whilst Freud's theory is about the unconscious leaking out thoughts during dreaming. Freud thought that everybody had a powerful unconscious and it is part of our nature. One difference between Freud's theory and Hobson and McCarley's theory is that Freud used case studies to understand meaning behind dreaming, whereas Hobson and McCarley used experiments and scanning to show activation of neurons. Both theories used different research methods.
5 One of the treatments carried out in a sleep disorder clinic is cognitive behavioural therapy. This helps the individual to uncover negative automatic thoughts that are affecting their behaviour and sustaining anxiety, resulting in sleep problems. The individual uncovers their negative thoughts and works with the therapist to resolve them. For example, someone might think they are not good enough, so a therapist can work with them to find evidence that they are in fact good at a lot of things. Anxiety can be reduced in this way which can help improve sleep patterns.

Know Zone: Topic C Exam Question Answers

1 Content analysis is a way of measuring the number of times something occurs in a form of media, such as newspapers, books or television.
2 Content analysis is used to measure how many times aggressive acts occur in different media forms. The researcher identifies what they believe is an act of aggression and then count how many times it happens over a period of time or occasions.
3 Content analysis can be biased if the sample of media used is not representative of what they are studying. For example, if the categories of aggressive behaviour are not valid, then a researcher may be measuring something they did not intend to or missing something they actually wanted to measure. Another problem is that the way a researcher interprets a behaviour may not be the same as another researcher. This can lead to unreliable findings.

4 Protection of participants relates to how participants of research are looked after, psychologically and physically, when involved in a study. We can protect participants by minimising any physical and psychological harm caused by the study. We should make sure that we consult other professions to ensure that we are correct in our belief that participants will not suffer harm. We should also try to get informed consent, offer the right to withdraw, debrief participants and offer any counselling if they may have been affected by the study.

Know Zone: Topic D Exam Question Answers

1 Nature means things like genetics and hormones that affect development and nurture means that what happens to you during your life affects your development.
2 A closed question only has a few possible answers like 'do you have a phobia?' yes/no. An open question has lots of possible answers, like 'how does it make you feel'?
3 Animals are simpler than humans so what we find out in animal experiments might not be the same for people. Some experiments cause animals to suffer, for example if they are in pain or deprived of something, so this needs to be used as little as possible.

Know Zone: Topic E Exam Question Answers

1 One biological explanation for criminality is the chromosome abnormality XYY. People with the chromosome abnormality XYY have an additional Y/male chromosome that can be identified by taking a blood sample. This is not an inherited defect, but it has been linked to criminal behaviour. People with an XYY chromosome pattern have been reported to have lower intelligence and to be more aggressive than the general population. Some notorious criminals, such as Arthur Shawcross and John Wayne Gacy were found to have the XYY chromosome.
2 One social explanation for criminal behaviour is the self-fulfilling prophecy. If someone is labelled a criminal and treated in a way that is consistent with the label, they might eventually behave in a way that conforms to the expectations of others.
3 The aim of Theilgaard's study (1984) was to see if there was a link between XYY chromosome abnormality and criminal and aggressive behaviour.
4 The purpose of offender profiling is to help the police narrow down a list of suspects so they can investigate a more manageable number. It suggests a list of probable features or characteristics about the person who committed the crime that may help officers identify and convict a criminal. It also suggests useful clues that can be used to aid an investigation, such as items that can be found at the criminals home. Because profiling offers a description of the person's character, it can be useful in suggesting interview techniques.
5 Attractiveness of a defendant is one characteristic that can influence jury decision-making. If a defendant is attractive they are seen as trustworthy and dependable. This leads the jury to believe that they are not guilty. However, this is not the case if the defendant has used their looks to commit the crime. In this case they are more likely to be seen as guilty. Sigall and Ostrove (1975) demonstrated this effect as participants gave the shortest prison sentence to an attractive person who committed burglary, but the longest sentence to the attractive person who committed fraud.

Glossary

activation-synthesis model: a model of dreaming proposed by Hobson and McCarley where the brain is active but no sensory information is coming into it. The brain puts the information it has together to make sense of it and this is the dream.

acupuncture: a therapy that uses needles and particular points in the body. It rests on ancient Chinese knowledge and understanding of the body.

adaptive: a structure or behaviour that makes an individual more likely to survive.

ADHD (Attention-Deficit Hyperactivity Disorder): where a child does not attend well to classwork, is hyperactive (lots of movement and activity), tends to be forgetful, impulsive and easily distracted.

adrenal glands: pair of glands (small organs) that release hormones, one of which is testosterone.

aggression: angry or violent behaviour or attitude.

aim: a statement of what a study is being carried out to find.

ambiguous figure: a stimulus with two possible interpretations, in which it is possible to perceive only one of the alternatives at any time.

amygdala: a brain structure involved in aggression.

antennae: the feelers on the head of an animal such as a moth or cockroach.

anxiety: a state of fear or worry.

association: the link between the neutral stimulus and the unconditioned stimulus that makes the neutral stimulus cause the same response.

authoritarian: a style of government where society's members have little input and have to accept the government's decisions.

axon: the 'cable' that leads from a cell body of a neuron down to the terminal buttons that hold the neurotransmitter

bar chart: a graph with separate bars. Usually there is one bar for each condition in an experiment.

bias: when decisions are not fair because of something in the situation or person's thinking, such as a response bias to a questionnaire.

binocular depth cues: information about distance that needs two eyes, such as stereopsis.

blindspot: the area of the retina where the optic nerve leaves. It has no rods or cones so cannot detect light.

British Psychological Society (BPS): the society that governs psychology in Britain and controls the profession.

case study: a research method studying an individual or a small group and gathering in-depth and detailed information using different means.

castration: surgical removal of testicles.

cell body: the inner core of a neuron where the impulse starts from.

censorship: preventing information from being circulated in some way.

central nervous system (CNS): the brain and the spinal column.

chromosome abnormality: a mutation of genetic material that results in a change in the number or structure of chromosomes.

circadian rhythm disorders: problems with the body's 24-hour sleep-wake cycle.

classical conditioning: also called Pavlovian conditioning, a learning process which builds up an association between two stimuli through repeated pairings.

claustrophobia: fear of closed spaces.

clinical psychologist: a psychologist who works within mental health and helps people with various disorders such as depression.

closed question: simple question with few possible answers.

closure: lines or shapes are perceived as complete figures even if parts are missing.

cognitive behavioural therapy (CBT): a very popular therapy at the moment and studies suggest that it is the most successful. The individual is encouraged to look at their thinking and perhaps change how they perceive things as well as change their behaviour.

collectivist: describes a culture that encourages group dependence, cooperation and group identity, e.g. Japan. People rely on each other to achieve together.

colour after-effect: an illusion caused by focusing on a coloured stimulus and perceiving opposite colours immediately afterwards.

competence: a psychologist's ability to conduct a study.

condensation: when many thoughts and elements from the unconscious are represented in the dream in one symbol.

conditioned response (CR): the action produced in classical conditioning after association has taken place, which is triggered by the conditioned stimulus.

conditioned stimulus (CS): a trigger for a behaviour called the conditioned response, which only produces this behaviour after association has taken place.

cones: light-sensitive cells in the retina that can detect colour.

confidentiality: an ethical guideline for studies that involve people as participants, which ensures that information gained must not be shared with others without permission. There are some occasions when confidentiality must be broken, however, if there are issues of safety for someone else. Confidentiality is linked to privacy.

conform: to adjust to expectations made of us.

consent: permission to take part in a study.

construct: a way of thinking about someone, formed from experiences.

content analysis: a research method used to measure the number of times something comes up in a book, newspaper article, television programme, etc.

Continuing Professional Development (CPD): a requirement of psychologists, that every year they submit a log to the British Psychological Society that shows they are furthering their own training and working suitably.

continuity: straight lines, curves and shapes are perceived to carry on being the same.

control group: a group that does not receive an experimental condition. This group provides a baseline against which to compare those participants who do experience a condition of the experiment.

controls: ways to keep variables constant in all conditions of an experiment.

correlation: a measure of an association or relationship between two factors or variables. For example, the factors of family size and crime can be correlated to see if there is a link between the two.

correlation study: a study that sees if there is a link between two variables, e.g. testosterone and aggression

counselling: a term for various forms of therapy, although in general, counselling is about listening to someone without judging them and allowing them to explore their lives and experiences in order to help them to work through their problems.

countertransference: when an analyst transfers feelings onto the client in response to transference from the client (when they transfer feelings of love or anger onto the analyst).

credible: when a theory or findings agree with our beliefs and understanding and/or come with evidence that we can accept.

criminal consistency: the idea that a person will commit a crime in a way that mirrors his or her own personality and ability, e.g. an organised person will commit an organised crime.

custom: a longstanding practice of a particular group of people.

debrief: being told the truth about a study when it is over.

deception: being lied to.

defendant: a person who has been accused of a crime and is now in court.

delinquency: breaking the rules in a minor way.

demand characteristics: when we change our behaviour to meet the demands of the situation.

dendrite: thread-like structures that spread out from the cell body and receive a neurotransmitter from the terminal buttons of other neurons.

dependent variable: the factor which is measured in an experiment.

deprivation: when we change our behaviour to meet the demands of the situation.

depth cues: the visual 'clues' that we use to understand depth or distance.

descriptive statistics: ways to summarise results from a study. They can show a typical or average score or how spread out the results are.

detachment: term that links with attachment theory, referring to a lack of an attachment figure, i.e. one or more close loving relationships, in early childhood. This can be harmful for an adult because it is said that adults base their relationships on their own early childhood relationships.

displacement: when something that seems to be unimportant in a dream is made central, to shift attention from what is really important.

distortion illusion: where our perception is deceived by some aspect of the stimulus. This can affect the shape or size or an object. For example, a distortion can make a figure seem bigger or smaller than it really is.

doctorate (PhD): the highest degree awarded. It is the next step up from a Masters degree.

dream analysis: a method used by Freud to help uncover unconscious thoughts, by analysing dreams and uncovering symbols.

dyslexia: difficulties with reading.

educational psychologist: works with children and their development, in particular their learning and schooling.

EEG (electroencephalograph): a machine with electrodes is attached to the head and can pick up brain activity, which can be shown in graph form on a monitor.

empathic listening: a way of listening to another person so that there is real understanding. It also involves responding in a way that shows that you have listened.

entrapment: when the law tries to force a person to commit an offence or implicate themselves in a crime they may not have committed.

ethical guidelines: advice to help psychologists solve ethical issues.

ethical issues: potential psychological or physical risks for people in experiments.

ethics: moral issues which are dealt with using guidelines and principles.

evaluate: identify the good and bad points, or strengths and weaknesses, of a theory or point of view.

evolution: the changes in organisms which occur because of natural selection. Animals that are better adapted live longer and have more young so their useful characteristics are passed on and become more common in the population.

experiment: a research method which measures participants' performance in two or more conditions.

experimental (participant) design: the way that participants are used in different conditions in an experiment. They may all do all conditions or different participants may do each condition.

exposure therapy: like systematic desensitisation as it has a fear hierarchy but not so much focus on relaxation – more on thinking.

extinction: the loss of a classically conditioned response when the conditioned stimulus is repeated many times without the unconditioned stimulus.

extraneous variables: any variables that might affect the results of the study that may not be controlled.

eyewitness: somebody who sees a crime or aspects of a crime scene and who helps the police to find out what has happened or to catch whoever was responsible.

false memory: any memory that is not true and can be given by someone else 'remembering' an event and telling another person, who then 'remembers' it as true. Freud's definition refers more to false recovered memory, where a childhood memory (e.g. of abuse) is suggested by the analyst and accepted, then later found not to be true.

family therapy: therapy that involves the family of the patient. The family is often thought to be relevant to the treatment of an individual because people do not function in isolation and problems that the patient has may be caused by or linked to problems within the family.

fear hierarchy: in phobia treatment, a listing of the least feared up to the most feared situation that can be used to tackle the phobia systematically.

fiction: an illusion caused when a figure is perceived even though it is not present in the stimulus.

figure-ground: a small, complex, symmetrical object (the figure) is seen as separate from a background (the ground).

flooding: a therapy that is occasionally used for phobias. It involves facing the person with their fear either in reality or using their imagination.

forensic psychologist: works with offenders and within criminal settings, e.g. courts and prisons, to focus on offender behaviour, for example.

free association: a method used by Freud in psychoanalysis where the patient is encouraged to express a flow of consciousness. The process helps to uncover links which can then be interpreted.

generalisable: refers to findings of studies and whether they can be said to be true of people other than those that were studied.

generalisation: when a conditioned response is produced to stimuli that are similar to the conditioned stimulus.

genes: units of hereditary information that control characteristics and are passed from one generation to the next.

Gestalt laws: perceptual rules that organise stimuli.

height in the plane: objects closer to the horizon are perceived to be more distant than ones below or above the horizon.

hierarchy of fears: a list of fears that are arranged from most to least feared.

holistic: taking into account the person as a whole rather than just one aspect, for example someone's snoring.

hormones: chemicals produced by the human body that send signals to organs around the body via the bloodstream.

hypersomnia: problems with sleeping too much.

hypnotherapy: a therapy that uses hypnosis to bring about a very relaxed state so that issues can be explored.

hypothesis (*plural* **hypotheses**): a testable statement of the difference between the conditions in an experiment. It describes how the independent variable will affect the dependent variable.

identification: a feeling of similarity with a role model that leads to the imitation of their behaviour – we believe we can be like them.

impulse: the electrical signal that travels from the cell body of a neuron to the terminal buttons, where it releases a neurotransmitter.

illusory contour: a boundary (edge) that is perceived in a figure but is not present in the stimulus.

independent groups design: different participants are used in each condition in an experiment.

independent variable: the factor which is changed by the researcher in an experiment to make two or more conditions.

individualistic: describes a culture that encourages independence, personal achievement, competition and individuality, e.g. the USA.

informed consent: an individual's right to know what will happen in an experiment, and its aims, before agreeing to participate.

insomnia: problems getting to sleep or staying asleep.

interventions: plans that list changes in behaviour or attitudes that are required to help ease problem situations or change problem behaviour.

latent content: the meaning underlying the dream. If the symbols from the manifest content are translated by an analyst, they can reveal unconscious thoughts.

Likert-style questions: statements with a ranked answer scale from 'strongly agree' to 'strongly disagree'.

limbic system: an area of the brain involved in emotion.

linear perspective: when parallel lines appear to converge (meet) in the distance.

longitudinal study: research that takes place over a long period of time. It is used to track changes in behaviour of the same children (or subjects) over a long period of time. However, it can be very time consuming and participants may drop out of the study.

mandatory: has to be done.

manifest content: what the dream is said to be about by the dreamer – the story the dreamer tells.

maternal deprivation: when the bond is broken between caregiver and child because of separation.

mean: an average that is calculated by adding up all the scores in a set and dividing by the number of scores.

median: an average that is the middle number in a set of scores when they are put in order from smallest to largest.

medical model: this refers to the idea in a society that problems are 'illnesses' and can be diagnosed and then treated. In our society we work within this model.

methodology: refers to how psychology works, including how data are gathered. It involves considering 'how do we know?'

mode: an average that is the most common score or response in a set.

modelling: observing, identifying with and copying the behaviour of a role model.

monocular depth cues: information about distance that comes from one eye, such as superimposition, relative size, texture gradient, linear perspective and height in the plane.

moral censorship: deciding what material is suitable for broadcasting or publishing and what material is not considered moral or suitable.

motion after-effect: an illusion caused by paying attention to movement in one direction and perceiving movement in the opposite direction immediately afterwards.

movement inhibition: the state, during REM sleep, when the body is paralysed and there is no movement.

narcolepsy: a brain disorder where people have sudden attacks of sleep in the day.

natural experiment: an experiment where the independent variable is naturally occurring and not set up by the researchers.

nature: what we are born with.

neuron: a cell in the body, including in the brain, that sends information using both electrical and chemical processes.

neurotransmitter: a chemical at the terminal button of a neuron, which is released by the impulse and then goes into the synaptic gap.

non-verbal information: information that we pick up from other people (or indeed animals) apart from their words. It includes facial expressions, gestures and physical movements/positions. Folded arms, for example, may indicate defensiveness.

nurture: what we learn from the way we are raised.

objective: where the researcher's views do not affect the information that is gathered.

obscene: considered to be morally objectionable by a society.

observational learning: the process of learning from watching others.

obsessive compulsive disorder (OCD): when someone has thoughts that they cannot banish from their mind no matter how hard they try, and they act out these thoughts even though they are very distressed by doing so. Common OCDs include washing hands repeatedly or repeatedly locking the door when leaving the house.

Oedipus complex: the idea that a boy from about the age of four years old will have unconscious feelings for his mother and want his father out of the way, though then fears his father and feels guilty too.

one-trial learning: learning a classically conditioned response in a single association between the neutral stimulus and the unconditioned stimulus.

open (-ended) question: question that asks for description and detail.

optic chiasma: the cross-shape where some of the information from the left and right eye crosses over to pass into the opposite side of the brain.

optic nerve: bundle of nerve cells that leads out from the retina at the back of the eye. It carries information from the rods and cones to the brain.

paranoia: a disorder in which a person is obsessively distrustful of others.

parasomnias: problems during sleep, such as nightmares and sleepwalking.

paternalistic: a style of government where decisions are made for the good of everybody else. This rests on the idea of the head of the household knowing what is best for everybody else in the household.

perception: the way the brain makes sense of the visual image detected by the eyes.

perceptual set: the tendency to notice some things more than others. This can be caused by experience, context or expectations.

personal construct therapy: a therapy where someone finds their own way of looking at people (their personal constructs) and uses those constructs not only to see how they judge the people they know but also to measure change after therapy.

phallic: term used to refer to anything that is related to or said to represent the male penis, or the term can refer to the penis.

phobia: an intense fear that prevents 'normal living' in some way.

pons: an area in the brain at the top of the brain stem/spinal cord.

preparedness: the tendency to learn some associations more easily, quickly and permanently than others.

primary sleep disorders: sleep disorders which are not related to any other problem, but are problems in themselves.

privacy: an ethical guideline for studies that involve people as participants, which ensures that their names must not be recorded and they must not be identifiable. Privacy is linked to confidentiality.

profile: a list of predicted abilities, personality characteristics, occupation, marital status, etc. that can be used to narrow down a list of suspects for a crime.

protection of participants: looking after the rights and welfare of participants to ensure no physical or psychological damage.

proximity: objects which are close together are perceived to be related.

psychiatrist: a medical doctor specialising in mental disease. Only psychiatrists can carry out diagnoses or prescribe medication – psychologists cannot.

psychoanalysis: Freud's therapy, designed to help release unconscious thoughts.

psychoanalyst: someone who uses Freud's views to help someone to unlock unconscious thoughts.

psychodrama: a therapy, usually involving a group, where one person's problems, issues or ambitions is the focus of a drama. Their story, or part of it, is acted out and focused on by the group to bring issues to light and to explore them.

psychological sleep disorders: problems with sleeping where the brain and mind are involved.

psychopath: person suffering from a chronic mental disorder with abnormal or violent social behaviour.

qualitative data: data involving stories or attitudes

quantitative data: data that involve numbers and statistics, such as percentages.

questionnaire: a research method using written questions

random activation: during REM sleep, when neurons are active randomly not deliberately.

range: a way to show how spread out a set of results is by looking at the biggest and smallest scores.

rank-style questions: questions with points either in order that can be chosen or that can be put in order.

recall: remembering with few prompts.

receptors: at the dendrites of a neuron that receive the neurotransmitter if the 'fit' is right.

recognition: remembering by choosing between possible alternatives, e.g. several pictures.

reconstructive memory: recalled material is not just a 'copy' of what we see or hear. Information is stored and when it is remembered it is 'rebuilt' so can be affected by extra information and by ideas (like schemas) we already have.

rehabilitation: the process of integrating a person back into the community. It refers to the process by which prisoners are treated during prison to ensure they can rejoin the community and not commit more crime. It can also be used to describe how therapy can be used to help a person rejoin their families after receiving care.

relative size: smaller objects are perceived as further away than larger ones.

relaxation technique: a strategy used to calm a person down in order to reduce anxiety and stress.

reliability: refers to whether findings from a study would be found again if the study was repeated.

REM sleep: stage of sleep that occurs about 5 times each night, where there is rapid eye movement (REM) which indicates that dreaming is taking place.

REM sleep disorder: problems with sleeping that are linked to dreaming and REM sleep disorders such as REM sleep behavioural disorder (RBD).

repeated measures design: the same participants are used in all the conditions in an experiment.

repeated reproduction: a task where the participant is given a story or picture to remember. They then recall it several times after time delays. Differences between each version are measured.

response: in classical conditioning, the reaction an animal or person makes to a stimulus. It can be an emotion or a behaviour.

response bias: the patterns that participants fall into when answering a questionnaire, for example by always saying 'yes' or trying to guess the aim.

reticular activating system (RAS): an area of the brain between the medulla and midbrain, near the pons.

retina: the light-sensitive layer at the back of the eye. It is made up of nerve cells called rods and cones.

right to withdraw: a participant's right to leave a study at any time and their ability to do so.

rods: light-sensitive cells in the retina that respond even in dim light.

role model: a person who is looked up to and copied.

sample: a collection of participants gathered to undertake a psychological research study.

schema (*plural* **schemas** or **schemata**)**:** a framework of knowledge about an object, event or group of people that can affect our perception and help us to organise information and recall what we have seen.

secondary elaboration: how the dreamer builds a story when telling what the dream is about, adding to and changing things, which makes analysis hard.

secondary sleep disorders: sleep disorders that stem from another problem.

self-esteem: the way we feel about ourselves, our self-confidence and self-opinion.

self-fulfilling prophecy: when the expectations of others affect our behaviour, so that it reflects those expectations

sensory blockade: during REM sleep, when no information enters through the senses.

serial reproduction: a task where a piece of information is passed from one participant to the next in a chain or 'series'. Differences between each version are measured.

similarity: figures sharing size, shape or colour are grouped together with other things that look the same.

size constancy: we perceive an object as the same size even when its distance from us changes.

slip of the tongue: when someone uses the wrong word for something. Freud analysed these slips to help uncover unconscious thoughts.

social desirability bias: when participants give the answers they think will be acceptable to other people to make themselves look better.

social learning theory: the idea that learning comes from the observation and imitation of role models.

social norm: a behaviour or belief that is expected and accepted in a particular culture.

social phobia: fear of interacting with others and being with others; perhaps an extreme form of shyness.

souvenirs: a keepsake or memento taken by an offender from their victim or the crime scene, usually to remind them of their crime.

special needs: refers to any difference in development that requires special attention or approaches to helping the development.

specific phobia: fear of an object or something specific as opposed to social phobia.

standardised test: a test that has been used often enough to find out what the results mean and to be sure that it measures what it claims to measure reliably.

standardised instructions: guidance for participants that is the same for everyone.

stereopsis: a binocular cue to depth. The greater the difference between the view seen by the left eye and the right eye, the closer the viewer is looking.

stereotype: a general view of a person based on limited or untrue ideas.

stimulus (*plural* **stimuli**): in classical conditioning, something that might trigger a response; in perception, a picture or other visual image that is used in an experiment to show to participants.

structured questionnaire: a set of written questions in a fixed order. All participants answer the same questions.

subjective: where the researcher is somehow affecting the information that is gathered, perhaps by their interpretation.

superimposition: a partly hidden object must be further away than the object covering it.

suspect: a person that the police think may be guilty of a crime, but who has not yet been found guilty in court.

symmetrical: if an object or image is divided in half, the two halves look alike – they appear to be mirror images.

synaptic gap: the gap between the dendrites of one neuron and the next.

synaptic transmission: what happens when a neurotransmitter released by an impulse of one neuron goes across the synaptic gap and is taken up at the dendrites of another neuron.

systematic desensitisation: a therapy that is used for specific phobias and involves pairing relaxation with the phobic object rather than fear.

tally: a single mark on a chart to show that a behaviour/ category has been found during a content analysis.

terminal buttons: at the end of the axon of a neuron that hold the neurotransmitter.

testes: testicles, the male sex glands.

testimony: the evidence given by a witness, expert, or a person the defendant knows well (a character witness).

testosterone: a chemical that produces male characteristics and is said to be involved in aggression in men.

texture gradient: an area with a detailed pattern is perceived to be nearer than one with less detail.

tradition: a practice that has been handed down through generations.

transference: when a client transfers feelings of love or hate onto their analyst as part of the analysis.

twin studies: research into the similarity of twins, particularly their criminal similarity, to investigate genetic links.

unconditioned response (UCR): the action produced in classical conditioning before any association has taken place, which is triggered by the unconditioned stimulus.

unconditioned stimulus (UCS): a naturally-existing trigger for a behaviour. It causes the unconditioned response.

unreliable: a one-off finding that may not happen again because of a lack of control in a study.

unrepresentative: limited so that it might not apply to everyone.

valid: refers to findings of studies and means that they are about real-life situations, real-life behaviour or feelings that are real.

verdict: a decision made by a jury. The verdict can be guilty or innocent.

vicarious reinforcement: learning through the positive consequences of other people's actions rather than firsthand – we are more likely to copy if they are rewarded.

victimisation: when someone is treated unfairly.

visual cortex: the area at the back of the brain that interprets visual information.

visual illusion: a conflict between reality and what we perceive.

watershed: term used to indicate a turning point. When applied to TV programming it is the 9 p.m. deadline before which programmes (including cable and satellite programmes) that contain certain levels of violence and/or sex cannot be broadcast.

XYY: a rare genetic pattern said to be linked to aggression and slow learning ability.

Index

Index